ALIEN
AND PHILOSOPHY

The Blackwell Philosophy and Pop Culture Series
Series editor William Irwin

A spoonful of sugar helps the medicine go down, and a healthy helping of popular culture clears the cobwebs from Kant. Philosophy has had a public relations problem for a few centuries now. This series aims to change that, showing that philosophy is relevant to your life – and not just for answering the big questions like "To be or not to be?" but for answering the little questions: "To watch or not to watch *South Park*?" Thinking deeply about TV, movies, and music doesn't make you a "complete idiot." In fact it might make you a philosopher, someone who believes the unexamined life is not worth living and the unexamined cartoon is not worth watching.

Already published in the series:

ALIEN AND PHILOSOPHY

I INFEST, THEREFORE I AM

Edited by
Jeffrey Ewing
and
Kevin S. Decker

WILEY Blackwell

This edition first published 2017
© 2017 John Wiley & Sons Ltd

The right of Jeffrey Ewing and Kevin S. Decker to be identified as the authors of the editorial material in this work has been asserted in accordance with law.

Registered Offices
John Wiley & Sons, Inc., 111 River Street, Hoboken, NJ 07030, USA
John Wiley & Sons Ltd, The Atrium, Southern Gate, Chichester, West Sussex, PO19 8SQ, UK

Editorial Office
9600 Garsington Road, Oxford, OX4 2DQ, UK

For details of our global editorial offices, customer services, and more information about Wiley products visit us at www.wiley.com.

Wiley also publishes its books in a variety of electronic formats and by print-on-demand. Some content that appears in standard print versions of this book may not be available in other formats.

Library of Congress Cataloging-in-Publication data applied for

Paperback ISBN: 9781119280811

Cover Image: © sololos / Getty Images
Cover Design: Wiley

Set in 10.5/13pt Sabon by SPi Global, Pondicherry, India

Printed in the United States of America

10 9 8 7 6 5 4 3 2 1

In memory of Kathleen Ewing, shining light and amazing mother.
You're always in my heart, and thank you for everything,
forever. — J.E.

To Phil Neale, philosopher and alien. — K.S.D.

Contents

Contributors
In Space, No One Can Hear Them Scream

Alejandro Bárcenas teaches history of philosophy at Texas State University. He is the author of *Machiavelli's Art of Politics* (2015) and a contributor to *The Daily Show and Philosophy* (Wiley Blackwell, 2007) and *The Ultimate Star Trek and Philosophy* (Wiley Blackwell, 2016). His research focuses on political theory and classical Chinese philosophy. He hopes one day to get a chance to discuss *Lawrence of Arabia* with David from *Prometheus*.

Adam Barkman (PhD Free University of Amsterdam) is an associate professor of philosophy and the chair of the philosophy department at Redeemer University College. He is the author of five books, including *Making Sense of Islamic Art and Architecture* (2015), and the co-editor of four books on philosophy, film, and pop culture, most recently *The Philosophy of Ang Lee* (2013). Adam has traveled to over fifty countries in his time, but still wants to see a pyramid in Antarctica (sans alien queens, of course).

Alexander Christian is a research fellow at the Duesseldorf Center for Logic and Philosophy of Science at the Heinrich Heine University in Duesseldorf, working in philosophy of science (demarcation problem) and research ethics (scientific misconduct, questionable research practices, responsible conduct of research in health sciences). Alex gave up his dreams of being an astronaut when he was ten years old and watched *Alien* for the first time alone on a tiny black and white TV. Although he thinks that his second career path is way more secure, he hides an M41A Pulse Rifle under his desk. Because they mostly come during office hours, mostly.

Daniel Conway teaches philosophy at Texas A&M University. He too has been deemed "expendable" by various employers, though not yet—as far as he knows—in the context of their pursuit of weaponized alien biotechnology. Needless to say, *that* decision would be understandable…

Kevin S. Decker teaches philosophy at Eastern Washington University, where he often lectures about the phenomenology of peaches and the rights of vampire citizens. He is the editor or co-editor of several anthologies of philosophy and popular culture, including *The Ultimate Star Wars and Philosophy* and *The Ultimate Star Trek and Philosophy* (with Jason T. Eberl) and *Philosophy and Breaking Bad* (with David Koepsell and Robert Arp). His book *Who is Who? The Philosophy of Doctor Who* saved his life recently when, the lights having gone out, he used it to wedge a door piston shut on the USCSS *Costaguana* to protect him from the predatory ship's cat, Smithey.

David Denneny's career as a graduate student in philosophy has just started at Southern Illinois University at Carbondale, and he's excited to dive right into some heavy-duty philosophy. His hobbies include playing funky music on bass guitar, being something of a political dissident, singing R&B on karaoke night, and referring to quotes from smarter people than himself when he wants to get a point across. Stay groovy comrades, and keep an eye out for Xenomorphs!

Jeffrey Ewing is a doctoral candidate at the University of Oregon, and has written chapters for various popular culture and philosophy books, including those on *Frankenstein*, *Jurassic Park*, and *Ender's Game*. He loves to write poems on natural subjects, such as Xenomorphs. "Roses are Red, Grass is Green. Where is the Facehugger? It's lunging at m – " *muffled scream*

Martin Glick is a doctoral candidate at the University at Göttingen studying legal philosophy. His research interests also include political philosophy, aesthetics, and trying to convince the general population that *Predator 2* should be considered one of the essential 90s action films.

Tim Jones, PhD, is an Englishman who wrote the final draft of his chapter while staying with his partner's family in America. He therefore knows what it's like to be an alien and manages to conduct himself without tearing to pieces everyone he comes across and desiccating their corpses, so can't see why the Xenomorphs are unable to behave themselves by following his example.

Chris Lay is a doctoral candidate and graduate teaching assistant at the University of Georgia and is deeply interested in issues of personal identity. He devours science fiction in all its forms: books, movies, video games—you name it. Chris un-ironically and shamelessly enjoys SyFy Channel original movies far more than he should. He has a serious problem; please help him.

William A. Lindenmuth is Associate Professor of Philosophy at Shoreline College. He received his MA in philosophy in New York City from the New School for Social Research, and his BA in English from Saint Mary's College in California. He's taught in New York, Las Vegas, Seattle, and Rome, Italy. He specializes in normative ethics and moral psychology, particularly through the mediums of literature and film, arguing that our stories show us both who we are and who we'd like to be. William has contributed to *The Ultimate Star Trek and Philosophy*, *The Ultimate Star Wars and Philosophy* (Wiley Blackwell), and the forthcoming *The Philosophy of Christopher Nolan*, *Jane Austen and Philosophy*, and *Romancing the Zombie*. He mostly philosophizes at night. Mostly.

Greg Littmann is a human—a sort of tube of soft tissue, composed mostly of water, and held semi-rigid by a calcium endoskeleton. Having an internal skeleton leaves his vital organs dangerously unprotected, but has two major advantages. Firstly, an endoskeleton provides great structural support, allowing him to grow almost two meters long—large enough to become Associate Professor of Philosophy at Southern Illinois University Edwardsville. Secondly, an endoskeleton permits sufficient joint articulation for fine manipulation like typing, enabling him to publish on the philosophy of logic, evolutionary epistemology, and the philosophy of professional philosophy, as well as writing numerous chapters for books relating philosophy to popular culture, including volumes on *Doctor Who*, *Jurassic Park*, *Planet of the Apes*, *Star Trek*, *Star Wars*, and *The Walking Dead*. Taxonomically, humans are a species of ape, most easily distinguished from other apes by their patchy hair and enormous buttocks.

Louis Melançon is a faculty member at the National Intelligence University. He's a doctoral candidate at the George Washington

University and has contributed various chapters on philosophy and popular culture topics including *The Avengers* and *The Hunger Games*. While it's true that in space no one can hear you scream, he now realizes that people can still hear you weeping in your office.

Robert M. Mentyka received his MA in philosophy from Franciscan University of Steubenville in 2011, and has since authored chapters in both *Bioshock and Philosophy* and *Lego and Philosophy*. He currently works overnight shifts as a legal document processor, but was recently cited by mid-level management for "excessive ethical thought while on the job." He is currently scheduled for transport to Fiorina "Fury" 161 for reeducation in company policy, but is confident that nothing eventful could happen at such a remote corporate outpost...

James M. Okapal is Associate Professor of Philosophy, Chair of the Department of Philosophy and Religion, and Chair of the Department of History and Geography at Missouri Western State University. His research explores the intersections of ethics and popular culture, especially in science fiction and fantasy. He's published articles on ethical issues in *Harry Potter*, *Star Wars*, and *Star Trek*. He often finds himself misquoting Call when he receives a phone call or email—"I can't respond now. I burned my modem. We all did"—and returning his attention to something much more enjoyable.

Bruno de Brito Serra, who has previously contributed to *Sons of Anarchy and Philosophy*, holds a PhD in philosophy from Durham University and, much to his own dismay, does *not* hold one of those awesome body-mounted machine guns that Vasquez and Drake carry around in *Aliens*—which would certainly come in handy to increase the persuasiveness of any philosophical arguments tossed around the table at the Philosophy Department...

Joe Slater is a doctoral candidate at St Andrews, Scotland. He works on moral philosophy and is particularly interested in how much morality demands of individuals. As a big sci-fi nerd who has occasionally been suspected of being an alien, he was naturally attracted to contributing to this volume.

Sabina Tokbergenova is an independent philosopher interested in ethics and social philosophy. Her most recent publication is a chapter in *Wonder Woman and Philosophy*. While she may not know how to operate a flamethrower, Sabina does know a thing or two about how to scorch her enemies in philosophical debates.

Seth M. Walker is a doctoral student at the University of Denver, studying religion, media, and popular culture. He regularly writes on topics in these areas—including volumes in the PCP genre on *Jurassic Park*, *Orange Is the New Black*, and *The Walking Dead*—and edits an online magazine that engages the intersection between religion and popular culture: *Nomos Journal*. He's been known to stand on the peaks of Colorado's beautiful 14ers, scornfully shaking his fist at the gods…and the impending Xenomorph invasion.

Andrea Zanin feels alien most days she wakes up and blames a combination of growing up in psychotic South Africa and mothering four children under the age of six (as we speak). She is a *cum laude* English honors graduate (with a random law degree to boot) currently living in London, where she spends her time writing, ranting, being a journalist, and trying to be more like Ripley and less like an acid-drooling Xenomorph. She rarely succeeds. Andrea has contributed chapters to various pop culture and philosophy books, including *Sons of Anarchy*, *Hannibal Lecter*, and *X-Files*.

Introduction: A Word of Warning...

Ironically, the first people scared by the Xenomorphs in *Alien* were the cast of the 1979 film themselves. All they knew of the infamous Chestburster scene in advance was that there would be an alien head, and it would have teeth. John Hurt (Kane) was lying underneath the table and "his" chest in the scene was artificial. Prosthetics weren't great in those days, so they filled the artificial chest cavity with animal organs from a butcher's shop. The studio started to stink of flesh. Of course, in some ways the cast should've known what would happen, since the crew were all wearing raincoats and the set was draped in plastic. Four cameras were rolling, and the cast could see the alien head pulsing under Kane's t-shirt. The cast leans in, curious about what's going to happen. Suddenly, the head rips out of the chest and twists around. Everyone panics. A stream of blood three feet long catches Veronica Cartwright (Lambert) straight in the mouth, and she passes out. Yaphet Kotto (Parker) went to his room after the scene and refused to talk to anyone. The whole cast were shocked and scared, the first casualties of the Xenomorph species. The next time you find yourself scared or shocked while watching *Alien*, one of the greatest sci-fi/horror/monster films of all time, remember you're in excellent company.

Beyond its effective fear-inducing potential, a lovely side-effect of watching a film as thought-provoking as those in the *Alien* saga is that it involves our relationship to radically disparate Others—the Xenomorphs, androids, the Engineers. The *Alien* series gives us grounds to wonder what makes us unique as a species. While we're

Alien and Philosophy: I Infest, Therefore I Am, First Edition.
Edited by Jeffrey Ewing and Kevin S. Decker.
© 2017 John Wiley & Sons Ltd. Published 2017 by John Wiley & Sons Ltd.

very much animals (and share much in common with them), as far as we know we do many things that no other earthly animal does—we file legal briefs, pay our Netflix bills, and pilot craft into space.

There are two features unique to being human, though, that are particularly relevant to the book you're about to dig into. First, no animal has devoted so much time towards voluntarily feeling and promoting the experience of *fear* as humans. We sky-dive, bungee jump, and take risks to feel a rush of adrenaline. We stay up late to read H.P. Lovecraft, Stephen King, Thomas Ligotti, and Richard Matheson. We pack into theaters to see *Alien*, *The Thing*, *Cloverfield*, *It Follows*, and hide behind the couch cushions for Netflix's brilliant *Stranger Things*. Second, no other species spends their time philosophizing in the ways humans have—what is the meaning of life? What is beauty? How do you define "art"? How should we treat one another? How do we *know* any of these things? We philosophize, and many of us *love* a good scare. The *Alien* series perfectly combines these two unique traits, inspiring deeper thoughts as much as it scares.

At a technical level, few horror films are as iconic as the entries in the *Alien* series. We owe the sleek menace of the elongated Xenomorph head (and its mouth-within-a-mouth) to the Swiss surrealist H.R. Giger's genius, the surprise of the first Chestburster scene to Ridley Scott's experimental direction. Then there's Ripley "negotiating" with the Xenomorph Queen using a flamethrower as leverage in *Aliens*, Ripley's dramatic sacrifice in *Alien³*, and her discovery of the horrific cloning program in *Alien: Resurrection*. The world of *Alien* is simultaneously horrifying and thought-provoking; as a science fiction/horror masterpiece, it can ask questions that other genres can't easily ask or fully answer.

This book features nineteen chapters that engage both the deeper layers of the *Alien* universe and what those layers *mean* on topics as diverse as identity and personhood, morality and the political and economic forces of the *Alien* universe, just war theory in going into battle against the Xenomorphs, the philosophy of horror, and feminist insights into Ripley's leadership style.

Questions about what is or is not a *person* are suggested by *Alien*'s diverse array of entities. Though androids like Ash and Bishop are not human, do they meet the criteria to be seen as *persons*? And if they are, what is their moral *status*? Do we have any duties to treat them well, or are they merely *things*? These questions have deep implications for the human future—how will we treat artificially intelligent AI or androids, and perhaps even extraterrestrial life?

These questions dovetail into major issues in ethics. Does the moral status of human persons imply that the way corporations like Weyland-Yutani treat their employees is inherently wrong? Philosopher, economist, and revolutionary Karl Marx attracts the attention of several of our authors to explore *why* Weyland-Yutani make harmful choices in favor of profit. We also highlight the *political* failings evident throughout the *Alien* series that free the corporate hand to grip its human employees more and more tightly.

These chapters also open discussion on a number of problems in the ethics of warfare. In a related vein, the orphan Newt's situation is used to highlight an often forgotten element of Plato's *Republic*—the argument that involving children in warfare may be, with the right guide, a positive part in their human development.

The *Alien* series allows us to examine the roots of many of our fears about the unknown, the corrupting, the predatory, and the unstoppable—we love a good scare, but why, and what does that mean? What does it show about what makes us afraid? The philosophy of cosmic horror perfected in the works of H.P. Lovecraft (a key inspiration for the series), the value of horror films as art, and themes of contagion and impurity are explored in a number of chapters.

The *Alien* series boasts Ellen Ripley, one of the bravest and most badass protagonists in film history, and Ripley makes a number of choices in the films that allow us to examine femininity and motherhood in depth. What principles animate Ripley's decisions, and what do they mean? Is she representative of a feminist ethics of care, or is there something else going on in her head? Beyond Ripley, *Alien* allows us to examine other concerns of feminist philosophy, such as interpreting Xenomorph violations of human bodies as a lens to examine the nature and effects of rape.

The saga is also illuminated through application of the insights of continental philosophy. Are Xenomorphs exemplars of Nietzsche's ideal of the Übermensch? What does the existentialism of Camus say about Ripley-8's decisions *not* to commit suicide despite the discovery of her cloned nature? And how does Jean-Paul Sartre's defense of revolutionary violence highlight our human-centered interpretation of the *Alien* series; do Xenomorphs have a right to resist us? Perhaps Xenomorphs would watch the *Alien* film as a horror movie about being one of their own born on a hostile spaceship, full of extraterrestrials trying to kill it!

The Xenomorphs are memorable for a number of their traits—their raw power, adaptability, their quick development, their hive mind.

As Ash put it, they are the "perfect organism," whose "structural perfection is only matched by its hostility." Likewise, we think that the *Alien* films are the "perfect" science fiction/horror series. Establishing a world equally filled with terror and depth, they are the ideal meeting of the two unique human traits we focused on in the beginning of this introduction—our love of a good scare, and of philosophical exploration.

We're proud to penetrate these questions with you, and hope that you feel the warm glow of philosophical insight hug your face, grow large in your chest, and take on a life of its own.

Part I

IDENTITY AND MORAL CONSIDERABILITY: "WE MADE YOU BECAUSE WE COULD"

"No Man Needs Nothing": The Possibility of Androids as Lockean Persons in *Alien* and *Prometheus*

Chris Lay

Most of us probably take it for granted that "human beings" and what philosophers and lawyers call "persons" are one and the same thing. The *Alien* franchise often challenges this idea, though. To first-time viewers of *Alien*, seeing Parker knock Ash's head clean off his shoulders while the android's body continues to fight back is just about as jarring as the Xenomorph Chestburster exploding out of Kane in the middle of the *Nostromo* mess hall. Why? Because, up until that point, Ash looked and acted like a perfectly normal *human person* (albeit an emotionally detached one). In *Aliens*, the synthetic Bishop balks at being called an android, demurring, "I prefer the term 'artificial person' myself." When someone else calling himself Bishop shows up on Fiorina 161 at the end of *Alien³*, Ripley elects to throw herself into the active smelter because she cannot be sure that this "Bishop" isn't an android sent by Weyland-Yutani to harvest the Xenomorph queen gestating inside her. Another android, Call, from *Alien: Resurrection*, both rejects and is disgusted by the fact that she is something that is less than human. However, the Ripley clone Ripley-8 seems to imply that Call's compassion for others supersedes her synthetic programming and allows her to transcend being a mere "auton."

Alien and Philosophy: I Infest, Therefore I Am, First Edition.
Edited by Jeffrey Ewing and Kevin S. Decker.
© 2017 John Wiley & Sons Ltd. Published 2017 by John Wiley & Sons Ltd.

In each of these cases from the *Alien* films, the franchise asks us to question both what it is to be human and whether or not beings are possible that are like humans, even if they are not biologically human. This is where a distinction between "human" and "person" comes in. Bishop wants to be treated like a human (despite the fact that he's not, biologically speaking, a human being). Call is ashamed of and appalled by her synthetic nature, but might Ripley-8 be right in thinking that certain features—such as her capacity to self-reflect—make Call more "human" than she realizes? If something shares certain relevant traits with humans (without being biologically human), we may be able to group that something and humans into a common category. Let's call this the category of "persons." For philosophers, deciding what belongs in this category and what doesn't is the *question of personhood*—that is, what makes something count as a person, and can there be persons who are not human?

Perhaps more than any other film in the franchise, the *Alien* quasi-prequel *Prometheus* directly engages this question of personhood. To the viewers, the android David at least appears to be a person: we see David play basketball, worry about his looks as he grooms himself in a mirror, and express his love of *Lawrence of Arabia*. These certainly seem to be things that bona fide persons would do. Yet, many of the characters in the film treat David as if he could not possibly be a person. In a hologram played to the crew of the *Prometheus* after they wake up from hypersleep, Peter Weyland, David's creator, says of his creation:

> There's a man sitting with you today. His name is David. And he is the closest thing to a son I will ever have. Unfortunately, he is not human. He will never grow old and he will never die. And yet he is unable to appreciate these remarkable gifts, for that would require the one thing that David will never have: a soul.

If we assume that Weyland is right and that David does not have a soul, why should that matter to whether or not David counts as a person? If "having a soul" is essential to being a person, and if devices, no matter how complex, don't have souls, then David definitely cannot be a person. On the other hand, the relevant features of David that make us think he *seems* like a person might not necessarily be attached to the idea of a soul. In that case, we might have good reason to say that David is a person after all.

"Well, I guess that's because I'm a human being, and you're a robot"

René Descartes (1596–1650) would have agreed with Weyland's take on David. Descartes thought that humans were made of two distinct substances: a body (made of physical stuff), and a soul (made of nonphysical stuff). It is the soul that gives us the features that make us persons, though. In his *Meditations on First Philosophy*, Descartes says:

> I know certainly that I exist, and that meanwhile I do not remark that any other thing necessarily pertains to my nature or essence, excepting that I am a thinking thing, I rightly conclude that my essence consists solely in the fact that I am a thinking thing [or a substance whose whole essence or nature is to think].[1]

Here, Descartes means that thinking is the one feature of himself that he can be absolutely sure of. So, for example, Ripley could hypothetically doubt that she has a body or that she has been safely rescued from the *Narcissus* (the *Nostromo*'s shuttle). In these cases she might just be dreaming, or, in the case of Ripley's dream of a Chestburster in *Aliens*, having a nightmare. However, she cannot doubt that she exists and that she thinks. Indeed, she would have to both exist and think in order to conjure up the dream! For Descartes, the upshot is that our mental features are part and parcel with the soul, or a "substance whose whole essence or nature is to think."

Of course, human beings also have bodies, but these account only for the biological features of humans. To Descartes, our physical features have nothing to do with our *essential nature*—as things that think—because the body is completely separable from the idea of thinking. Thoughts are not physical things and bodies are. The two are thus wholly different in kind. Since for Descartes the essential features of humans are mental features, and mental features are features exclusively of souls, this means that the criteria for personhood—those essential features that other things might be able to share with humans—are only features of souls. Lots of things have bodies, but only souls (and, by extension, things that have souls) can think. So, for example, Descartes claims that animals are "automata" whose behavior, though similar to that of humans, can be explained entirely "as originating from the structure of the animals' body parts."[2] Animals don't have the ability to think because they don't have souls.

The same argument can, I think, be extended to androids like David. Androids appear to act like human persons—they communicate, evidently emote, and are outwardly human in nearly every way. However, their behavior is strictly mechanical. Without a soul, David cannot think. Without thought—*the* essential Cartesian criterion of personhood—David cannot be a person. He is just missing the right sort of features. This is exactly how David is treated by the other characters in *Prometheus*. Weyland explicitly points to David's lack of a soul in his speech to the *Prometheus* crew. A despondent, half-drunk Charlie Holloway condescends toward David while shooting pool, all the while noting that David is lucky that he—an unfeeling android—cannot experience disappointment like a real person could. Even the generally optimistic and kind Elizabeth Shaw sees David as nothing more than a sophisticated machine. At the film's end, when a bodiless David wonders why Shaw is so eager to track down the Engineers and seek answers from humanity's creators, she matter-of-factly asserts, "Well, I guess that's because I'm a human being, and you're a robot." These characters apparently adopt the Cartesian view of persons in denying David personhood. David cannot feel emotions like disappointment or empathize with those who have a desire for answers because he does not have a soul, which is the seat of such capacities.

"Technological, intellectual, physical…emotional"

The Cartesian take on personhood is not the only way to read *Prometheus*, though. In a promotional short film for *Prometheus* called "Happy Birthday David," David is introduced as an "Eighth generation Weyland TIPE: technological, intellectual, physical…emotional."[3] Two of these qualities are primary features of persons, according to John Locke (1632–1704). In contrast to Descartes, Locke believes that what makes something a person is not tied up with having a soul. Indeed, a "person" is something completely different from a "human," or any other animal, for that matter. The primary feature of animals—including humans—is, for Locke, a certain functional organization of their bodies. That is, their organs work together in particular ways to make sure that the being can perform basic life functions.

At the same time, we can distinguish persons from mere animals with a certain functional biology. Locke defines "person" at two points in *An Essay Concerning Human Understanding*. First, he says that a person "is a thinking intelligent Being, that has reason and reflection, and can consider it self as it self, the same thinking thing in different times and places."[4] So, persons are able to think, can be rational—or follow some set of logical rules—and have the capacity to self-reflect. This last idea is especially important. If something is to be considered a person, it must have the ability to see itself as a thinking thing that persists over time. "Person," Locke later adds, "is a Forensick Term appropriating Actions and their Merit; and so belongs only to intelligent Agents capable of a Law, and Happiness and Misery."[5] What Locke is getting at here is that the category of "persons" is crucial for identifying who deserves praise or blame (morally, legally, and otherwise). For the label "person" to act as an identifier for something having moral status, persons have to be capable of rationality (acting in observance of laws) and moral emotions (happiness and misery). In other words, a person must be able to understand why she is being held accountable and that her actions have consequences in terms of emotional effects.

To sum up, the picture of a person we get from Locke is of an intelligent, rational, self-reflective, and emotional being. Anything that can have all of these features must count as a Lockean person. Ripley's cat Jonesy may exhibit a sort of intelligence and even feel to some limited degree. Yet, the cat can neither act according to some set of rules—that is, he is not rational—nor can he self-reflect. Thus, Jonesy is not a person. The human characters of the *Alien* franchise do seem to have all of these characteristics. So does the clone Ripley-8. What about androids like David, though? Do they have what it takes to be persons according to Locke's definition?

"The trick, William Potter, is not minding it hurts"

We have four criteria of personhood to work with here: intelligence, rationality, capacity for self-reflection, and emotionality. In the case of David and other androids, I think that only three of these are really up for discussion. No one questions whether or not androids are rational—in fact, the problem often seems to be that they are *too* rational; they cannot do anything *but* follow rules and commands. Taking intelligence next, David surely appears to be capable of thought, understanding, and other mental operations (which is just what intelligence is for Locke). David can communicate (he even learns the Engineers' language, more or less) and respond to both instructions and environmental changes. But this is only what Locke calls a "passive" power of thought or intellect: David enjoys certain mental operations, but only in a responsive way, like how a basketball only moves if something else picks it up or throws it. He is programmed to have certain thoughts and the like. This might count as a sort of limited intelligence, but to self-reflect, David would almost certainly need to be able to *actively* think. He would need to be able to generate novel thoughts himself, independently of his programming.

It seems clear that David is able to do this. He is plainly aware of himself, as he models his behavior, speech, and appearance after Peter O'Toole in *Lawrence of Arabia*—whom David idolizes. This demonstrates a concern with not just how he sees himself, but how he would like others to see him as well. David also seems to be painfully aware of himself when Weyland notes that David has no soul. His dejected expression tells of a being that suddenly regards itself as "less-than." David is, in Weyland's speech, made cruelly aware that he will forever lack something that could put him on equal footing with everyone around him. So, if we believe that David is self-reflective, we should identify some self-generated mental features (products of active thinking) that make this self-reflection possible.

One very telling example of such a mental feature is David's judgment about his desires. Although David tells Shaw that "want" is not something that he, as an android, can experience, he immediately follows this up with the line, "That being said, doesn't everyone want their parents dead?" But to kill Weyland and—as David himself puts it—to be free of Weyland's programming is hardly David's only desire. David wants to be accepted by his creators (both Weyland and other humans) as much as Weyland does in his pursuit of the Engineers. This is why David deflates during Weyland's speech and beams when the freshly awoken Engineer caresses his head (just before violently ripping it off)—for a moment, he thinks that *something* has accepted him. Given David's imitation of Peter O'Toole, it is also probably fair to say that he desires to look, act, and be perceived a certain way, as well. David judges all of these desires to be worthwhile and hence pursues them. Locke argues that our desires determine our will to act in some given way, but this determination is constrained by our active judgments about whether we ought to see those desires through or not.[6] In fact, for Locke, this is precisely what makes human actions "free": that they're in accord with our judgments. David's choice to pursue these desires shows then that he has an active power of the intellect—free from the bindings of his programming—that explains the apparent self-reflection that we observe as viewers.

Lastly, we have the possibility of David's emotionality. Is David "capable of happiness and misery"? Locke defines emotions—or "passions"—in terms of pleasure and pain. So, it might be objected that all Locke is talking about as a criterion of personhood here is *sentience*, or conscious experience of sensations like pleasure and pain. Given that David is beheaded and does not seem to mind it all that much, it may look like he can't have these sorts of experiences. David is quite adamant that he does not have any sort of feeling. Further, in "Happy Birthday David," David states directly that he cannot feel human emotions (though he understands them and can respond accordingly).

Locke also points out, however, that there is "pleasure and pain of the Mind, as well as the Body."[7] David certainly seems to take pleasure in things—he enjoys films like *Lawrence of Arabia* and delights in being called a "son" by Weyland. Likewise, while watching the holographic map of the universe in the orrery room of the Engineer ship, David is overcome by a sense of wonder. He is also apparently pained when Weyland says that David lacks a soul and by the scorn of his human companions. His relationship with Holloway in particular reveals David to be capable of the pain of emotional resentment. Just before Holloway is infected with the black liquid, he says to David with a sneer, "I almost forgot, you're not a real boy," and, after Holloway pejoratively remarks that humans made androids for no other reason than to satisfy their own curiosity, he laughs off David's suggestion that the two are not so different. David does little to disguise his contempt for Holloway throughout the scene. Note that it is only *after* their exchange that David decides to contaminate Holloway's drink—making it quite plausible that he does it partly out of spite.

While learning how to act like Peter O'Toole in *Lawrence of Arabia*, David repeats the line from the film, "The trick, William Potter, is not minding it hurts." David seems to adopt not only O'Toole's mannerisms, but also his character's mantra—this is how he inures himself against the emotional pain of being rejected as sub-human by those around him. And this explains the caustic personality he develops toward say, Holloway. Case in point: when the *Prometheus* crew first enters the Engineer ship, Holloway jokes, "They're making you guys pretty close," to which David replies (with no shortage of snark), "Not too close, I hope." Based on the above, it seems clear that David is intelligent, rational, and capable of self-reflection and emotional feeling.

He fits the Lockean definition of a person. David can therefore feel the hurt of being denied his personhood. The trick is ignoring it. Or, as Locke says, making a judgment about the desire to rid oneself of the pain—the judgment to accept the pain and do something with it.

"I repeat, all other priorities rescinded"

Even if it looks like David can count as a person on Locke's definition, this does not mean that all androids are persons. Ash, the Science Officer of the *Nostromo* in *Alien*, serves as a nice counterpoint to David. Whereas David is treated much differently than his human colleagues, Ash is—quite mistakenly—seen by the rest of the *Nostromo*'s crew to be just like them. Yet when we ask if Ash is intelligent, rational, self-reflective, and emotional, I think we get a very different answer than we do for David.

Again, let's take it for granted that Ash is rational. He is also obviously intelligent in at least a passive way, as he communicates with the rest of the crew and can adapt apparently spontaneously to situations. For instance, Ash makes the decision to allow Kane back onto the ship with a Facehugger coiled around his neck. This isn't because Ash was specifically ordered to do this by Weyland-Yutani, but because his doing so falls in line with dispositional or background orders from the company to return any life-forms the crew may find on the planetoid LV-426. Ash is reactive, and as such has Locke's passive power of thought.

Rationality and a limited intelligence alone, though, don't make Ash a Lockean person. Ash patently does not seem to have an active power of thought and so cannot engage in any sort of self-reflection. Remember that, for Locke, active thoughts (like judgments) allow us to choose to act on our desires (or to refrain from so acting). Desires, in turn, determine our wills toward some action. Unlike David, who could actively decide to pursue some of his desires, Ash seems able to follow only the strict rules of his programming. When Brett and Parker balk at checking out the distress signal originating from LV-426, Ash simply parrots rules in the crew's contracts that would bind them to investigate. He tries to kill Ripley by shoving a magazine down her throat because Weyland-Yutani has directed him to preserve the Xenomorph specimen for study—*at all costs*. As Ash's severed head is interrogated by Ripley, Parker, and Lambert about this overriding "special order," Ripley asks, "What about our lives?" Ash replies, with eerie calm, "I repeat, all other priorities rescinded." Ash can passively respond to commands and carry out his orders, but never shows himself capable of the active power of thought.

In his discussion of freedom, Locke says that a "Tennis-ball, whether in motion by the stroke of a Racket or lying still at rest, is not by anyone taken to be a *free Agent*" because the tennis ball cannot think.[8] Although Ash can think, he cannot think *for himself*, or in an active way. He is, then, much more like the tennis ball (or Johner's basketball in *Alien: Resurrection*). Just as the basketball's movement is limited to what Johner or someone else does with it, Ash's thoughts are limited to that range of possible responses programmed by the company that created him. This means that he cannot see himself as a "thinking thing in different times and places" but only as an instrument of Weyland-Yutani.

Ash also does not seem to exhibit any sense of emotional feeling in *Alien*. Keeping consistent with Locke's definition of emotions as varying degrees of pleasure and pain, nothing seems to bring Ash pleasure *or* pain. He has no connection with any of his human crewmates—we see him sitting on his own at the mess hall table in the Chestburster scene. To Ash, the crew are expendable resources for the company, and he seems to have no desires independent of the company's goals. The closest we get to any sort of emotion from the android is mockery in his last words to the crew: "I can't lie to you about your chances, but…you have my sympathies." Ash, then, lacks the Lockean criteria of personhood on two counts: he is incapable of self-reflection and cannot feel. Even if David meets the Lockean requirements of personhood, not all androids do by default. Ash, for one, is not a Lockean person.

"There is nothing in the desert, and no man needs nothing"

We have seen that there are a couple of ways to determine whether or not androids in the *Alien* series—and especially David from *Prometheus*—can be persons. On the Cartesian view, David is not a person because David does not have a soul. Locke challenges this idea with a picture of a person that does not tie the important features of persons to some particular substance, like a soul. While Descartes gives us a quick and simple "no" to the question "Is x a person?," in the case of androids like David, Locke's answer is more complicated.

David appears to qualify as a Lockean person, but Ash, for one, does not. The Lockean view leaves open the possibility that there might (currently or in the future) be things that human beings create that could have the same moral status as we do.

When the crew of the *Prometheus* first arrive on LV-223 and see a rocky wasteland, David whispers another line from *Lawrence of Arabia*: "There is nothing in the desert, and no man needs nothing." To say that "no man [that is, no human] needs nothing" is equivalent to the claim that "all humans need something." In other words, defining features of humanity are needs, wants, and desires. David also has desires and needs (among other emotions): he wants to be accepted as a son and as an equal of sorts to his colleagues, and he wants to be free of the control of the Weyland Corporation. David very much sees himself as someone ostracized by those around him—just like O'Toole as T.E. Lawrence. And he certainly arrives at this idea of himself by a process of self-reflection. If the nonhuman David does think rationally, self-reflect, and feel like human persons, this ostracism is both arbitrary and cruel. It is hardly different from the pride of the gods that led them to eternally torture the Titan Prometheus when, as Weyland says, the Titan only "wanted to give mankind equal footing to the gods."

Notes

1. René Descartes, "Meditations on First Philosophy," in *The Philosophical Works of Descartes*, trans. Elizabeth S. Haldane (Cambridge University Press, 1911), 28.
2. René Descartes, "To More, 5.ii.1649," in *Selected Correspondence of Descartes*, trans. Jonathan Bennett (2010), 215.
3. "Happy Birthday David," along with other illuminating short films used to promote *Prometheus* prerelease, is available as a special feature on the *Prometheus* DVD and Blu-ray, and is also easily accessible on YouTube.
4. John Locke, *An Essay Concerning Human Understanding*, ed. Peter H. Nidditch (Oxford University Press, 1975), 335.
5. Ibid., 346.
6. Ibid., 283.
7. Ibid., 258.
8. Ibid., 238.

Androids: Artificial Persons or Glorified Toasters?

Joe Slater

You have a moral status. By this, I mean that *you matter*. For example, there are things it would be *wrong* for you to do. There are also things it would be wrong for me to do to you. You have *rights*. What makes you the type of thing with this moral status? Is it just being human? Does the creature discovered by the crew of the *Nostromo* in *Alien* have moral status? Can it be *wronged*? Maybe you think that even though we might reasonably hate those creatures, and certainly not want to be anywhere near them, it would still be wrong to torture them. And what about synthetics? Do androids like Ash in *Alien* have rights?

Philosophers have tried to answer this type of question in several ways. In this chapter, we'll look at a few of these different ways, thinking about some cases that might be surprisingly difficult to explain, like why babies matter, whether animals have moral status, and what we should think about synthetics (or "artificial persons," as Bishop prefers to be called) in this regard.

"He was programmed to protect human life"

One way we might try to answer these questions is by saying that only human beings have moral status. This is a nice, simple answer to the question. Because this rule for moral status doesn't depend upon intelligence or ability, it lets us say that even human babies (who are notoriously not very bright!) matter, morally speaking. That's great, because generally speaking, we do think it's wrong to go around kicking babies.

Alien and Philosophy: I Infest, Therefore I Am, First Edition.
Edited by Jeffrey Ewing and Kevin S. Decker.
© 2017 John Wiley & Sons Ltd. Published 2017 by John Wiley & Sons Ltd.

Thinking about it this way would have some consequences we might not like, however. If all that matters in being "human" is having the right genetic code, then it seems that a human embryo should be considered as having the same status as a fully grown adult. In a similar vein, a human being who is completely brain-dead, but still alive, would deserve moral consideration. While many people do think embryos and those in persistent vegetative states have some rights (and thus have some kind of moral status), whether their status is equal to that of a normal adult is controversial.

Another type of problem case we might consider involves categorizing what is and what is not a human being. In *Alien: Resurrection*, for instance, Call notes that the resurrected Ripley isn't human. "Wren cloned her because she was carrying an alien in her," Call explains. The Ripley clone seems to be a hybrid—mostly human, but part alien as well. If she gets moral status by being very similar to human beings, how far does that extend? Does the Xenomorph that's born at the end of *Resurrection*, a creature that possesses some human DNA—and recognizes Ripley as its mother—fit into the moral community too?

These cases—embryos, the brain-dead, and human–alien hybrids— might give us reason to reconsider the view that it's only human beings that matter. There are also things that seem to warrant moral consideration which wouldn't be included in that formulation, such as animals. Whether or not we're pet owners or vegetarians, presumably we think certain animals matter in our decision-making. Ripley goes to extreme lengths to save Jones the cat in *Alien*. This must be because she thinks Jones matters somehow, and that it would be bad if Jonesy was to be killed.

Australian philosopher Peter Singer argues that it is *speciesist* to treat human beings as the only things worthy of moral status.[1] He thinks speciesism, like racism and sexism, is morally abhorrent. While most people in the western world have acknowledged that racism and sexism are bad, Singer thinks we haven't properly appreciated the moral status of other species. It's difficult to see why it's justified to say that humans are special *just because* they're human beings; it just seems arbitrary. The charge of speciesism seeks to expose a bias underlying our moral thinking and to make us think about what facts really matter when asking whether it's okay to treat someone (or something) a certain way. We can imagine some intelligent animal or alien species— perhaps even the ones in the *Alien* films—or forms of synthetic life that would have some moral rights. So simply drawing the line at whether something is human doesn't seem to do the job.

Autonomy

Instead of simply belonging to a species, maybe there is some special ability or trait that makes something matter morally. We could then say it's forbidden to treat anything that has that trait or ability in certain ways. Animals, aliens, or androids might be in the class of things having moral status. *Autonomy* is one trait some philosophers, including Immanuel Kant (1724–1804), have thought is a good candidate for conferring moral status. It is difficult to define autonomy, but for now we can think of it as the ability to consider options, evaluate them, and freely choose to act in accordance with them.

Kant thinks autonomy determines moral status because he thinks that the only thing that's good in itself (rather than only good as a means to other good things) is a *good will*. We can think of this as good intentions. You act morally, according to Kant, if you can frame and make yourself obey moral laws, which you can only do if you have autonomy. One reason we might think of autonomy as the supreme notion of moral status is the role it plays in fixing the meaning of other moral ideas. Advocates of autonomy suggest, for example, that you can't see other moral agents as intrinsically valuable unless you're autonomous yourself. With this understanding, we don't need to know whether the Ripley-8 clone from *Alien: Resurrection* is human or not in order to know whether she matters morally. If she can consider options for her future and choose to do the right thing, then she matters. The same goes for synthetics and "artificial persons." If Bishop is autonomous (for example), then it would be wrong for us as moral agents to use him *just* as a tool.

This account seems to have problems, though. Not only does the reliance on autonomy exclude ordinary, non-autonomous animals from moral consideration, but also it leaves out babies. Babies don't deliberate about their options and choose rules to follow when they do stuff. Those who accept autonomy as an ultimate moral principle suggest that there isn't anything intrinsically wrong about treating babies or animals in ways that might be forbidden to treat autonomous moral agents. Instead, they say, the reason it's wrong to hurt babies or animals is because of something it does to *us* moral agents. Going around torturing babies might be bad because it's bad for their parents, or because it makes us vicious and therefore more likely to ignore or violate moral laws.

Another approach that retains the moral status of babies is to count anything with the *potential* to become autonomous as having moral status. While this would keep babies in the mix, it would also force us to count embryos as having moral status, and maybe even individual sperm cells or eggs because they all seem, in one way or another, to have the potential to become autonomous beings. Perhaps more problematically, this type of view can't account for why animals matter. You don't have to be a vegetarian to think it's wrong to be arbitrarily cruel to animals. Generally, all of us think animals have some moral standing. When Ripley saves Jones the cat in *Alien*, there is *some* reason to do so (I think she actually goes way too far, risking her life *a lot*. Come on, Ellen—it's just a cat!). Similarly, when Murphy's dog Spike dies in *Alien³*, it's not completely crazy to be sad about that. And it does seem like a serious limitation for a moral theory if it can't explain at all how the lives and suffering of animals matter.

"Because pain hurts"

Another obvious candidate for whether something has moral status is the theory that focuses on whether a thing can experience pain and pleasure. In ancient Greece, the followers of Epicurus held this type of view. More recently, Jeremy Bentham (1748–1832) defended it when he outlined the ethical position of *utilitarianism*. When asking why creatures have rights, he asked:

> Is it the faculty of reason or perhaps the faculty of discourse? But a full-grown horse or dog, is beyond comparison a more rational, as well as a more conversable animal, than an infant of a day or a week or even a month, old. But suppose the case were otherwise, what would it avail? The question is not, Can they *reason*? nor, Can they *talk*? but, Can they *suffer*?[2]

This probably strikes most of us as pretty sensible. The reason it'd be wrong to kick Jones the cat, or babies, or you or me is because we experience pain, and as Ripley reminds Johner when advising him to get away from her—"pain hurts" (*Alien: Resurrection*). That by itself gives us reasons to avoid it.

For traditional utilitarians like Bentham, the *only* things that matter to morality are pain and pleasure. So, anything that can experience pain or pleasure has moral status. This neatly includes normal human adults, babies, and most animals. It clearly doesn't include plants, brain-dead people, or embryos. One difficulty we might find is whether to include synthetic beings. In *Alien*, after being decapitated, the android Ash shows no sign of being in pain. Indeed, what would be the point in making synthetics that experience pain? We might note that there is a difference between experiencing pain and noticing that you're damaged in some way. While the former is a sensation that makes you want to alleviate it as soon as possible, the latter is simply a diagnostic recognition. If you're anesthetized, you can notice that your leg is broken, but you won't feel pain. We might well imagine that synthetics are like that.

As it happens, Bishop does seem to be able to experience pain. When Ripley manages to reactivate his mangled torso in *Alien*[3], he says, "I hurt. Do me a favor. Disconnect me." If we're to take that literally, then synthetics—at least of Bishop's type—would have moral status according to Bentham's picture. That would suggest that we could have obligations to androids, but the idea is problematic in the *Alien* universe. After all, Bishop is ordered around like a slave, and Burke says "it's been policy for years to have a synthetic on board."

For the sake of argument, I'm going to assume that synthetics don't really experience pain. Maybe Bishop was speaking figuratively. In any case, the type of synthetic life that doesn't experience pain—which does seem possible and may be the case for Ash—offers an interesting problem. Do beings like that just not matter, morally speaking, at all?

Agents and Patients

Up until now, we've just looked at one kind of moral status. While the fact that it's wrong to treat you in certain ways means you've got moral status, we might also think there's another important type of moral status. A normal human being can both be wronged and *commit* wrongs. This difference picks out an important distinction. On one hand, there are things that can *act* morally or not, things that can act rightly or wrongly. Philosophers call these *moral agents*. On the other hand, there are things that can have moral acts done *to* them, that can *be* wronged or treated rightly. These are *moral patients*.

According to this view, normal human beings are both moral agents and moral patients, but babies are not agents—babies don't seem to be able to act in ways that are good or evil. Yet it seems to most of us like it's wrong to do certain things to them. The same goes for most animals.

We might think that the two answers to the question of moral status we've looked at so far—autonomy and the ability to feel pleasure or pain—address these separate moral situations of agency and patiency. The ability to analyze potential choices and select from among them in moral terms seems like the sort of ability that creatures that can act rightly or wrongly should have. If you have no choice about what you do, you can't be blamed for what you do. If the Xenomorphs always act purely on instinct, not evaluating options and choosing freely from among them, then they don't appear to be moral agents. They might be more like predatory creatures such as lions or snakes. It doesn't make much sense to blame them for acting the way they do.

As for moral patiency, we might think that just being able to experience pain or pleasure suffices for this. The fact that something could feel in pain if you act a certain way to them does seem to give you a good reason not to do it, and the fact that something would get pleasure if you do something for them is a reason in favor of acting so. Of course, you might still be right to decide that inflicting pain on (or killing) moral patients is sometimes the right thing to do. Sometimes you might have to nuke a colony full of aliens from orbit, just to be sure, because the alternatives are even worse.

"It's a robot! A goddamn droid!"

Where would this leave our synthetics? If we think they don't really experience pleasure or pain, they aren't moral patients on this view. Perhaps they're just moral agents. Synthetics do seem to weigh options and decide between them. If that's right, they can wrong others, like Ash, when he screws over the crew of the *Nostromo*; they can't *be* wronged, though.

This also doesn't seem quite right, for this reason: the notion of pain and pleasure we've been talking about so far is simply *physical* pain or pleasure. Being stabbed or shot, or enjoying food or sex are examples. Even if a synthetic can't experience that sort of thing, why should it matter? A lot of human suffering or joy comes from other, nonphysical sources. In *Aliens*, when Ripley comforts Newt, who's struggling to get to sleep, it's obvious that Newt can suffer from having bad dreams. However, as Newt reminds us, her doll Casey can't suffer because "she's just a piece of plastic." Having a bad dream isn't a physical pain, but it's definitely *bad* for whoever goes through it. Surely it's *that* sort of difference—what separates things with preferences, likes and dislikes, from mere objects like plastic dolls—that matters when you consider whether it's right or wrong to act toward a moral patient.

So, do synthetics have this feature? Do they have hopes or dreams, desires or predilections? It seems like they do. Even if Bishop can't feel pain, he still seems to have *interests* of some sort. He makes this clear when he reluctantly volunteers to leave his relative safety to remote-pilot the ship, saying, "I'd prefer not to. I may be synthetic but I'm not stupid." In *Alien³*, he expresses a desire to be turned off, saying, "I could be reworked, but I'll never be top-of-the-line again. I'd rather be nothing." Perhaps this means that he has some pride, and that if his desire to be top-of-the-line can't be satisfied, he'd prefer not to go on at all. Even Ash seems to have desires or preferences, perhaps most obviously borne out in his weird fetish for the alien: "The alien is a perfect organism. Superbly structured, cunning, quintessentially violent…How can one not admire perfection?"

Though we probably don't share all the desires of synthetics, they are the sort of thing that gives a life meaning. A more modern version of utilitarianism, called preference utilitarianism, looks at these sorts of things. It cares more about the *interests* of beings. Preference utilitarianism says we should do whatever satisfies the most preferences, whether they are the preferences of animals, human beings, or androids. However, one needn't take such a strong view as this; it could be said that just having preferences makes you a moral patient. You might want to say, for example, that although they were all moral patients, the interests of Lambert, Parker, and Ripley were more important than those of Jones the cat because of the type of interests they are or whether these are good things to be interested in.

When we think about interests this broadly, it seems that we can have duties toward synthetics. That might not seem like a big deal generally speaking, but if true artificial intelligence (AI) is invented in the not too distant future, this is an issue that will need serious consideration. With that in mind, synthetic life-forms can count as moral patients. Perhaps, like us, Ash and Bishop would then count as both moral agents and patients. We might, however, still doubt that androids can really be moral agents. It might be strange to think of an android as a moral agent, considering that it is simply a computer program running through a piece of hardware. As Bishop jokes, he's "just a glorified toaster." It seems very strange to think that something running on your laptop could be morally responsible for its outputs.

Actually, it's not that clear that Bishop would count as autonomous. It's important for autonomy that you are actually able to *choose* what to do. Bishop makes it very clear that his programming limits that choice. After he hears about Ash's turning against the crew of the *Nostromo*, he tries to explain that it couldn't happen with him: "That could never happen now with our behavioral inhibitors. It is impossible for me to harm or, by omission of action, allow to be harmed, a human being." This takes away some of the choices he could make, and this could be seen to threaten his autonomy. Autonomy, it seems, requires free will, and unbreakable rules that restrict your choices limit the freedom of will.

But is this really so different from us? People have psychological conditions that stop them doing certain things: paralyzing phobias, depression, or just treating some actions as unthinkable. These might make it effectively impossible for you to do something, just as Bishop couldn't do anything to hurt humans because of his own limitations. So, is there any real difference—one that should *make a difference* in how it's permissible to treat them—between artificial persons and human beings? One challenge is identifying when a system can actually have interests, and when it is able to consider options for the future. Clearly a toaster can't do these things, but unless there's something truly special about human beings that can't be replicated by a machine, one day we are likely to create artificial persons. If what I've speculated about here is correct, it would be wrong to treat them with cruelty, or as tools or slaves, as seems to happen in *Alien* and *Aliens*. But then, what else would you expect from the Weyland-Yutani Corporation?

Notes

1. As discussed in *Animal Liberation: A New Ethics for our Treatment of Animals* (HarperCollins, 1975).
2. Jeremy Bentham, *An Introduction to the Principles of Morals and Legislation*, second edition (Pickering, 1823), 236.

3

"All Other Priorities Are Rescinded": The Moral Status of Employees in the *Alien* Franchise

James M. Okapal

Charlie Holloway believes the Weyland Corporation's Prometheus mission is about discovering the origins of human life on earth. Given the marketing materials published by the company, this seems reasonable. The promotional website for the Weyland Corporation states, "we have uncovered exciting new information which may ultimately redefine the entire narrative of human existence. Help us unearth the truth."[1] By the time the mission lands on LV-223, Holloway asks Meredith Vickers, the company's representative on *Prometheus*, whether Weyland Corporation is pursuing an unknown agenda. She patronizingly replies, "My company paid a trillion dollars to find this place and to bring you here. If you had raised this money yourself we would happily be pursuing your agenda. But you didn't. And that makes you an employee." This theme—that of a company devaluing its employees and their interests—permeates the narrative of the *Alien* franchise. It is part of why Weyland Corporation, and its descendants, embodies the notion of the evil corporation.

The evil corporation is a common trope throughout science fiction. As Angela Allen recently put it, "It's become so cliché to have faceless, heartless, and soulless corporations conspiring against their employees and consumers that the concept is considered simple and digestible enough for inclusion in children's movies" such as *Wall-E*.[2] She even mentions the *Alien* franchise, pointing out that the corporation

Alien and Philosophy: I Infest, Therefore I Am, First Edition.
Edited by Jeffrey Ewing and Kevin S. Decker.
© 2017 John Wiley & Sons Ltd. Published 2017 by John Wiley & Sons Ltd.

founded by Peter Weyland routinely "privileges profits over its own employees…who are ultimately expendable."[3] But what lies behind such callous attitudes? Are the expendability of employees and violations of their supposed rights things that can be justified?

You Will Get What You Deserve

The narrative world of the *Alien* universe is shot through with self-interested motivations, many of which focus on money. The dialogue in the first half of *Alien* is monopolized by discussions of the shares—i.e., money—that Brett and Parker are going to receive. When the signal arrives from LV-426, Parker complains that the *Nostromo* isn't a rescue ship and demands more of a stake in the operation. In *Aliens*, Carter Burke, the voice of the Weyland-Yutani Corporation, sends out wildcatters at Hadley's Hope to look for the ship mentioned by Ripley in her log. The family that finds the ship, Newt's family, are motivated by the "big score" that will result from the find. Burke later admits that he sent them because he was worried that alternative courses of action would leave no one with exclusive rights, and thus no money. When Ripley suggests nuking Hadley's Hope, Burke's first response is to mention the cost of building the terraforming facility. In *Prometheus*, we get a hint of this attitude in Fifield's response to Millburn's attempt at befriending him: "I ain't here to be your friend. I'm here to make money." This last instance is perhaps the most telling: it highlights the profit motive *and* maverick individualism that infects almost everyone in the franchise.

In this narrative world, then, individualism, self-interest, and profit are the motivations of almost everyone but Ripley. Such attitudes, assumed as background when we ask the question, "What is the purpose of the corporation?," support what's known as *stockholder* or *shareholder* theory. In a famous essay, Milton Friedman (1916–2006), an advocate of this theory, writes, "A corporate executive is an employee of the owners of the business. He has direct responsibility to his employers. That responsibility is to conduct business in accordance with their desires, which generally will be to make as much money as possible."[4] But the idea that the purpose of a business is to maximize profits predates Friedman, and has been traced back the ideas of Alfred A. Berle (1895–1971). Berle writes:

> It is the thesis of this essay that all powers granted to a corporation or to the management of a corporation, or to any group within the corporation, whether derived from statute or charter or both, are

necessarily and at all times exercisable only for the ratable benefit of all the shareholders as their interest appears.[5]

These two quotes sum up the idea of the stockholder view. To Friedman and Berle, the sole purpose of the corporation is to maximize profit for its stockholders. If we object that such a view is too narrow-minded, defenders of stockholder theory might then employ an important article of faith that "the invisible hand" of the market will create benefits for all while the managers act to maximize profit for the owners.[6] The problem here is that an individual corporation will behave much like the very visible hand of the murderous android Ash in *Alien* and routinely attempt to endanger or suffocate non-stockholders to achieve its ends.

Why might we think that Friedman's and Berle's way of understanding the purpose of a corporation is morally wrong? To answer, it will help to look at the notion of moral status. In discussions of moral status, the concept of moral considerability is important. If you are morally considerable, then you have a type of moral value that imposes obligations on others. At a minimum, it requires others to take your interests into account when making decisions.[7] Some beings that are morally considerable are referred to as "persons." Persons are those beings who have Full Moral Status (FMS). If a being has FMS, there is a very stringent moral presumption against interfering with that being. For example, since we would consider Ellen Ripley a person, it would be morally wrong to kill her, experiment upon her without her consent, or directly cause her suffering.[8]

Though there is a lot of controversy about which things are or are not persons, Agnieszka Jaworska and Julie Tannenbaum note that, "It is usually taken for granted that all adult cognitively unimpaired human beings have FMS."[9] In other words, most of the human characters in the *Alien* films should be considered to have FMS. Interesting test cases of beings that might be morally considerable but lack FMS include all of the androids in the movies—Ash, Bishop, and David, as well as the auton Call—since they are not human. Given this, we can understand why Bishop prefers to be referred to as an "artificial person" in *Aliens*: it keeps him from being treated as less than a member of the crew—perhaps as a tool—by elevating his moral value. Other androids like Ash and David might be viewed as cognitively impaired in that they apparently lack any moral restraints and are merely extensions of Weyland (David) or the Weyland-Yutani Corporation (Ash), while Call seems to have complete autonomy. Additionally, if we take a strict genetic view of humanity (that "genetically human" equals "person"), this leads to concerns about the moral status of several characters in the series. First, the Xenomorph/Ripley hybrids in *Alien: Resurrection* would also lack FMS since they are chimeras. Second, all the YY-chromosome inmates of Fiorina in *Alien³* would lack FMS. If the definition of being a human includes having exactly forty-six chromosomes, then having an extra Y chromosome would, by definition, make the inhabitants of Fiorina nonhumans and thus they'd lack FMS. Finally, also in *Alien³*, the character of Francis Aaron, aka "85," may fall below the acceptable level of human cognitive ability due to his low IQ scores and so he might also lack FMS.

So let's say that most of the adult humans outside the inhabitants of Fiorina in *Alien³* have FMS. This would mean that any corporate decision that might affect them negatively should include, as part of the decision-making process, their individual interests, especially their interests to avoid being destroyed, experimented on, or caused to suffer. To do otherwise is to treat them as lacking FMS and possibly as having no moral value at all. If they completely lack moral value, then they are merely things with instrumental value.

Consider the debriefing scene in *Aliens* as an indication of how little the Weyland-Yutani Corporation thinks about the interests and lives of its employees. Ripley is brought in front of a group of executives to explain why she destroyed the *Nostromo*. The executives point out that she destroyed a $42 million ship and all of its cargo. What's more interesting, though, is what they do *not* mention during this scene. Even though data on the individual crew members flit across the screen behind Ripley, the executives never mention them. It's as if the crew and their lives are of no importance to the executives, which Ripley finds exasperating. This omission seems to be the result of adopting stockholder theory. As Jaworska and Tannenbaum point out, "historically the moral status of people falling into a group perceived as 'other,' such as foreigners, racial minorities, women, the physically disabled, etc. has been routinely denied."[10]

This is the root of the problem with stockholder theory. In effect, everyone who is not a stockholder is "other" and is thus denied FMS in the eyes of the corporation, as Vickers forcefully points out to Holloway in *Prometheus*. The key implication of stockholder theory is that no one besides the owners of the corporation has FMS. This clears the way for the managers of the corporation to do whatever it takes to maximize profit for the stockholders. Note how employees, as a result of adopting stockholder theory, have a strange status.

Employees do not have FMS, but from the point of view of managers they are valuable assets, i.e., have instrumental value for what they can do to maximize profits. From the point of view of the accountants, however, employees are not merely assets, but also financial liabilities to a corporation in terms of wages and benefits. When taking into account both of these viewpoints, the FMS of employees is ignored and they are only positively valued as long as they can increase profits relative to the costs they impose on the bottom line. So, any way that a company can suppress wages and benefits (such as having employees die once they no longer contribute to the increase of profits) would seem, at first blush, to be justified by stockholder theory. Viewing employees as mere instruments seems to be a basic operating principle of every iteration of Weyland Industries. The result is that the company is always willing to sacrifice employees to pursue the interests of the owners.

The company, or its agents, repeatedly violates the stringent restrictions on harming beings normally considered to have FMS. There are indications that Burke tried to impregnate Ripley in *Aliens* by pushing a Facehugger onto her in the lab. David, as an extension of Weyland and the Weyland Corporation in *Prometheus*, spikes Holloway's drink to infect him, leading to Shaw being impregnated by the Chestbuster. This mere instrumental valuing of employees is most explicit in *Prometheus* when Weyland tells one of the Mercs, "If [Shaw] opens her mouth again, shoot her." We can see that as an employee, Shaw only had instrumental value in finding the Engineers. After Weyland has made contact, Shaw's value disappears. And of course, there is the moment in *Alien* when Ash finally tells the crew about his secret mission to return the Xenomorph. When Parker asks, "What about our lives, you son of a bitch?," Ash's reply is merely, "I repeat, all other priorities are rescinded." In other words, the FMS—in fact the entire moral considerability—of these cognitively normal adult human beings is ignored by the Weyland Corporation. This allows the company to violate with impunity, at least according to stockholder theory, the stringent moral constraints against destroying, experimenting on, or directly causing harm to employees. On stockholder theory, where only stockholders have value or moral status, employees are not part of the moral community, and with these presumptions all of the actions of the company could be justified. The employees thus get exactly what they (theoretically) deserve, that is, no consideration whatsoever in the decision-making process of the owners of the corporation.

Employees are Stakeholders

What sort of protections would the crews of the *Nostromo*, *Sulaco*, and *Prometheus* have if stockholder theory were rejected? An alternative view, most closely associated with R. Edward Freeman, is called stakeholder theory.[11] Stakeholders are "groups and individuals who benefit from or are harmed by, and whose rights are violated or respected by, corporate actions."[12] The most important stakeholders are employees, customers, and suppliers who are integral to the basic functioning of any firm. Stakeholder theory entails that stakeholders have "a right not to be treated as a means to some end, and therefore must participate in determining the future direction of the firm in which they have a stake."[13] When a corporation adopts this theory, then, employees have moral considerability and perhaps even FMS. Whatever the level of moral significance possessed by an employee, it is often presumed that employees are treated according to basic and stringent rights not to be destroyed, experimented upon, or made to suffer; an employee can make a rights claim against his or her employer to ensure these rights are not violated.[14] In order to ensure that they're not violated, a series of derivative rights come into play. Two of the most important are the right to a safe, healthy work environment and the right to participate in matters affecting employees.[15] As Ronald Duska points out, once these rights are recognized, they "would necessarily override the right of shareholders to profit maximization."[16]

These rights are, of course, violated by the company. According to Denis Arnold, "Broadly construed, worker safety includes both injuries that occur as a result of violent workplace events…and diseases and injuries that are the result of exposure to toxic substances or repetitive motion."[17] When it is not feasible to eliminate all such hazards, "an employer has an obligation to inform workers in advance regarding workplace hazards so that individual workers can make informed decisions about the work and the work conditions they find acceptable."[18] In *Alien*, Special Order 937 to bring back the Xenomorph is for the eyes of the science officer only. This implies that none of the crew, even those like Dallas and Ripley who outrank Ash, are to have knowledge of the secret mission to acquire the Xenomorph. It becomes clear in *Aliens* that the United States Colonial Marines are told nothing about their mission to LV-426 until they are revived from cryosleep. Finally, in *Prometheus*, the crew has apparently been kept in the dark about both the overt and the covert missions. Just before the briefing on the overt mission, one of the crew says, "It is corporate run, they're not telling us shit"; they do not know about Shaw's and Holloway's interest to find out about human origins. With regard to the covert mission, not even Shaw and Holloway know Peter Weyland is alive and on the ship with the intent of finding a way to extend his life.

Now, the Xenomorphs are clearly akin to toxic substances and are the cause of violent workplace events, what with their acid for blood, a reproductive cycle that destroys the host, and a ravenous appetite for any biological entity that is not used for incubation. Given that the Weyland-Yutani Corporation knows of the existence of the Xenomorphs in *Alien* and *Aliens*, and that in *Prometheus* the point is to make contact with the Engineers, a race of biological organisms that could expose the crew to significant injury, stakeholder theory implies that the company should have made all of this information known to the crew before they contracted to go on the missions. By not doing so, the Weyland Corporation kept the employees from being able to make informed decisions about the full range of risks they could face on the missions. According to stakeholder theory, it's clear that the managers of each company did not take into account the interests of its employees and thus morally wronged them.

In Space No One Can Hear You Scream

So far we have two different ways of evaluating the actions of the various iterations of Weyland Industries. One excuses the actions by eliminating employees from moral consideration. The other condemns the company for violating basic, stringent constraints on how to treat beings with FMS. But could there be a third option that recognizes the FMS of employees and yet would excuse the actions of the company? Tibor Machan (1939–2016), a libertarian, thinks so and focuses on employer–employee relationships as the result of freely chosen activities specified in a contract.[19] The employee agrees to provide labor for the employer in exchange for pay and benefits. As is pointed out in *Alien*, the crew of the *Nostromo* have each individually agreed to a contract that spells out the financial and other obligations of both parties. Libertarians usually assume that employers still have an obligation to disclose valuable information to employees, as would be true according to the stakeholder theory. When this is violated, the employee can take various actions in response to the discovery. Machan suggests leaving the firm, organizing and bargaining with the firm for improvements, or purchasing the firm.[20] Another option, pointed out by Denis Arnold, is to sue the firm. As Arnold explains, according to the libertarian view, "workers who do not sue their employers, and who do not quit their hazardous jobs, may be assumed to have weighed the relevant costs and benefits and decided that keeping the hazardous job was in their best interest."[21] Since none of the employees of any iteration of Weyland Industries in the films either sued or quit the job—the crew of the *Nostromo* could have foregone all their shares and not investigated LV-426, the crews of the other ships could've just refused to do their jobs after the briefings, and the people at Hadley's Hope could've returned to Earth—we must assume that following through on the contracts was accepted and so no moral wrongs were committed.

The problem with the libertarian attempt to find a middle ground is that in the *Alien* franchise some underlying libertarian assumptions are violated. One obvious assumption that is violated is that the employees, as individuals with FMS, have a right to full information about the nature of the jobs they are being offered. In the case of the crew of the *Nostromo*, the important information is deliberately hidden from them both before and during their mission. In the cases of the crews of the *Prometheus* and *Sulaco*, the information is withheld until it is effectively impossible for the crews to refuse to continue with the missions. This violation is tied to another key assumption that the libertarian is relying upon to explain the nature of employee–employer relationships. This assumption is that employees have at least one, if not both, of the strategies of "exit" and "voice" available to them, as understood by Albert Hirschman (1915–2012).[22] An exit strategy is carried out when a member of an organization leaves the organization. This might be illustrated through Parker and Brett willingly giving up their shares, or the crew of the *Sulaco* and *Prometheus* deciding to not commence their missions once the briefings have ended, or the residents of Hadley's Hope returning home. The use of "voice" occurs when the member makes known his or her "dissatisfaction directly to management or to some other authority to which management is subordinate or through general protest addressed to anyone who cares to listen."[23] In other words, the employees can go to management and complain; they can attempt to make their complaints known to regulatory agencies like Occupational Safety and Health Administration (OSHA), ask their union to bargain for changes in employer's actions, or sue the corporation. The only occurrence of the voice strategy in the films is Ripley yelling during the debriefing after she is rescued in *Aliens*.

The relationship between these two strategies when an employee is faced with upsetting or immoral practices of an organization is quite complicated. What is important here is that given the nature of the missions—in deep space with limited communication with either the company or the society at large—the employees have neither exit nor voice options. Despite Parker's protestations, he had no choice but to follow Dallas and the rest of the crew to LV-426. He couldn't have left the ship and his voice, as an employee who works below the rest of the crew both literally and figuratively, was ignored. Likewise, the crews of the *Sulaco* and *Prometheus* can't quit working for either the Weyland-Yutani Corporation or Weyland Corporation once they know about the nature of the mission—they're already on the ship with nowhere to go. The people of Hadley's Hope seem to have no means of leaving the planet. In each of these cases, the people are also cut off from the rest of society and political-legal infrastructure through limited communications across the vast distances of space. In other words, the employees have no ability to try to convince the company to change policy.

Here's what the libertarian attempt at finding a middle way misses: in the working situations found in the films, and perhaps more often in real life than is imagined by abstract models used to describe the behavior of employees, neither exit nor voice are truly available options. In order for a voice strategy to work, the threat of exit must be meaningful.[24] But consider the number of obstacles to making a threat of exit meaningful. If the local unemployment rate is high, then the employer knows that there are plenty of people willing to take the job without complaint and can ignore the complaint of the employee. If there are very few employers in an area or perhaps only one, then the employee has nowhere else to go for work. While there is always the *theoretical* possibility of looking for work globally, that possibility has many restrictions. A citizen of one country, especially if that citizen has few skills or limited education, is unlikely to be able to enter any other country to find work. Even if a person is able to leave one community for another in the same country, such a choice is risky. When a person does move, deep ties to family and community support are strained, possibly broken. These ties support individuals through difficult times created by economic or health issues that are not entirely controlled by individuals. When these real-world situations are considered, employee–employer relations are akin to a totalitarian regime in which "the absence of the possibility of either voice or exit spelled absolute control."[25] Going back to the fictional examples of the films, the fact that no one either quit working for the company once their mission began or pursued any voice strategies is not evidence that the employees willingly accepted their contract and all the consequences that came as a result of accepting. To have done so willingly, the crews must have been afforded both the exit and voice strategies. Since it is basically impossible to use the exit strategy in space, one also loses one's voice. In other words, in space no one can hear you scream.

This is Rumor Control. Here are the Facts!

There are at least three different theories we can use to evaluate how each iteration of Weyland Industries treats its employees in the *Alien* films.[26] These include stockholder theory, libertarian theories, and stakeholder theory. Stockholder theory condones the questionable behavior of corporate managers by treating employees as if they have no moral status and no moral considerability whatsoever. Since employees are not within the moral community, they are not owed information about the nature of the jobs and they do not have protections against unreasonable risks of injury, death, or being experimented upon by the employers. Employees have only instrumental value and are therefore expendable. In the case of libertarian theories, the employees do have moral status but libertarian assumptions about the way employee–employer relations work are violated. Most notably, the employees are unable to use the strategies of voice or exit to change the behavior of the employer. Thus, libertarian theories seem to allow immoral behavior by the employer whenever an employee remains on the job. By contrast, stakeholder theory both accords FMS to employees and recognizes that employer actions can violate the rights of employees regardless of whether an employee expresses dissatisfaction with the employment situation. While stakeholder theory is not without problems, as illustrated throughout the *Alien* franchise, only stakeholder theory makes sense of our intuition that Weyland Industries and its descendants are paradigmatic examples of a faceless, heartless, and soulless corporation, and that the way they treat their employees is morally wrong.[27]

Notes

1. "Discover New Worlds" from Weyland Industries, http://www.projectprometheus.com/newworlds/
2. Angela Allen, "How the 'Evil Corporation' Became a Pop-Culture Trope," *The Atlantic*, http://www.theatlantic.com/business/archive/2016/04/evil-corporation-trope/479295/ (accessed April 25, 2016), para. 1.
3. Ibid., para. 13.
4. Milton Friedman, "The Social Responsibility of Business Is to Increase Its Profits," in *Ethical Theory and Business*, eds. Tom L. Beauchamp and Norman E. Bowie (Pearson Prentice Hall, 2004), 51. This article was originally published in *New York Times Magazine*, September 13, 1970.
5. A.A. Berle, "Corporate Powers as Powers in Trust," *Harvard Law Review* 44 (1931): 1049.
6. Andrew L. Friedman and Samantha Miles, *Stakeholders: Theory and Practice* (Oxford University Press, 2006), 20.
7. For more on moral considerability, see James M. Okapal, "Of Battle Droids and Zillo Beasts: Moral Status in the Star Wars Galaxy," in *The Ultimate Star Wars and Philosophy: You Must Unlearn What You Have Learned*, eds. Jason T. Eberl and Kevin S. Decker (Wiley Blackwell, 2015), 183–192.
8. Agnieszka Jaworska and Julie Tannenbaum, "The Grounds of Moral Status," in *The Stanford Encyclopedia of Philosophy*, ed. Edward N. Zalta (Summer 2013 Edition).
9. Ibid., 3.
10. Ibid.
11. The first extensive attempt to develop such a theory was in R. Edward Freeman, *Strategic Management: A Stakeholder Approach* (Cambridge University Press, 1984). Since this time, there has been an explosion in research regarding stakeholder theory. See Friedman and Miles, *Stakeholders*, for an extensive overview of these developments of, as well as historical antecedents to, stakeholder theory since the publication of Freeman's book.
12. R. Edward Freeman, "A Stakeholder Theory of the Modern Corporation," in *Ethical Theory and Business*, eds. Tom L. Beauchamp and Norman E. Bowie (Pearson, 2004), 58.
13. Ibid., 56.
14. Ronald Duska, "Employee Rights," in *A Companion to Business Ethics*, ed. Robert E. Frederick (Blackwell, 2002), 262.
15. Ibid., 264.
16. Ibid., 265.
17. Denis G. Arnold, "Working Conditions: Safety and Sweatshops," in *The Oxford Handbook of Business Ethics*, ed. George G. Brenkert (Oxford University Press, 2009), 629.

18. Ibid., 630.

19. Tibor Machan, "Human Rights, Workers' Rights, and the 'Right' to Occupational Safety," in *Moral Rights in the Workplace*, ed. Gertrude Ezorsky (State University of New York Press, 1987). Machan lists the title of this article as "Rights and Myths in the Workplace" and it is sometimes referenced with this alternative title.

20. Ibid., 49.

21. Arnold, "Working Conditions," 633.

22. Albert O. Hirschman, *Exit, Voice, and Loyalty: Responses to Decline in Firms, Organizations, and States* (Harvard University Press, 1970).

23. Ibid., 4.

24. Ibid., 82.

25. Ibid., 83.

26. One interesting alternative way to evaluate the actions would be to use integrative social contracts theory. For an overview of this alternative see Thomas Donaldson and Thomas W. Dunfee, "Toward a Unified Conception of Business Ethics: Integrative Social Contracts Theory," *Academy of Management Review* 19.2 (1994): 252–284.

27. I'm grateful to Jeffrey Ewing, Kevin Decker, and William Irwin for the comments and corrections made to earlier drafts of this chapter.

Part II

ETHICS: "I DON'T KNOW WHICH SPECIES IS WORSE"

4

Disposable Assets: Weyland-Yutani's Special Brew of Business Ethics

Bruno de Brito Serra

In some developed nations—perhaps most famously, in the United States—corporations are today legally regarded as "people." But if that were literally true of the Weyland-Yutani Corporation in the *Alien* franchise, the least it would deserve is a swift left-hook to the jaw from Ripley and the few unfortunate bastards who survive with her in each of the movies. After all, as far as "the Company" is concerned, employees seem to have a moral status somewhere between slave and a thing in a petri-dish, useful only as means to an end—and disposed of afterwards without any sort of remorse.

Throughout the franchise, Weyland-Yutani's actions have been bad enough to force a change in our reaction to the phrase "the Company" whenever it pops up in dialogue. While its first mention in *Alien* is innocuous, in later films our reaction is likely, "Holy crap, is the Company involved here? What sort of evil, sadistic plot are they up to this time?" In fact, the Company can even be regarded as the true villain of the stories. They are the ones who always knowingly send people to kick the hornets' nest, while the hornets are mostly reacting to it with characteristic viciousness. Granted, the "hornets" in this case happen to be body-snatching Xenomorphs with acid for blood and a flair for dramatic murder, but the analogy still holds. In a sense, the Xenomorphs are just doing what's in their nasty biological nature, but the Company—comprised of people capable of moral thought—should know better than to systematically doom fellow human beings to a likely horrific demise.

Alien and Philosophy: I Infest, Therefore I Am, First Edition.
Edited by Jeffrey Ewing and Kevin S. Decker.
© 2017 John Wiley & Sons Ltd. Published 2017 by John Wiley & Sons Ltd.

Unless they shouldn't…because, at the end of the day, what they're doing might actually just be "good" business.

Greedy as a Space Pig

The question of what constitutes good business practices is, in a nut-shell, what business ethics is all about. Beyond this simple definition, however, things get a bit more complicated. First of all, what does "good" even mean in that sentence? Are we talking here about good in a *moral* sense (as in "I will not send employees to investigate a potentially dangerous alien ship under the assumption that they are expendable, because that is wrong")? Or is it meant in the *economic* sense (as in "I will use employees as disposable incubators for a potentially profitable alien species, because money, baby!")? More often than not, *profitable* business practices are treated as synony-mous with "good" business practices, which sort of makes sense: companies and corporations are, after all, founded assuming that they will produce profits for investors and shareholders. This fact, of course, does not automatically mean that such companies will always behave unethically in the pursuit of profit. It can, however, pose a serious ethical problem if the pursuit of profit comes to be regarded as something that must be done by any means necessary and *at any cost*. And it is precisely here that the moral sense of "good" factors into the equation.

Ethics, simply put, aims to give us tools to distinguish right from wrong. As any of us should know, this is hard enough to accomplish when you're trying to make a decision that only affects you or maybe a handful of other people. Business ethics, however, increases the scope of the question and makes it even more complex. The actions of a company as large and influential as Weyland-Yutani, for instance, will inevitably have an impact on thousands or even millions of people. Now, does that make it proportionally more important to correctly discern between right and wrong in business ethics? Arguably yes: the more lives a decision stands to affect, the more importance should be given to it. (There's a distinction between how *deontological* and *utili-tarian* ethics handle this, but we'll get into that in the final section.) Nevertheless, the fact that the scope of a decision like that is so much harder to grasp (can you really conceive of the consequences your action might have for a *million* people?) also leaves a door open for more "creative" interpretations of right and wrong.

To really understand these issues, let's make a quick detour through another iconic movie and one of those great characters everyone loves to hate: Gordon Gekko from 1987's *Wall Street*. For those of you not familiar with the movie, Gekko is a Wall Street financier during the 1980s who is (not so shockingly) involved in a lot of shady dealings. What interests us here, however, is a speech he delivers to morally justify his despicable conduct, summed up by one of the most iconic movie lines ever: "Greed, for lack of a better word, is good." At this point, I can almost hear those of you who never saw the movie ask, "What's Gekko getting at there? How the hell can greed be good?"

Gekko's argument is straightforward. Simply put, greed can be defined as a longing for more and better things. It drives us to get out of bed in the morning and work towards improving our lives. More importantly, from an evolutionary standpoint, greed is what motivated the human species to push forward, to achieve progress, and ultimately become the most advanced species on Earth. If greed provides us with so many advantages, it cannot be bad; and therefore it must be *good*.

Now, there are a lot of holes in this reasoning, but its significance lies in the fact that it seems to sum up Weyland-Yutani's worldview and understanding of business ethics throughout the *Alien* films. Profit is always the immediate goal. It is often stated that the company wants the Xenomorph so it can be studied by its bioweapons division (in *Alien*, *Aliens*, and *Alien³*), presumably in order to then market a packaged version of it to the highest bidder. But at the end of the day, because there are (luckily) very few people who are *totally* devoid of any sort of moral conscience, some pseudo-moral justification always enters the picture—for instance, a flimsy notion that progress in military technology always finds a way to trickle down to civilian applications, and thus will improve humanity's existence as a whole. (Bishop II's desperate plea for Ripley not to kill the Xenomorph she is carrying at the end of *Alien³*, asking her to "think of all we can learn from it," certainly hints at this sort of rationalization.) All in all, it would seem that "greed is good" is a mantra that can work in outer space as well as on Wall Street.

"I work for the Company, but I'm really an OK guy"

While we're on the topic of greed, the character of Carter Burke, skillfully played by Paul Reiser in 1986's *Aliens*, fulfills a crucial role beyond his contribution towards the advancement of the plot: he provides a face for our hatred of and disgust for "the Company." Burke is the quintessential corporate weasel, and in many ways it's almost as if Gordon Gekko was transported into science fiction. He begins by throwing Ripley to the wolves during the inquiries regarding the events of *Alien*, only to later blackmail her into accompanying the mission to investigate the fate of the settlers on LV-426. Constantly bitching about the monetary value of the installation, he even defends the moral duty to not exterminate an alien species that is clearly "important." And as the cherry on top, not only do we find out that he knowingly sent the settlers to their doom, but also that he released the surviving Facehuggers on Ripley and Newt as they slept. His motivation for all this? On his own admission, the millions that he could make by delivering the alien specimens back to the Company.

Now, don't get me wrong: Burke is a despicable person, dangerously close to (if not already embodying) the financial division psychopath deprived of a moral conscience that we alluded to earlier. But I can't help but feel that he, much like the characters of Ash and Mother in *Alien*, is there to represent Weyland-Yutani in a broader sense, high-lighting another one of the big problems concerning business ethics: *accountability*. You see, one of the key components of moral judgments is finding out whether or not there is someone who could—and should—be held accountable for the action being judged. It's a basic moral principle that if you do something that you couldn't help but do, if your free will and ability to make a decision were not at all involved in the action itself, then you shouldn't be held accountable for it. That's why the plea of insanity is used in all those cop shows. If you are insane, then you're presumably not *in complete control* of your body or your actions—and therefore shouldn't be held fully accountable for them.

Why does this matter for business ethics? Well, have you ever taken a call from a telemarketer? Being on the receiving end of a telemarketing call is pretty much a universally hated experience. If you've ever been there, you probably did one of two things: either you sat through entirely too much of what felt like a soul-crushing spiral of boredom, or you lost it, shouted some profanities into the phone, hung up, and then felt guilty about it sometime afterwards. In both those instances, there's usually a common theme. The reason *why* you sat through it or felt guilty about behaving like an angry fool tends to be the same: you realized that the person on the other end of the line was just doing their job, that they probably don't like it anymore than you do, and that they just do it to put food on the table. (If you're more imagi-natively masochistic, you might also imagine a sick granny or three hungry children, but I'll leave that up to you.)

If that is the case, however, a question still remains: who *can* you blame and get justifiably angry at for the harrowing experience of a telemarketing call? The supervisor at the call center? No, her job is not to target you specifically, just to make sure that the call-center operators are as efficient and professional as possible. The guy who writes the script for the operators? Nope, he's probably just an English major who couldn't find any other paying jobs. The owner of the call center? For all you know, she could be a hardworking single mother of two, who managed to rise in the competitive world of call centers despite everything she had to overcome—and all while trying to raise her children. Continuing along this line of reasoning, you'll probably just end up getting angry at an abstract idea and grudgingly muttering under your breath: "damn telemarketing...."

The problem of deferring accountability is unavoidable in any large company, and Weyland-Yutani is no exception. Of course, companies are made up of people, each of whom should be held accountable for their actions. But when a company is large enough that each employee just performs a very specific role, without having a complete understanding of the whole that their role contributes to, how can any of them be held accountable for the actions of the company itself? This problem can also be exploited by those who recognize it. Say an employee takes the initiative to do something he knows to be immoral—as Burke apparently did in *Aliens*. It's still possible to circumvent accountability on similar grounds. It's a shame that Burke cowered his way into karmic retribution at the hands of a Xenomorph before he had the chance to tell us some sob story about how "the corporate world is dog-eat-dog," how "if he didn't do it someone else would," or even "how the company forced his hand by making his job security depend on such projects." These would have been weak rationalizations, but not necessarily false ones. These rationalizations are clearly shown in *Alien*. There are several moments when the tragic fate of the crew could have been avoided, but ultimately they follow the orders of the company either because doing so would lead to a sizable bonus in their salary, or because doing the opposite would make the company dock their pay. The crew thus found themselves in a situation where the company held both the carrot and the stick, being herded down a different path than one they would've otherwise taken.

In such situations, you could, of course, try to attribute the responsibility to the company itself. But just think about the cases you're aware of when a big company is found to be at fault. What usually happens? And, in light of that, what do you think would've happened if Ripley went back to Earth after her many dealings with the company and proceeded to expose them to the press? In all likelihood, Weyland-Yutani would have found some scapegoat within its ranks—another Burke, his supervisor, his division—in order to sacrifice it in public, and, at the end of the day, keep the profits. Corporate accountability works both ways: the company can always argue that, due to the extensive dimensions of its operations across space and time, it cannot fully monitor *everything* that each of its many employees is doing. It can only—and usually does—vow to remove the guilty party and do a better job with supervision in the future.

In a sense, companies like Weyland-Yutani operate as *sentient machines*: they are built with the purpose of maximizing profits, their internal logic is one of cost–benefit analysis, and each of their components is geared towards fulfilling that purpose as efficiently as possible. Characters like Ash and Mother, as well as Burke (to a lesser degree), provide the most telling embodiment of the Company in the *Alien* franchise. What makes them such perfect antagonists is the fact that their thought processes transcend that of our heroes, not only in the qualitative sense—following cost–benefit considerations rather than moral ones—but also in terms of the framing of the problem—what we might call "seeing the bigger picture." This too is characteristic of a company that understands itself as living on *beyond* the people who comprise it at any given time, and therefore it must operate under different assumptions than they do.

Special Order 937—Crew Expendable

We've just said that Ash and Mother operate a cost–benefit form of reasoning, rather than subjecting their decisions to moral concerns. In *Alien*, Ash admits a certain admiration for the Xenomorph's existence free from any "delusions of morality," a feature that makes it a more "perfect" being than the humans he had been forced to blend in with. Cost–benefit reasoning, however, is not something completely foreign to the field of ethics.

As mentioned earlier, there are two major approaches to ethics that can help us to understand the extent to which cost–benefit reasoning is ethical. The first, defended and popularized by Immanuel Kant (1724–1804), is *deontology*. Deontology tends to deal in moral absolutes, identifying moral principles that are timelessly true—so much so that Kant, for instance, famously argued that it is *always* morally wrong to lie, even if an axe-wielding killer turns up at your doorstep asking the location of your loved ones. Lying even in this extreme scenario, he argues, would still be wrong, because if we determine that *everyone is allowed to lie whenever circumstances seem to call for it*, the world would eventually degenerate into an uninhabitable mess.

This is the sort of moral reasoning we sometimes see coming from people like Ripley and Bishop—who, despite being an android like Ash, had luckily been upgraded to feature something close to Isaac Asimov's "Three Laws of Robotics." As he explains to Ripley in *Aliens*, it is absolutely impossible for him to harm a human being or to allow a human being to be harmed by omission of action (something he clearly shows later in the movie, when he uses the surviving dropship to rescue Ripley, Hicks, and Newt rather than just save his own synthetic skin). In a nutshell, a deontologist would likely criticize Ash's behavior and Mother's "Special Order 937" on the grounds that it is always and absolutely wrong to cause the death of a human being, whether for profit, scientific advancement, or even to save another human being. For these reasons, deontologists don't accept cost–benefit reasoning as ethical.

The second major approach to ethics is *utilitarianism*, whose most famous early proponent was John Stuart Mill (1806–1873). Utilitarianism shies away from absolutes and demands that each situation be analyzed in terms of its predictable consequences. It deems morally right any decision that maximizes good consequences for the greatest number of people. In light of this, it's no surprise that utilitarianism lends itself to be interpreted (and often misinterpreted) as a sort of cost–benefit analysis. Let's not be too quick, though, to dismiss utilitarianism as the hallmark of evil androids (technically, they're amoral). In fact, our very own Ellen Ripley engages in utilitarian moral reasoning in *Alien* when Kane is brought back to the ship by Dallas and Lambert. While the latter are desperately trying to get Ripley to open the airlock in order to get Kane to the medbay, Ripley insists that quarantine must be enforced for the safety of the *Nostromo* and everyone else inside it—this is the greatest good for the greatest number. If Ash hadn't caught Ripley off-guard and opened the hatch himself, we would've been robbed of a great movie (and the remaining crew would've been spared horrible deaths).

Even though the central idea of utilitarianism can certainly be subverted to fit our own agenda—as was the case with the Gordon Gekko speech—it seems that it's not without merit after all. Ripley would be

willing to sacrifice one to save six. Most of us would probably agree
that is a sound decision to make (under the circumstances, at least).
But what about later in the movie, when Parker has a choice to fire the
flamethrower at the Xenomorph as it's holding Lambert? Ultimately,
he decides not to, presumably because he's not willing to also kill a
fellow crewmember in the process. But how would you choose in that
situation? Would you see Lambert as acceptable collateral damage to
save the rest of the crew? And, when it comes down to it, is your life
more important than anyone else's because it's your own?

Regardless of your answer to these questions, one thing is certain:
Weyland-Yutani regarded their employees as expendable, given the
possibility of securing a Xenomorph specimen. Was the reasoning
behind that utilitarian, and maybe even morally right at a level that
Ripley could not comprehend at the time? Let's be honest: probably
not. But it could be presented as such: we could, for instance, argue
that study of the Xenomorph would lead to breakthroughs in medicine and civilian applications that stood to benefit the lives of millions
or billions of people. Would the mere possibility of that be worth the
lives of Ripley and the people who met an untimely end throughout
the *Alien* franchise? What if the benefits were, in fact, a certainty?
Don't worry if you can't answer with absolute confidence; most philosophers can't either.

At the end of the day, what the story of *Alien* should teach us about
business ethics is that the latter *must* be a concern of ours. The point
of large companies like Weyland-Yutani is not to be morally good and
spread kindness; it's to make money and maximize profits. If they
operated in a vacuum without pressure from their employees or consumers, there would be absolutely no incentive, from a strictly busi-
ness-only standpoint, to harbor any kind of ethical concerns. As such,
it is also up to us, as citizens of a world in which such companies exist
and operate, to at the very least demand accountability and business
practices that conform to our sense of morality. Granted, that provides no guarantee that businesses will be ethical. But it's definitely
better than doing nothing at all. And, who knows, if companies that
behave unethically find their profit margins diminished by a popular
reaction against them, there might actually be a chance to persuade
them to at least try to care.

Alien is set in a science fiction universe, in which Weyland-Yutani's
far-reaching tentacles and evil agendas are obviously exaggerated for
dramatic effect. But considering that we already live in a world in
which corporate lobbies increasingly determine the nature of political

agendas, the lessons taught to us by "the Company" should ultimately boil down to a simple fact: if we don't take business ethics seriously, we may find ourselves living in an economic and social reality not unlike the one portrayed in *Alien* movies. And in that reality, even if we don't come across any particularly nasty Xenomorphs, we may nonetheless find ourselves quite familiar with the feeling of being ripped open from the inside out—namely, after reading the latest demand letter from our bank or insurance company.

5

Corporate Greed and Alien/ation: Marx vs. Weyland-Yutani

Alejandro Bárcenas

"You know, Burke, I don't know which species is worse.
You don't see them fucking each other over for a goddamn percentage."
—Ripley to Burke, *Aliens*

In *Aliens*, Ripley is miraculously rescued after drifting in space for fifty-seven years. Once she's recuperated from the long hypersleep and gets back to the routine of daily work, she spends the rest of her time at home, sitting by herself, in a tiny and messy apartment with a cigarette in her hand. The smoke rises slowly while she stares into the void. Contrary to all odds and in spite of losing the entire crew of the *Nostromo* to an aggressive alien, she's alive and well. She's brought news of the existence of a hostile and deadly species in order to warn both the Weyland-Yutani Corporation and, hopefully, humanity in general against trying to make contact with the Xenomorphs in space. She is working at the docks and getting her life back together again. So why does she feel lost—as if she has no purpose in life?

To Have and to Consume

Despite impressive technological developments, there is something that doesn't seem to have changed in the future of the *Alien* saga: capitalist society. Capitalism seems to have triumphed over other economic models and, as the author of the most sophisticated diagnosis

Alien and Philosophy: I Infest, Therefore I Am, First Edition.
Edited by Jeffrey Ewing and Kevin S. Decker.
© 2017 John Wiley & Sons Ltd. Published 2017 by John Wiley & Sons Ltd.

of the flaws of capitalism, Karl Marx (1818–1883), explained, the consequence of its triumph is that all of its problems and deficiencies are exacerbated. The capitalist mode of production—defined as unlimited accumulation of capital for its own sake—was largely triggered by one of the most important events in the history of humanity: the Industrial Revolution. As Marx and his longtime friend and collaborator Friedrich Engels (1820–1895) explained in the widely read *Communist Manifesto*, the Industrial Revolution and its new social class of bourgeoisie changed the old feudal world into a society with a capacity to produce without precedent in human history.[1]

At the time, the development of powerful steam tools generated a great deal of optimism. It was believed that modern technology would put an end to many dreadful jobs and, hence, bring a conclusion to centuries of abuse and exploitation. Slavery in particular would rapidly disappear, and the new era would finally bring about universal freedom from oppression. Marx did not share such optimism. He was among those who realized that, even though capitalism allowed for the construction of projects only imaginable in the past, it also brought along a dangerous element of dehumanization.

In the *Alien* films the worst tendencies of capitalism seem to drive the Weyland-Yutani Corporation's decisions, confirming Marx's fears that people would not be at the center of the process of capitalist production. It is clear the Weyland-Yutani Corporation has taken its goal of acquisition of profit at all costs very seriously, as demonstrated by Special Order 937. This is made explicit in *Alien* and *Alien*[3] in which people—the crew of the *Nostromo* and the prisoners and staff of penal colony Fury 161—are considered disposable if they get in the way of acquiring an alien form of life that could be studied for profitable military or biological applications. If greed is the main motivation for a corporation, Marx would not be surprised that the vast majority of their decisions would not have anything to do with the improvement of the quality of human life for its own sake. As a result, many of the characters in the *Alien* franchise display features of what Marx described as "alienation."

Alienation is one of Marx's key ideas. Like many elements of his philosophy, he developed and reconsidered it throughout his life. Here we will mainly focus on alienation as it is described in a series of notebooks written in 1857–1858, also known as the *Grundrisse*. The *Grundrisse* attracted a great deal of attention after their publication in the late 1930s because they serve as a window to Marx's creative process and some of his most interesting insights, such as what it means to live a good life. In those early studies, Marx realized that the capitalist system made people live a form of "alienated life" in which all passions and all activity are submerged in avarice.[2] As a consequence, workers only want to live in order to have and consume, and not because they are concerned with a life that fulfills their humanity. Their motivation is that of Parker, who asks in *Alien*, "and what about the money? If you wanna give me some money, I'll be happy to oblige." Alienation also might explain why in *Prometheus* the geologist Fifield tells Millburn, "I ain't here to be your friend. I'm here to make money." This kind of interaction is the effect, Marx explains, of a capitalist system in which people do not know how to relate with each other when a relationship is not aimed at the pursuit of profit. This is the predictable result when money is considered the only thing of value: it destroys what human relations are supposed to be. In other words, Fifield doesn't know how to "exchange love for love, trust for trust,"[3] as Marx wrote, but wishes to have a relationship only if it results in money. In Fifield's mind, no other relationships are worth pursuing, alienating himself in the process from his own humanity in order to seek an external thing.

Work: The Alien Plague

Marx explains that in a capitalist system "work is avoided like the plague."[4] This is no surprise because, Marx observes, when exploited workers toil for hours, their humanity is denied and they become the equivalent of machines. At work they have no space to actually have a life: they spend all their physical energy at work, while ruining their brains doing mindlessly repetitive jobs. Therefore, Marx concludes that workers are at home with themselves as human beings when they are *not* working, and when they *are* working, they are not at home with themselves as human beings.[5] Work of this kind ceases to be voluntary and becomes forced labor, according to Marx. Such work doesn't satisfy the need to become a fulfilled individual, but rather is only a *means* to try to satisfy other needs. Thus, Marx writes, "its alien character is obvious from the fact that as soon as no physical or other pressure exists, labor is avoided like the plague."[6] No wonder Pvt. Frost, after he is awakened from hypersleep upon the *Sulaco*'s arrival at LV-426, grumbles, "I hate this job!"

In the *Grundrisse*, Marx comes to the conclusion, based on insights from ancient Greek and Hellenistic philosophers, that the good life should be one of active self-realization and autonomy.[7] While that is the proper goal for every human being, the capitalist system offers the possibility of such a pursuit only to a few, those who have the free time, while denying it to the vast majority, who labor in ruinous ways. The *Grundrisse* also expands the way to understand alienation. For Marx, self-realization means individuals freely developing their particular talents, capacities, and abilities[8]—as, for example, certain pre-industrial artisans did. Alienation, though, produces the opposite of self-realization. Alienation results from a coercion to develop only those skills that are valued by the capitalist system. Furthermore, people are caught in a process that gives shape to their desires, while not understanding the origin of their desires. As a result, their own desires are alien to their unique individuality, and people lead frustrated lives.

In addition, the values that the capitalist system promotes revolve around a desire for consumption. Compulsive consumption fuels a longing for money, which ends up defining all human relations. Consequently, Marx writes, "people place in a thing (money) the faith which they do not place in each other."[9] The desire of money for its own sake and the exchange of activities and products for money transform relations from social connections between persons to relations mediated and defined by something alien to their nature: money. When a society is defined in such terms, that is, when "all values are measured in money,"[10] and not by considering the development of humanity itself as the goal of society, then the activity of commerce stands opposed and indifferent to and, therefore, alienated from individuals. Parker realizes this in *Alien* once he has become aware that the company has rescinded all priorities, including the preservation of life, because of greed. Feeling outraged, Parker complains to Ash, "The damn company! What about our lives, you son of a bitch?"

For Marx, this adds another feature to alienation: the disposability of the individual. Individuals are not special or considered important in themselves, but instead are treated as commodities that can be bought and sold.[11] As we've seen, in the state of alienation the person's capacities are not developed towards becoming a self-realized human being. That's because the capacities no longer belong to the worker, but are developed only to be inserted in the process of the production of capital. We see this in *Prometheus* when Vickers tells Dr. Shaw and Dr. Holloway, "I think there might be some confusion about our relationship." Vickers clarifies that Shaw and Holloway aren't on LV-223 to pursue their research agenda, and therefore they "will do nothing but report back to me." Since Shaw and Holloway did not pay for the operation to take place, Vickers announces, "that makes you an employee."

The Real Enemy: Pure Capitalists

Marx thought that the laws of capitalism could be conceived in their pure form, but he never used the specific term "pure capitalism."[12] Rather, he recognized that cultural and historical differences complicate the analysis of capitalism. Among the prominent scholars who analyzed the term "pure capitalism" are Rosa Luxemburg (1871–1919), who applied it to explain the eventual economic collapse of the capitalist system in her book *The Accumulation of Capital*, and Henryk Grossman (1881–1950), who used it in his *The Law of Accumulation and Collapse of the Capitalist System*, a work that was published in German right before the Stock Market Crash of 1929.[13]

For Marx, in spite of the different obstacles in the way of the actual practical application of a "pure" capitalist system, "it is nevertheless accomplished at an increasing degree with the advance of capitalist production and the subordination of all economic conditions under this mode of production."[14] Clearly, there are certain characters in the *Alien* films that seemed to represent what a "pure capitalist" might look like: someone only concerned with the interests of the Corporation regardless of the cost to human life.

One might think first of Carter Burke in *Aliens*, whose decisions are all based on preserving the value of the colony on LV-426 or on the profit he could gain by bringing the Xenomorphs back to Earth. But it is the android Ash in *Alien* who seems to be a manifestation of what the Corporation would like to have as their perfect capitalist operator. It is no surprise that Ash admires the Xenomorph for its "purity" and because it is "unclouded by conscience, remorse, or delusions of morality." He would like to mimic its ruthless way of acting so that he could rescind other priorities, such as human life, in order to carry out the orders of keeping the alien alive so that it could be used for commercial purposes. It is clear that the Corporation has tried to make humans blind to ethical choices by encouraging them to only follow orders that further the goals of the Corporation. As Captain Dallas says to Ripley, "standard procedure is to do what the hell they tell you to do." In other words, as Marx explains, because the ethics of political economy is acquisition, there arises a dichotomy, "Whom should I believe? Political economy or ethics?"[15] The alienation of individuals from their ethical consciousness happens because, in the words of Dallas, "that's what the company wants to happen." But how can a person make ethical choices if their life is solely dedicated to the accumulation of capital? What the Weyland-Yutani Corporation seems to have figured out is that the "pure capitalist" is someone with no conscience or remorse, and only someone, like Ash, who is not a human being could be that way.

The End of History?

The future depicted in the *Alien* films seems to support not Marx's prediction that the inherent contradictions of the capitalist system would make it unsustainable, but rather the prediction of the political scientist Francis Fukuyama. In his book *The End of History and the Last Man*, Fukuyama wrote that "the end point of mankind's ideological evolution" and "the logic of modern natural science would seem to dictate a universal evolution in the direction of capitalism."[16] Interestingly enough, the *Alien* films do not question the merits of Fukuyama's argument. Instead they assume its premises and design a future in which all of humanity will apparently live under some form or another of capitalism. Fukuyama's book, published originally in 1992—that is, after the fall of the Berlin Wall—was meant to address the traumatic experiences of the Soviet Union, China, and other highly centralized economies during the twentieth century by providing an alternative view of the times to come.

All of a sudden, after the collapse of the Soviet Union, Fukuyama's vision of the future appeared to come into existence. Capitalism showed itself to have triumphed as the only viable economic system on the world stage. But if the future takes the form of capitalism, then, as a consequence, its deficiencies and problems persist. This is where Marx's ideas have gained new relevance. Marx's comprehensive analysis continues to bring light to both the present—as has been recently shown by the best-selling French economist Thomas Piketty in his book *Capital in the Twenty-First Century*[17]—and the possible future depicted in the *Alien* films.

If the *Alien* films are correct, we might face a future ruled by ruthless corporations perpetuating alienation, perhaps relying on synthetics to carry out their goals in order to avoid the dichotomy between political economy and ethics. If that is the case, then the Weyland-Yutani Corporation will have won the fight concerning whether to have a society aimed at the pursuit of greed or a society aimed at the cultivation of humanity for its own sake. Let's just hope that perhaps the ghost of Marx will be haunting the spaceships of the future, fighting alienation with the help of Ripley.

Notes

1. Karl Marx and Friedrich Engels, *The Communist Manifesto* (Penguin, 2002), 222.
2. Robert C. Tucker, ed., *The Marx–Engels Reader* (W.W. Norton, 1978), 96.
3. David McLellan, ed., *Karl Marx: Selected Writings* (Oxford University Press, 2002), 119.
4. Lawrence H. Simon, ed., *Karl Marx: Selected Writings* (Hackett, 1994), 62.
5. McLellan, *Karl Marx*, 88.
6. Simon, *Karl Marx*, 62.
7. Jon Elster, ed., *Karl Marx: A Reader* (Cambridge University Press, 1986), 49.
8. Ibid., 54.
9. Ibid., 51.
10. Ibid.
11. Ibid., 61.
12. Karl Marx, *Capital: A Critique of Political Economy. Volume III: The Process of Capitalist Production as a Whole* (Kerr, 1909), 206.
13. For more on Marx's legacy, see Leszek Kołakowski, *The Main Currents of Marxism* (W.W. Norton, 2005).
14. Marx, *Capital*, 168–169.
15. Tucker, *The Marx–Engels Reader*, 97.
16. Francis Fukuyama, *The End of History and the Last Man* (Free Press, 2006), xv.
17. Thomas Piketty, *Capital in the Twenty-First Century* (Belknap, 2014). Published originally in French as *Le capital au XXIe siècle* (Seuil, 2013), the book addresses the question, based on data from two centuries, posted originally by Marx: "do the dynamics of private capital accumulation inevitably lead to the concentration of wealth in ever fewer hands?" Piketty, *Capital*, 1.

6

The Public and its Alien Problem

David Denneny

"It seems to me that the most widespread assumption of our time is that if a thing can be done, it must be done. This seems to me wholly false. The greatest examples of the action of the spirit and of reason are in abnegation."

—J.R.R. Tolkien[1]

Alien and its sequel *Aliens* pit small groups of humans against a foe that knows only violence. The constant presence of this single-minded, parasitoid adversary reveals something much more fundamental, though, than just the historical persistence of thoughtless, instinctive violence. Both films carry their horrified audiences toward the spectacle of social disintegration, from the destruction of small groups to that of the greater public at large. The Xenomorphs are nasty creatures, easy to blame, but both of these films ask us to consider who is *really* responsible for the mayhem. Political forces are at work behind the on-screen events, and most of the characters are ignorant of what truly affects their fates.

Actually, much of what goes wrong in these films is due to confused beliefs the characters hold. In this chapter, we'll use the approach of an American philosophical school of thought known as pragmatism, and its foremost defender John Dewey (1859–1952), to critically address this problem. Pragmatists insist that the actions we take are more important than the beliefs we hold. A belief, in fact, is only meaningful if it's a habit of action.[2] Pragmatists think that doubt creates inaction, so to cast off doubt, we focus on ways to move past doubt and so "fix" our beliefs. Belief in a proposition means that,

Alien and Philosophy: I Infest, Therefore I Am, First Edition.
Edited by Jeffrey Ewing and Kevin S. Decker.
© 2017 John Wiley & Sons Ltd. Published 2017 by John Wiley & Sons Ltd.

given the appropriate circumstances, we would act as though the proposition were true. If a belief makes no difference in our decision to act (or even *think*), then the belief means nothing at all.

Through *Alien* and *Aliens*, we can apply pragmatism to political philosophy, and in particular we can see how John Dewey's philosophy in *The Public and Its Problems* serves to illustrate the social and political failings we viscerally experience in these films.

Alien as Political Dystopia

First, let's take a look at *Alien*. Within its first fifteen minutes, we find the crew of the *Nostromo* debating whether they should investigate a distress call. The android, Ash, eventually interjects that "there is a clause in the contract etc. etc...." Ash's insistence on obeying rules and regulations trumps any further dialogue. This is how all the really important decisions will be made throughout much of the film: Ash's subtle yet overriding influence leads to Kane being let back on board after being attacked by the Facehugger. Even Ash's refusal to freeze the alien, and Kane with it, gives us the impression that Ash might not be the most competent resident scientist. It's obvious that *some* alternative measures could've been taken to remove the Facehugger without killing Kane. The crew, under Ash's guidance, even leaves Kane and his parasitoid alone for a short time. Ripley questions Ash's judgment, but Ash never provides any satisfactory explanations.

We later discover that Ash's mission was to recover an alien to study; the human crew of the *Nostromo* were officially "expendable." It seems that an indirect political force is orchestrating the events of this film. Thus, the most important "actor" or "character" in this movie is never seen by us or the crew, who are caught in an impersonal, political tidal wave. And the later films give us no reason to think things get any better in the *Alien* universe.

This dystopian future is something that John Dewey wanted desperately to avoid. In 1927, Dewey wrote *The Public and Its Problems*, a book that attempted to diagnose the most pressing dilemmas facing the American public. In fact, the political problems of Dewey's time are reminiscent of the problems encountered in the first two *Alien* movies. In *Public*, Dewey deals with many issues, including the role of expertise in politics and how mistaken beliefs about the role of science and economics in political life can ruin a democracy.

The crew of the *Nostromo* were victims of a political regime unable to control corporate interests that failed to fully assess both the direct and indirect consequences of their actions: people died, and horribly, as a result. In his own time, Dewey was forced to witness two world wars. The first of these was a war that revealed, more than anything, that "non-political forces" (for example, culture and the world economy) "are the expressions of a technological age injected into an inherited political scheme which operates to deflect and distort...[the] normal operation [of non-political forces]."[3] The political scheme of the *Alien* universe is equally unfit to contend with the injection of an unhealthy dose of Xenomorphs, especially considering that Weyland-Yutani was planning to study and use the Xenomorph in their bio-weapons division. Dewey was faced with a technologically advanced, mechanical form of warfare, while the crew of the *Nostromo* and the space marines were faced with a new kind of deadly organism.

What makes this scenario more challenging is that it's probably *not* true that there was a diabolical plot hatched by a handful of politically powerful individuals to use the *Nostromo* to retrieve the alien. Those who represent the interests of others, rarely, if ever, actually want to unleash forces that could threaten humanity as a whole (witness the success of Cold War détente and disarmament). It's easy to blame individuals, or small groups of people, for catastrophic events that no single group or individual could have foreseen. We know that the crew of the *Nostromo* and the space marines were under the governance of the "United Americas," a state comprised of the former nations of North, Central, and South America.[4] It's fair to surmise, given the facts on screen, that this was the political state that dealt with a potential threat to humanity in a haphazard manner that invited a Xenomorph getting loose amongst a large human population. The United Americas was only eighteen years old when the events of *Alien* took place, and it doesn't seem like this government has much control of the Weyland-Yutani Corporation. Yet, both the United Americas and Weyland-Yutani seem negligent in the extreme.

This diffusion of blame invites a common reaction from citizens of liberal democracies. When it seems impossible to point the finger of blame at someone in particular, it's often assumed that human nature must be to blame! Maybe it's human intuition that compels us to self-destruction? But these thoughts arise out of irrational desperation. Dewey rejects the appeal to human nature when he reminds us that "alleged instinct and natural endowment appealed to as a causal force themselves represent physical tendencies which have been shaped into habits of action and expectation by means of the very social conditions they are supposed to explain."[5] We are usually referring to socially ingrained habits, not something intrinsic and "natural," when we cling to the idea that our nature is to blame.

In fact, Dewey thinks our tendency to refer to "essences" or "natures" as the root of certain troubling phenomena is a holdover not from politics, but from a surprising source, Plato's theory of Forms. Thanks to Plato and his static world of Forms, our theory of knowledge is poorly suited to dealing with the real world of politics. In Dewey's words:

> the theory of knowledge has been systematically built up on the notion of a static universe, so that even those perfectly free to feel the lessons of physics and biology concerning moving energy and evolution, and of history concerning the constant transformation of man's affairs (science included), retain an unquestioning belief in a theory of knowledge which is out of any possible harmony with their own theory of the matters to be known.[6]

The idea of a static universe meshes well with a politically inflexible conservatism that can't respond constructively to new technologies like those unleashed in World War I (or newly discovered creatures like Xenomorphs, for that matter!).

Politics as a Science?

When trying to understand the roots of the political dystopia in *Alien* from a fresh perspective, one should first consider Dewey's suggestion that, "if one wishes to realize the distance which may lie between 'facts' and the meaning of facts,…one [should] go to the field of social discussion."[7] No dinner party is safe from the wildly disparate beliefs of the attendees regarding subjects like ethics, economics, religion, art, and other "cultural" subjects. This kind of discord is only manageable if we realize that the idea of a "pure science" of politics or society, just like the idea of a pure Form, is mistaken. The last testimony of Ash helps us understand why. As the android is dying, Ripley asks how to kill the alien, and Ash insists that "you can't…you still don't know what you're dealing with, do you? A perfect organism." Ash declares this with an air of objectivity baffling in its arrogance; he seems to be treating this subjective value judgment as though it's another scientific "fact" that the simpletons aboard the *Nostromo* just don't understand.

We make a similar mistake when we treat the findings of science as entirely removed from their social context. Science is always concerned with using *means* to secure *ends*, but acceptable means and ends are always wrapped up in values chosen from outside of the practice of science. This raises a contentious philosophical debate, but from the perspective of the pragmatist, it's one with serious political stakes. If the myth of "pure science" with certain conclusions is dispelled, then we can get on with removing the institutional barriers that exist between scientific knowledge and the culture at large. Dewey explains the situation poetically when he states:

> Man, in understanding of himself, has placed in his hands physical tools of incalculable power. He plays with them like a child, and whether they play harm or good is largely a matter of accident. The instrumentality becomes a master and works fatally as if possessed by a will of its own—not because it has a will but because man has not.[8]

It seems natural to us to make an observation about social facts (like poverty or racial tensions) and then proceed to *immediately* judge whether they are beneficial or harmful based on our personal, limited experience. But wider experience (and the scientific method) shows us that our judgments are more sound when their *consequences* are taken into account. A *consequence*, for Dewey, is much more than a mere objective causal connection. We decide to initiate certain consequences instead of others when they are seen as *meaningful* to us in relation to a larger web of values.

Personal, immediate judgments, while limited, are an essential starting point for deliberation. To the person who objects that we shouldn't bother assessing consequences, since there are potentially infinite consequences to our actions, two things could be said. First, we don't really know how far we can take our assessments of consequences until communities give it their best effort—remember, the pragmatist says we "cash out" our beliefs by taking action. Also, the point of assessing consequences is hypothesis creation. Better hypotheses do a better job of predicting consequences. We can either be at the mercy of chance, or we can focus on the meaning of the consequences in our overall experience that bring us closer to the goals the community would cherish.

So, the points of view of the individuals actually facing the aliens are most important when constructing a method to deal with the Xenomorphs. The "interests" of the crew members would be impossible to determine without looking at their nuanced, lived environment, and so taking into account everyone's interests must include the broader cultural context. Taking cultural meaning into account also entails the deliberate use of an intelligently applied method of problem solving that takes into account the interests of everyone affected. No single political aim, isolated from the broader cultural context, can be said to encompass all possible consequences. Yet Weyland-Yutani erases the *value* of the *Nostromo* crew's perspectives by conducting a crude cost–benefit analysis with their lives. The deaths of the crew members mean nothing, and not just in a sentimental sense, but in a literal sense as well. This erasure of the *meaning* of the lives of individuals is one of the symptoms of a state that can't direct political action in an intelligent and participatory manner. A disorganized government that lacks the institutions, resources, or even the ideas to provide an avenue for the public to have a voice can't necessarily be blamed for what it is structurally incapable of doing.

Such a government can only sit and watch as other, more focused, organized, and determined institutions, like Weyland-Yutani, drive forward in a limited way that only represents what Weyland-Yutani perceives to be their self-interest. The tragedy is that their so-called self-interest is so narrow that it hardly concerns itself with the public's dilemmas at all. This does nothing to help Weyland-Yutani's future security, and if they really assessed the consequences of their actions they would see that, despite making some immediate monetary gains, they are actually pulling the rug of shared cultural meanings out from under the public. The individual isolation that results will then almost certainly create discontent in the extreme among those separated from powerful, single-minded institutions like Weyland-Yutani.

For Dewey, a healthy state is formed to respond to the needs of *publics*: a "public consists of all those who are affected by the indirect consequences of transactions to such an extent that it is deemed necessary to have those consequences systematically cared for."[9] When the Weyland-Yutani Corporation, with the explicit backing of its national allies, sends employees and citizens to their doom without publicly acknowledging the consequences of these actions, the state, for all practical purposes, ceases to be a legitimate one, Dewey would say. For Dewey, the state's defining function is its ability to assess the indirect consequences of actions, via political, social, and economic research. It must then test through action hypotheses, based on social facts, ways to alleviate the worst effects of those consequences on the public. If the state fails in this capacity, it devolves into a mere collection of contending interest groups that can only be reactionary; it never can act as a genuine representative of the public.

Alien provides us with a picture of a governmental failure. Weyland-Yutani, with or without oversight from the United Americas, failed to assess the true threat that the alien presented. And the initiative to retrieve the alien was not conducted with the interests of the public in mind. In fact, it's hinted that the alien may be used as a weapon if successfully retrieved, even if this means sacrificing many of those whom the state ought to protect. Finally, Weyland-Yutani's decisions were "abstract" in the worst possible sense; that is, the decision to acquire the alien was based on aspirations that had no useful information about the aliens and their abilities. The lesson Dewey would take from this is that we ought to focus on refining our *methods* of problem solving and, at the same time, ensure that our ideas are in line with direct experiences of the objects of our study—that is, to confirm by experience, rather than rely on conjecture.

Furthermore, given that we know Weyland-Yutani, rather than the United Americas, made the calls in the first movie, it's highly likely that society in this movie is in the process of dissolving or already has dissolved. While blaming Weyland-Yutani entirely for the catastrophes of both movies would be valid, the Company seems to be merely filling the void left by a state that has already eliminated the public's ability to act collaboratively in its own defense against predatory corporations by using an intelligent method. Without intelligent political method, Weyland-Yutani will simply focus on doing what they do best: pursuing profit in a market economy. In the absence of other effective political social institutions, Weyland-Yutani's agenda could come to dominate the whole society. Of course, from the Company's perspective, they're acting in an organized, intelligent manner. The trouble is that no other social institutions seem to exist to give voice to the broader concerns of the public.

Weyland-Yutani's dominance is direct evidence of the state's failure. The United Americas exists to create and test social policies. If Weyland-Yutani decided to retrieve a Xenomorph for further military study (*definitely* a momentous political act) without government being part of the process, then it is clear that this government is ineffectual. Corporate interests are often pitted against the interests of the public at large (as we see in *Alien* and *Aliens*). But, if a state cannot leverage political authority over corporations in an intelligent way, or even mediate conflicts between corporate and public interests, then such a state is breaking down. The public will find a means to voice its ever more serious concerns, even if the result is violence.

Aliens: Transforming the Social into the Economic

By the time of *Aliens*, Carter Burke is a representative of the financial interests of Weyland-Yutani Corporation, and he clearly cares more about the financial stability of those he represents than the safety of those actually in contact with the aliens. Why is it that sometimes financial interests outweigh the value of human lives? The easy way out is to blame Burke and stop there. But again, the problem is deeper than that, Dewey tells us, pointing to the way human society has developed in the industrialized world:

> The newer forces [of industry] have created mobile and fluctuating associational forms. The common complaints of the disintegration of family life may be placed in evidence. The movement from rural to urban assemblies is also the result and proof of this mobility. Nothing stays long put, not even the associations by which business and industry are carried on. The mania for motion and speed is a symptom of the restless instability of social life, and it operates to intensify the causes from which it springs.[10]

Aliens presents us with a universe in which digital technology and space travel have increased the number of "mobile and fluctuating associational forms." But greater mobility also keeps people from forming meaningful attachments to others. When attachments are fleeting and serve narrow purposes, it soon becomes clearer why Carter Burke would forsake his peers for the good of his more stable relationship with the Corporation. A whole web of relationships provided Burke with vested interests that put him in his situation. For Dewey, the only antidote is to look for the consequences of often-subtle social forces, how they are created and sustained, and how they impact us all.

Earlier we saw that nonpolitical forces outstrip society's ability to rebuild itself. And so another serious problem relating to our mobile, industrial societies can be found in the claim that big business actually rules the political arena. Someone who believes that people like Burke will *always*, in every circumstance, use money to effectively control the levers of politics, believes in "economic determinism." But this is a position that's difficult to defend. Dewey reminds us that "most of those who hold these opinions [economic determinism] would profess to be shocked if the doctrine of economic determinism were argumentatively demonstrated to them, but they act upon a virtual belief in it."[11] The result? There is a chasm between the theories some people hold and what they practice. The values Burke holds inform him that profit is the supreme value. If pursuit of profit is held in the highest regard, then our political institutions and practices will reflect this. A belief that money inevitably controls our actions, especially our political actions, binds many people to the belief that profit is worth pursuing more than anything else, so we find ourselves in a vicious circle. Pursuit of profit held as the highest good leads to a social situation in which our institutions reflect this belief. Profit-driven institutions then perpetuate and reinforce this belief. And so the cycle goes on. The trick is to publicly assess the negative consequences of these beliefs, so we can more effectively address the influence of money in politics through institutional reform. Reforming our institutions is certainly more promising than falling back on blaming "human nature" for our big business troubles yet again!

The real source of belief that big business runs the whole show is a very popular, yet very outdated (and now destructive) idea of "individualism." Old-fashioned "rugged individualism" is, for Dewey, a relic of American pioneer culture.[12] The individualism of the past created a means for associating with one another that was effective in conquering nature and breaking down unnecessary traditional institutions (like monarchies and control by religion), but this old individualism is ill-suited to contemporary circumstances. We now live in a society in which individuals are defined by a narrow notion of financial success created (for most of us) by consumer influences. Dewey notes that "the chief obstacle to the creation of a type of individual whose pattern of thought and desire is enduringly marked by consensus with others, and in whom sociability is one with cooperation in all regular human associations, is the persistence of that feature of the earlier individualism which defines industry and commerce by ideas of private pecuniary profit."[13]

It is this mistaken, rustic individualism, tied to a money-driven concept of success, that produces the prejudice that a corporation is justified in its successes because of its owners' and shareholders' past activities or investments. In fact, freedom conceived solely as financial independence destroys all hope for harnessing methods for dealing with problems through cooperative political action. The fact is, Weyland-Yutani is trapped in this old "individualism" just like the rest of the public.

Recall that for a pragmatist, actions can be clues to habits of belief. The Weyland-Yutani Corporation, and the state it seems to effectively control, both behave as though the freedom of individuals is of little importance; they also act as if it's unimportant for those involved in a particular problem situation to be part of the decision-making process. So *no matter what* Weyland-Yutani and the state may claim, they do not hold a belief in principles of free enterprise, democracy, or self-determination. If Weyland-Yutani and the United Americas hold economic determinism as an ideal, they would undoubtedly treat such principles as negligible fictions anyway. Weyland-Yutani's real principles can only be found by observing their actions, a particularly important thing to remember when professed beliefs fail to coincide with actions taken.

If belief and action can't be so easily separated, we can see just how important it is to discover whether or not the economic determinist is mistaken. Dewey argues against economic determinism, saying, "For it is their belief that 'prosperity'—a word that has taken on a religious color—is the great need of the country, that they are its authors and guardians, and hence by right the determiners of polity."[14] The individualistic and money-driven belief in a destiny of prosperity (which is a *very* powerful belief in the United States today) can lead the public to hand control of the economy over to business interests. After all, why care when it's not in your control?

The power of big business and the ineffectiveness of the political system are actually symptoms of the diffusion and splintering of the public's political voice. It is the separation of the interests of the public from the political system, and the resulting apathy towards politics, that have increased capitalist power such that the necessity of economic domination is a plausible position for many. The fact that most individuals have such little influence in contemporary politics is a result of the way in which political institutions are organized. If the political process were more engaged in assessing the actual hopes and needs of individuals locally, and less with *manufacturing* hopes on a broad scale (usually by galvanizing the public through fear and sensationalism), we could find ourselves better able to tackle immediate problems in an intelligent way. The more elected representatives feel responsible for, and to, their electorate, the less alienated the public will feel.

Hope for the Future

The *Alien* universe, with its diabolical pact between the United Americas and the Weyland-Yutani Corporation, provides us with a worst-case scenario of the future. It doesn't look like the political machinery in that universe is much worse than our own, but we ought to recognize that better choices can be made to improve our situation. Institutional reform is necessary if the public is to find its voice again. Dewey insists that "governmental institutions are but a mechanism for securing to an idea [like democracy] channels of effective operation."[15] In the future, necessity may compel us to make more drastic institutional changes, but these changes must involve and be agreed to by more of us. This is because historically, "life has been impoverished, not by a predominance of 'society' in general over individuality, but by a domination of one form of association, [whether the] family, clan, church, economic institutions, over other actual and possible forms."[16] Our key task is to reorganize and reenergize channels for collaborative and collective effort to unlock the potential of as many individuals as possible. We can't do this by merely hearkening back to ideal "golden ages." Instead, we should think experimentally, make changes, assess their consequences, and move forward in a way that enriches the lives of individuals by giving them the opportunity to form many more meaningful, productive relationships.

Alien and *Aliens* tell us what we ought to avoid. Watching these two films is like witnessing what happens when our current political and ideological deficiencies are put to the test in a futuristic, doomsday-like environment. Yet we'll hopefully be better equipped than the crew of the USCSS *Nostromo*. Dewey's way forward is to recognize that "the problem of a democratically organized public is primarily and essentially an intellectual problem in a degree to which the political affairs of prior ages offer no parallel."[17] We have to reintegrate the public through institutions in order to dispel the apathy that leads to a dissolution of society like that of the *Alien* universe. The task is enormously difficult, but to say that the task is *impossible* is to believe in a static universe—that society's ideas cannot change. The Xenomorph is not the big bad enemy of the first two *Alien* movies. The enemy is our own ineffectual political forms. This is both comforting and disturbing. It's comforting because it places responsibility in our hands; it's disturbing because our concerted efforts, or lack thereof, are all that's left to blame.

Notes

1. J.R.R. Tolkien, April 1956 letter to Joanna de Bortadano, in *The Letters of J.R.R. Tolkien*, ed. Humphrey Carpenter (Houghton Mifflin, 2000), 246.

2. Charles Sanders Peirce contends that beliefs are habits of action in his influential essay "The Fixation of Belief," in *The Philosophical Writings of Peirce*, ed. Justus Buchler (Dover, 1955).

3. John Dewey, *The Public and Its Problems* (Swallow Press/Ohio University Press, 1954), 129, parentheses added.

4. This regime was founded in 2104 and the USCSS *Nostromo* was destroyed in an explosion in 2122. "United Americas," *Xenopedia*, http://avp.wikia.com/wiki/United_Americas.

5. Dewey, *The Public and Its Problems*, 10.

6. John Dewey, *The Philosophy of John Dewey*, ed. John J. McDermott (University of Chicago Press, 1981), 210.

7. Dewey, *The Public and Its Problems*, 3.

8. Ibid., 175.

9. Ibid., 15–16.

10. Ibid., 140.

11. Ibid., 118; parentheses added.

12. See Dewey, "Toward a New Individualism," in *The Philosophy of John Dewey*.

13. Ibid., 615.

14. Dewey, *The Public and Its Problems*, 118–119.

15. Ibid., 143; parentheses added.

16. Ibid., 194.

17. Dewey, *The Public and Its Problems*, 126.

Cross My Heart and Hope to Die: Why Ripley Must Save Newt

William A. Lindenmuth

Aliens concludes with a dilemma: how much should Ripley risk for Newt? In the previous film, she lost her crew, her ship, and cargo (worth $42,000,000 "in adjusted dollars") after being attacked by a creature "never recorded once in over 300 surveyed worlds." She is found adrift fifty-seven years later by a salvage crew. This trip out, the colony on planet LV-426 (Hadley's Hope) has been overrun by these creatures. The Marines sent to rescue them die one by one, and by the end, all that's left is an untrusted android, a wounded Marine, our scrappy protagonist, and a frightened little girl. Should Ripley risk the ship, everyone's lives, and the information about what's transpired to attempt to rescue one young colonist? Many philosophers would say no, claiming that "everybody [is] to count for one, nobody for more than one."[1] This would mean that no one is worth more than anyone else—I wouldn't ever be justified in looking out for my own child *instead of* another child I'm not related to, one who lives on the other side of the world.[2]

But don't you feel that your own loved ones deserve exceptional treatment? Do you think that any argument could convince you otherwise? Ripley doesn't. She made a promise, and intends to keep it. As we'll see, Ripley's exceptional treatment of Newt shows that the virtues of care and compassion should sometimes override universal rules of justice and fairness.

Alien and Philosophy: I Infest, Therefore I Am, First Edition.
Edited by Jeffrey Ewing and Kevin S. Decker.

"My name's 'Newt'"

Among the deleted scenes from the theatrical version of *Aliens* is a short sequence in which we learn about Ellen Ripley's daughter, Amanda. We see that the surprised, crushed, and devastated Ripley had promised to be home for Amanda's eleventh birthday...which took place fifty-seven years earlier. Amanda died childless, age sixty-six, two years before the events of *Aliens*. This explains why Ripley feels so connected and responsible to the only surviving colonist of Hadley's Hope, second-grader Rebecca Jorden, known as "Newt." We can surmise that Newt represents a stand-in for Ripley's deceased daughter and a second chance at motherhood.

The fact that director James Cameron chose to omit this scene, though, is interesting. Maybe he decided that Ripley's bond with Newt had to develop organically, and that presenting Ripley as a "failed" mother detracted from their relationship. Perhaps it made things too obvious. Regardless, moviegoers were left without it, and have had to understand the relationship between the surrogate mother and daughter on its own.

Left without this explanation, why does Ripley care and risk so much for Newt? The girl is young, innocent, and afraid. She's also the only person in *Aliens* who isn't on LV-426 by choice. Ripley promises the girl, who fears abandonment above all, that she won't leave her. But should everything be risked to save Newt's life?

"Those two specimens are worth millions to the bioweapons division"

In *Alien*, we find out that Ripley's unlucky blue-collar shipping crew have, unbeknownst to them, been sent to retrieve a new alien life-form. In *Aliens*, Ripley explains, "We set down there on company orders to get this thing [alien life-form], which destroyed my crew—and your expensive ship." Ripley had learned of this from reading a communiqué to the android science officer, Ash, from their corporate bosses. Ash's priority-one order is to return the organism for analysis, with "all other considerations secondary. Crew expendable." This is disheartening news. But from a cost–benefit perspective, the discovery of a new form of alien life—and all of the promise that discovery holds—*could* be worth a handful of lives.[3]

In one of the introductory scenes of *Aliens*, we see that the corporate heads of Weyland-Yutani don't believe Ripley's story and seem
disappointed about their loss of profit. In the time since, between
sixty and seventy families have been sent to terraform the LV-426,
"building better worlds." Only in another deleted scene do we see the
living colonists. Newt's family are shown as a "Mom and Pop survey
team," and we observe them in a sort of moon-buggy headed toward
the downed craft that carries the Xenomorph eggs. We see Newt and
her brother watching their parents enter the ship, and we hear Newt
let out a piercing scream when her mother abruptly returns and calls
for mayday as her husband lies immobilized and helpless with a
Facehugger clinging to him.

This scene was also cut. So, as viewers, we first meet Newt much
later in the film. Ripley is asked to return to the planet, as they've lost
track of the colony. She reluctantly returns on two conditions:
Lieutenant Gorman's "guarantee" of her safety, and the company representative Carter Burke's response to this query: "Just tell me one
thing, Burke. You're going out there to destroy them, right? Not to
study. Not to bring back. But to wipe them out." He answers, "That's
the plan. You have my word on it."

Jaws in Space

Given how *Alien* played out, we are meant to be on Ripley's side. But
can we imagine this scenario acted out in our modern world? Whether
it be people, an animal species, even a *virus*—we now hesitate to
"wipe out" anything. There's a tradition in rhetoric of presenting our
enemies as "too dangerous to be kept alive." But historically this has
been a perspective tied to racist, elitist, exclusivist worldviews, not the
pluralistic democracy we seem to be headed towards. These days we
tend to avoid saying that someone or something ought to be utterly
eradicated from existence.

Consider Steven Spielberg's *Jaws* (1975). The film portrayed sharks
as monsters, and so shark fishing and competitive tournaments became
popular. As a result, shark populations were decimated.[4] Eventually, a
backlash led to understanding and concern, study, and appreciation of
the feared beasts.[5] Not only for the maintenance of ecosystems, but
also for ecotourism, sharks are more valuable alive than dead.[6]
Regarding extinction, contemporary philosopher Peter Singer has
weighed in with the idea of "speciesism," that we can't treat one species

as inherently more valuable than others. Do humans hold the moral right to eliminate one species (say, wolves in rural regions of the west) because of their supposed threat to other species?

Alien, famously pitched as "*Jaws* in space,"[7] can certainly be seen as presenting a threat *much* different, and much more dangerous, than one great white shark. No one saw *Jaws* and became concerned that sharks would threaten the human race as a whole. *Jaws* simply warns, "Don't go in the water." By contrast, the Xenomorphs of *Aliens* seem not just adept at preying on us, but perhaps even engineered or evolved to do so (*Prometheus* and the future of the franchise have much more in store for us). At the debriefing in the beginning of *Aliens*, Ripley reports there are thousands of alien eggs on LV-426. She soon must shout over the objections of the corporate heads, "That's not all! Because if one of those things gets down here then that will be all, then all this [*grabs documents of proceedings*], this bullshit that you think is so important, you can just kiss all that goodbye."

If Ripley were given the option of simply pushing a button that would eliminate every last Xenomorph, she would push it without hesitation. Is this morally defensible? If the thinking was merely about comparing numbers, it would all be much simpler. The math suggests that if we could save five lives with one person's organs, we should harvest them, like it or not. But this is not an accepted practice. When it comes to other species, though, we often place our safety and comfort at a premium. If we want to eat a chicken sandwich, enjoy a vermin-free home, have our children play in a pest-free yard and our cats and dogs frolic in a neighborhood without coyotes, we must sacrifice members of other species. We wipe out wasps without a second thought—and isn't the eponymous race of *Aliens* like advanced, predatory wasps?

"A survivor"

Ash describes the alien in the first film as "A survivor...unclouded by conscience, remorse, or delusions of morality." Does this describe Ripley as well, doing whatever it takes to survive? In fact, she does something more: she *cares*. She cares about her cat, crew, job, duty, the colonists, the truth, the Marines, the mission, and, most importantly, her biological daughters. The alien Queen, though, also displays intelligence and care for her eggs. When Ripley destroys them, the Queen immediately sets out for revenge on Ripley. This is not so different from the motivation for Ripley's return to LV-426. As James Cameron explains in an interview: she's like a soldier returning to battle to work out her demons.[8] Ripley is shown to be vengeful towards Mother (the AI mainframe aboard the *Nostromo*), the Xenomorph in *Alien*, and the Queen in the sequel. All get called "bitch."

Towards the end of *Alien*, while preparing to destroy the ship and escape, Ripley goes after her cat, Jones, risking her life and those of the remaining crew to save it. This is caring, but is it also selfish or foolish?

"Standard procedure is to do what the hell they tell you to do"

To settle this, we should see what other sources of ethical wisdom offer themselves on the two missions. Besides Ripley, the crew of the *Nostromo* consists of the opportunistic Parker and Brett, who want to check out the distress call only if it adds to their paychecks; the terrified-of-everything Lambert; Kane, who sticks his head in an alien egg; the murderous android Ash, who relentlessly lies and deceives to get the alien back home; and Captain Dallas, who brings the alien aboard and makes one poor decision after another.

Aliens begins with the deep salvage team that finds Ripley and is disappointed she's alive: "Well, there goes our salvage, guys." The first sequel also gives us the ruthless Weyland-Yutani Corporation; the conniving, dishonest Burke; the overconfident, reckless, unsym-pathetic Marines (there to rescue "dumbass colonists"); and the inexperienced and opinionated Lieutenant Gorman. Compared to other protagonists, Ripley's never shown as extraordinary in any way except her resilience. She's pragmatic and a good leader, but she's never put in charge until the "proper" commanders are indis-posed—usually fatally. In *Alien*, third-in-command Ripley is ignored when she demands that quarantine procedures be followed before bringing the alien on board. Seeing the danger, she wants to destroy it rather than take it back for study.

In the second film, she again assists to eliminate the threat, but is not taken seriously and is neglected. "Look, man," PFC Jenette Vasquez says to her, "I only need to know *one* thing: where they are." Ripley confronts her: "Are you finished? I hope you're right. I really do..." At this point Gorman juts in, seemingly thinking that Ripley doesn't know how to talk to these people and he does. She interrupts his interruption and makes sure her voice—and *message*—get across. "Because just one of those things managed to wipe out my entire crew in less than twenty-four hours. And if the colonists have found that ship then there's no telling how many of them have been exposed. Do you understand?" She won't let Gorman represent her, or replace her voice.

"Why don't you put *her* in charge?"

In the next scene, Ripley demonstrates that she wants to contribute, and in one of the film's most memorable instances of the "Chekhov's gun" rule, adroitly operates a large robot power loader to their amusement and delight. Even in 2179, women showing physical prowess are still remarkable. It's only after saving the squad from the massacre in the processing station (where Gorman loses all control) that Ripley is able to wield more influence over the group. She suggests that they "take off and nuke the entire site from orbit," while Burke reminds them of the "substantial dollar value" attached to the colony, and that he cannot "authorize that kind of action." Ripley claims that Corporal Hicks is now in charge, and Hicks agrees with Ripley's plan, quoting her directly. He does this at other junctures in the film, and, after the destruction of the dropship, watches as Ripley runs the show. She calms the troops down, makes plans, and issues orders.

Soon after they're sealed in the compound, Hicks gives Ripley a locator that he can track. Clearly, Hicks cares about her.[9] But in the very next scene, Ripley gives it to Newt. Hicks cares about Ripley, and Ripley, believing she can handle herself, but also perhaps in an extension of caring, bestows it upon "her" little girl. After it becomes clear to Ripley just how deep Newt's fear of abandonment runs (she doesn't want Ripley to leave the room while she sleeps), she swears to her, "I'm not going to leave you, Newt. I mean that. That's a promise." "You promise?" Newt implores. "I cross my heart," Ripley responds, and they finish the oath together, "and hope to die." At this moment Newt embraces Ripley, and Ripley hugs Newt back, kissing her head. A bond is forged. Ripley has made a promise to never leave Newt, and intends to take it seriously. Is the fact that she singles Newt out for such a promise a sign that she's acting unjustly?

"You don't need me. I'm not a soldier"

Immanuel Kant (1724–1804) would have thought so; he argues that the application of morality must be impartial and universal. This means that moral duties apply to everyone equally, and that what applies in one situation applies in every similar situation. A proponent of utilitarianism, John Stuart Mill (1806–1873) says that morality requires us to be "as strictly impartial as a disinterested and benevolent spectator."[10] And James Rachels (1941–2003) says that impartiality "is at bottom nothing more than a rule against treating people arbitrarily. It forbids us from treating one person worse than another when there is no good reason to do so."[11] But aren't there good reasons sometimes to treat some differently from others? Is it odd that I'm more responsible for my children than I am for yours? If there were a sinking ship, each parent would first and foremost look out for the safety of their children. The idea that you could say "Please neglect your child to save mine instead" is ridiculous. Don't we look out for our friends and family in ways we do not for strangers or even neighbors? In many adventure films, the hero manages to save their family and other families as well, but real life is not like that. Our intentional bias is not for lack of time or interest, either: we can't, and don't *want*, to care for everyone the same way. Why would we think otherwise?

American psychologist Lawrence Kohlberg (1927–1987) helps us begin to understand why. His extensive research explored the moral development of children. He held that there were six stages of moral growth, starting when a child treats morality as little more than threats and rewards, leading up through a stage based on maintaining social relationships, to the sixth and final stage of morality: the duty to impartial, universal justice. One of Kohlberg's students, Carol Gilligan, saw that girls rarely "advanced" past the third stage. Females tended to focus on cooperation, sympathy, specificity, and care when dealing with moral issues, whereas males often thought in terms of abstract justice. Females rejected viewing cases as black and white, or seeing all topics as subject to universally applicable rules.

Females were not morally deficient in some way, unable to reach the morally superior sixth stage, Gilligan discovered. The problem was with the levels of Kohlberg's moral development scale itself. Justice, she observed is not always the most important thing, and perhaps partiality is appropriate in certain cases. Yes, many philosophers esteem justice and objective views, but just maybe it's because they are all *men*. Gilligan also came to see that girls were less assertive or aggressive about their views, being more willing to compromise and work things out. In her book *In a Different Voice*, she reasons, "Sensitivity to the needs of others and the assumption of responsibility for taking care lead women to attend to voices other than their own and to include in their judgement other points of view."[12] Gilligan argued that these realities don't imply weakness or wrongness, just a different form of moral expression. A *care-based ethic* simply emphasizes different qualities than traditional ethical stances, like those held by Kant, Mill, and Rachels. Care ethics gives priority to benevolence, relationships, mercy, and family. For Gilligan, the ideal ethical authority is not an impartial judge, but a loving mother.

"Oh, yeah. Sure. With those things running around?"

It's important to note that Gilligan is describing female moral *dispositions*, and not inherent qualities of women. She doesn't say that men could *not* think this way, or that *all* women do. Rather, she discovered a moral voice that had not been much heard historically—like Ellen Ripley's—despite its validity. In *Aliens*, Vasquez is portrayed as having traditionally masculine traits: she is bellicose, uncompromising, competitive, stubborn, and honor-focused. While these traits contribute to her toughness, they don't win in the bad-to-worse situation that is LV-426. By contrast, Ripley's realism, practical thinking, and care win the others over and eventually run the show.

Consider how Newt and Ripley problem solve their way out of an almost impossible situation, locked in a room with two Facehuggers. While cuddling Newt, Ripley spots the empty containers. After quickly ascertaining the situation, she alerts Newt without any fanfare, "Newt, wake up. Be quiet! We're in trouble." She reaches for her gun, but it's not there. She flips the bed onto the attacking creature and creates distance, while swinging Newt towards the door. It doesn't open, so she tries to pry it open. Then she attempts to get the attention of the team through the CCTV, which Burke turns off. Newt's suggestion to break the glass doesn't work. She finally comes up with the idea to use her lighter to set off the sprinkler and therefore the fire alarm, which gets the Marines headed their way. One could argue that this is what anyone would do, but it's another authoritative example of Ripley using openness and flexibility to get through a situation, and of protecting her ward. Compare this with the "Eek, a mouse!" trope about women from earlier motion pictures. This is a far cry from the beginning of the film, when she is overlooked and not taken seriously. Ripley has to demonstrate that she can navigate this male-dominated world better than they can. It is fitting that the aliens are ruled by a queen with no king; a significant point of these films is that stereotypically female qualities are what contribute to survival.

Ripley is constantly thinking of alternatives and compromises, and this isn't just because she's a woman. She is clearly not comfortable around guns (she jumps when Hicks pumps a grenade launcher), but learns how to use one anyway: "OK. What do I do?" In this situation, she's demonstrating not just practicality, but also sensitivity to Hicks and the desire to build a relationship with him. When Gorman can't act, she takes matters into her own hands and saves the team. When there is a threat of an overload after the dropship crashes, she comes up with another solution. After the crash, Hudson sees fit—as he so often does—to remind everyone how they are going to die. Ripley reminds him about Newt's very different strategy for enduring: "This little girl survived longer than that with no weapons and no training...Hudson, just deal with it because we need you and I'm sick of your bullshit." It seems as if Hudson cannot fathom a response that doesn't feature open combat. When that fails them, he sees no other alternative. Ripley instead emphasizes the importance of working together. An important aspect of care ethics is that caring reminds us how dependent we are on one another, as opposed to the stress laid on individual autonomy that deontological ethicists like Kant make. Care ethicist Nel Noddings states, "The approach through law and principle is not the approach of the mother. It is the approach of the detached one, of the father."[13]

Contrast the leadership styles of Gorman and Ripley. His emphasis on the mission impedes his ability to see the individuals he depends on. Ripley cares about people, relationships, and what's happening in front of her; it's only that intimate concern that allows her to succeed. Because Gorman doesn't see the team as a family, he doesn't even bother to learn their names. He's the soldier and commanding officer, she's the civilian; their behavior indicates otherwise.

"I don't want to hear about it, Bishop. She's alive. There's still time!"

Elizabeth Hirschman says this about Ripley:

> The character of Ripley actually stands in opposition to two evil foes: a violent, predatory space monster that devours human life and an inhumane, profiteering corporation that is willing to sacrifice people for money. Ripley—an androgynous female figure—is depicted in the narrative as the appropriate choice to overcome both evils. She is courageous and intelligent enough to defeat the monster; she is also compassionate and sufficiently moral to resist the lures of material gain.[14]

Ripley also has another function: being a loving parent. Loving parents don't do what they do out of a sense of duty, nor are they impartial. They are partial and caring about their children. Some moral thinkers, like Gilligan and Noddings, have put forth the notion that it's precisely this kind of nurturing and attentive relationship that is the cornerstone of ethics. They claim that morality isn't based on abstract principles or commands that hold regardless of person or place. Instead, the ethics of care prioritizes the particular identities, roles, and relationships involved.[15]

Noddings explains in *Caring: A Feminine Approach to Ethics and Moral Education* that living only by rules hewn in stone that apply always and everywhere is a good way to misrepresent a situation, and a deficient and neglectful way to help us navigate the specificity of ethical decisions. Ethics is complicated—why, then, are we interested in abstracting from the things that help us make more informed decisions? Who is involved, why, how, and what are the relationships to be considered? As Gilligan points out, it is a gift that females tend to be more attentive to these sorts of things, rather than a weakness and deficiency to be corrected by stereotypically masculine considerations that are hypothetical and removed.

Newt is not Ripley's biological child, but does this make a difference, morally speaking? Ripley has taken on the mantle of motherhood and made a promise. The sole survivor of a destroyed world, Newt has no one else, and Ripley, the lone survivor of a distant past, likewise has no one to care for. Noddings describes the fundamentals of a caring relationship as between the "carer" (one caring) and the "cared for," the person receiving the care. This relationship requires three things: the carer caring for the cared for, the carer acting on this, and the cared for being aware of this.[16] Ripley and Newt embody this perfectly.

Ripley's deep care for Newt is not a case of justice; it's not based on Newt's ability to "pay it back." It's not conditional, and Newt never even asks for it. In fact, she didn't want to be "rescued" in the first place. She resisted the Marines taking her in, biting Hicks in the process, and Ripley had to grab her to calm her down. Ripley asks her, "Don't you think you'd be safer here with us?" She shakes her head. "These people are here to protect you. They're soldiers." "It won't make any difference," Newt replies. All the machismo, machines, and weapons don't make Newt feel safe or even human. Only the love of someone who would duct-tape two guns together and go down into the hive with nineteen minutes to spare can do that. "I knew you'd come," she tells Ripley after they escape the planet. Newt acknowledges the care through a type of recognition Noddings characterizes as "completed in the other."[17]

Not Bad, for a [Wo]man

Ripley is going to save Newt whether she likes it or not. Philosophers love to consider "trolley problems," in which one must choose whether or not to throw a switch that would divert an out-of-control trolley speeding toward five people to travel down another track, killing one instead. On paper, it's reasonable to hit the switch, because saving more lives is superior to fewer lives. But what if the one person to be killed was your child? Does that make the whole rationale go out the window? Or do you save your child, and "reason, impartiality, and universality" be damned? The very same person who writes off the lives of two Marines who are still alive, but "cocooned just like the others," seemingly can reject that way of thinking when it comes to a little girl, *her* little girl. Can you imagine the film with Ripley *not* going back for Newt? Although the subsequent films don't emphasize this, part of the power of *Aliens* is that it's important that Ripley has something to live for other than herself, and that safety and redemption are possible. Suffice it to say, whether or not certain philosophers would think Ripley made the right choice, filmmakers and moviegoers do. Nel Noddings would argue that to not save Newt would, in fact, be *evil*. As she says in *Caring*, if "one intentionally rejects the impulse to care and deliberately turns her back on the ethical, she is evil, and this evil cannot be redeemed."[18]

"My mommy always said there were no monsters, but there are," Newt says. "Yes, there are." Ripley is forced to admit. "Why do they tell little kids that?" Newt asks. "Most of the time it's true," Ripley replies, and straps a locator on Newt's wrist. She is the embodiment of ultimate value to Ripley, representing almost everything good there is to live for. Knowing Newt, caring about Newt, Ripley would rather die than let anything bad happen to her. The powerful point of *Aliens* is that this is not a moral failing or lack of consideration, but a deep commitment and serious decision. Ripley's oath to rescue Newt is specific, and it is partial. But it's not *wrong*. There *are* monsters, and the only way we can sleep is if we know Mom and Dad will stop at nothing to protect us from them.

Notes

1. John Stuart Mill, *Utilitarianism*, http://www.gutenberg.org/files/11224/11224-h/11224-h.htm.
2. For another perspective on this, consider Peter Singer's drowning child example, found here: http://www.utilitarian.net/singer/by/199704--.htm.
3. Indeed, a utilitarian philosopher like Jeremy Bentham, who famously said in defense of animals "The question is not, Can they reason? nor Can they talk? but, Can they suffer?," might use this to argue for the rights of the aliens to exist. We only have the example of the alien queen, but she *clearly* suffers when Ripley destroys her eggs. Jeremy Bentham, *An Introduction to the Principles of Morals and Legislation* (Clarendon Press, 1907), note 122.
4. Stefan Lovgren, "'Jaws' at 30: Film Stoked Fear, Study of Great White Sharks," http://news.nationalgeographic.com/news/2005/06/0615_050615_jawssharks.html.
5. Nancy Knowlton and Wendy Benchley, "The State of Sharks, 40 Years After *Jaws*," http://www.smithsonianmag.com/science-nature/state-sharks-40-years-after-jaws-180952309/?no-ist.
6. Denise Chow, "Why Sharks Generate More Money Alive Than Dead," http://www.livescience.com/37048-shark-economic-value.html.
7. Matthew Hays, "A Space Odyssey," https://web.archive.org/web/20080905074007/http://www.montrealmirror.com/ARCHIVES/2003/102303/film1.html.
8. Randy Lofficier, "Interview with James Cameron and Gale Ann Hurd on *Aliens*," http://www.lofficier.com/cameron.htm.
9. He's also the only person other than Ripley to show care for Newt. He says, "Don't touch that. It's dangerous, honey," when she reaches for a grenade. In another scene, she is trying to see while they are collected around a table-top map. While Burke seems almost repulsed by her, Hicks helps her to sit on and get off the high table. In fact, she could be

dead without him. When the Marines first encounter her, Drake fires (thinking her a threat), and it's Hicks who leans into him to cause him to miss. In the script Drake remarks, "Let her go, man. Who cares?"

10. Mill, *Utilitarianism*, http://www.gutenberg.org/files/11224/11224-h/11224-h.htm.

11. James Rachels, *The Elements of Moral Philosophy*, sixth edition (McGraw-Hill, 2010), 13.

12. Carol Gilligan, *In a Different Voice* (Harvard University Press, 1982), 16.

13. Nel Noddings, *Caring: A Feminine Approach to Ethics and Moral Education* (University of California Press, 1984), 2.

14. Elizabeth C. Hirschman, "Consumer Behavior Meets the Nouvelle Femme: Feminist Consumption At the Movies," *Advances in Consumer Research* 20 (1993): 41–47, http://www.acrwebsite.org/volumes/9834/volumes/v20/NA-20.

15. For example, take the "original position," as argued by John Rawls, who thinks that fairness and justice have to be gauged by an impartial, uninvolved, and rational spectator.

16. Nel Noddings, *Starting at Home: Caring and Social Policy* (University of California Press, 2002), 19.

17. Noddings, *Caring*, 4.

18. Ibid., 115.

Part III

MORAL PSYCHOLOGY: "UNCLOUDED BY CONSCIENCE, REMORSE, OR DELUSIONS OF MORTALITY"

Nuking the Colony to Save It: Colonial Marines and Just Wars

Louis Melançon

Whether you call it LV-426 or Acheron, it's a desolate, ugly hunk of rock. When its atmosphere processing plant's fusion reactor exploded, it turned it into a desolate, ugly, *irradiated* hunk of rock uninhabitable by humans for thousands of years. This did not improve property values. The explosion itself can be considered a *force majeure* (well, maybe a *deus ex machina*), but it wasn't far off from what the surviving humans in *Aliens* were planning anyway: nuke the site from orbit. After all, this is the only way to be sure the Xenomorphs don't survive. But for purposes of a philosophical thought experiment, let's adjust the script a smidge: after the initial fight the surviving humans withdraw to the *Sulaco* without further incident. Once on board, they shoot everything that will explode down the gravity well until LV-426 becomes glass. That makes boring cinema (because it eliminates dramatic conflicts), but it also raises a question: in a conflict, is it morally acceptable to "go nuclear," or is there value to demonstrating restraint? As with most things in life, the answer varies with whom you ask. If you asked the Engineers, they would rip your head off. So they don't see value in demonstrating restraint. But that's not the only perspective out there.

When Aliens Stop Being Polite

To set the stage for considering the military decisions of Colonial Marines from an ethical perspective, strap in like it's a simulated

Alien and Philosophy: I Infest, Therefore I Am, First Edition.
Edited by Jeffrey Ewing and Kevin S. Decker.

combat drop from low orbit because we're going to bounce around through time. Before looking at the *Aliens* future of the twenty-second century, we need to stop by the fifth century BCE at another rock: the Aegean island of Melos. Back in the day, Athens and Sparta had some problems with each other known as the Peloponnesian War. Consider it the original East Coast/West Coast feud. One of its incidents involved Athenian troops rolling up to Melos and demanding that the Melians not only ally with Athens against Sparta but also pay for the privilege of doing so. The Melians saw themselves as kin to Spartans, yet wanted to be neutral in this entire beef. Thucydides (460–400 BCE), recognizing the importance of this event, left us the Melian dialogue, a dramatization of the negotiations. His record contains the famous line, "the strong do what they will, the weak do what they must."[1] This is the core of *political realism*.

In political realism, power is what matters. Power keeps you alive; it allows you to do what you want or need to do. If you don't have it, you need it; if you have some, you want more; eventually, in competition with others, you want more than anyone else.

Being a very astute reader you're probably thinking, "Hey, political realism is based on the existence of states, groups of humans in a political setting. But what we see in the Alienverse are, mostly, acts of individuals." You make a valid point, so let's make an assumption that can carry this issue. Although we see individual creepy creatures with acid for blood, ten-foot-tall weirdos with snow white tans, and scared humans, let's consider each group a state and the actions of the individuals as emblematic of the society and state they represent. Take the Engineers: they clearly have an advanced society with language, art, and music. Oh, and interstellar space ships! Can't forget that. We can think of them as a state. Same goes for the Xenomorphs; they form some sort of society, even if it's one that humans have difficulty recognizing or understanding.[2] Don't get me wrong, they are dangerous, terrifying, killing machines; but they aren't *mindless* killing machines. They use tools, and they cooperate and communicate among themselves. Let's consider them another state. Finally, it shouldn't matter much if they're a colonist, Marine, or a Weyland-Yutani corporate yes-man: the humans can be lumped into a monolithic group for ease of consideration.

Swapping "strong" Athenians and "weak" Melians for our three futuristic states, the Engineers are the strong; they do what they want. I'm not just talking about ripping off the head of an android who pulled you out of the stasis chamber (have a little empathy, who hasn't been cranky when abruptly awoken from a REALLY good nap?).

Let's take it to a larger scale. As we saw in *Prometheus*, the Engineers spurred the creation of mankind. Yet two thousand years before mankind achieved space flight, the Engineers were getting ready to wipe the Earth clean with some gnarly biological weapons. Why do that when there was no threat? The answer is simple: because they could.

The Xenos are realists too. From the human perspective, it seems like the Xenos are the strong. But maybe they perceive themselves as the weak, a perception that might drive their actions. After all, it looks like their first concern is survival: every time Xenos encounter a different form of life they are greeted with bullets or fire. And some screaming. First contact encounters, from the Xeno perspective, are high-threat environments, so engaging with violence has a very low threshold of risk. Sure they kill a lot, I mean a LOT, but it's not indiscriminate. They preserve and select some humans as incubators, eliminate high-threat individuals, and although we don't see it, likely kill for food (can we agree the Xenos probably aren't vegans?). The Xenos are aggressive because, on some level, they know that if they are not they'll be destroyed. That's the mindset of the weak doing what they must to survive.

For humans, it's a dangerous, scary galaxy out there beyond the third planet in the Sol system, so there's no question about being weak. They are surrounded on all sides by stronger creatures with no compunction about doing whatever they want or feel they need to do. If you're one of the *Nostromo* crew and you run into Xenos, you get away however you can. If you're Meredith Vickers, you turn a crew member who's been exposed to Engineer black goo into a Human Torch cosplay. You do whatever it takes to survive.

It might seem then that realism is an amoral position, but that's not entirely accurate. Within all the varieties of realism, there's room for ethical and moral considerations in making decisions. It's just that those considerations can't hinder the preservation of one's own security or power. The difficulty comes when people (or Engineers, or Xenos) lose sight of that and begin to conflate realism and its goal of survival with war and pure destruction for destruction's sake. The Melians understood this and tried to point it out to the Athenians. By allowing Melos to remain neutral, the Melians argued, the Athenians wouldn't really be losing anything from their alliance. But destroying Melos would show the rest of the Greeks that the Athenians were jerks. Athens didn't listen, and in the end they slaughtered or enslaved the Melians. In *Aliens*, we see the same kind of conflicts happening in the back of the armored personnel carrier (APC) on LV-426.

The Burkian Dialogue

After the first tragic encounter with the Xenos in *Aliens*, the remaining humans are trying to figure out their next steps in the back of the APC. Everybody left is in a pretty bad state, damaged either physically, emotionally, or both. Things went horribly wrong: ambushed by Xenos leading to cook offs (thermal ammunition explosions), heavy injuries, and most of the Marines dead or missing. What on screen is a significant emotional debate becomes, from the perspective of this chapter, a look into the decision-making process of one of our states (you rarely get to see this in the real world). A few active options are discussed: rolling in nerve gas, nuking the site from orbit, changing into clean underwear. Ok, that last one wasn't mentioned but, come on, don't we all suspect that Hudson soiled himself? Just a little bit?

Hudson, recognizing that they just got their butts kicked, suggests that the humans leave and call it even. This suggestion has a pretty good realist grounding: it acknowledges that one party is stronger than the other, and that the best way to stay alive and intact is to get away as fast as possible. This represents the opposite side of the Melian coin: although the Marines are, ironically, not in the position of strength, realism claims there is value in not fighting, at least in this case.

At this point Burke (slimy, slimy Burke) steps in with the following suggestion: "This is an emotional moment for all of us, I know that. But let's not make snap judgments. This is clearly an important species we're dealing with and I don't think you or I have a right to arbitrarily exterminate them."

Wow, Burke is trying to talk people away from the genocidal ledge! Is he suddenly developing a conscience? Not really. His first line of argument is as welcome as a goodnight kiss from a Facehugger: "This installation has a substantial dollar value attached to it." Then, being slimy but clever, he shifts his appeal to the ethical fiber of the other humans: humans don't have the inherent right to deprive the Xenos of their lives, scary as they may be, if they're not actively seeking to kill the humans. Burke is appealing to the notion that humans want to do more than just survive. From a position like this, there seems to be definite value in fighting in certain ways and not others. Let's take a look at that perspective to see if a tension with realism actually exists, and how this might impact the folks debating in the APC.

Still Searching for Answers

Should a sentient species seek more than just survival? It sure seems that we, together with the humans on the planets LV-223 and LV-246, think we should. The motivations behind the *Prometheus* expedition explicitly reflect this, asking why we were created and finding, if possible, a way of staving off the decay of time. It didn't work out so well for that crew, but as Dr. Shaw said in the final log entry, she's "still searching for answers." If survival alone isn't sufficient, our Xeno, human, and Engineer states would need to consider things like whether actions are just or unjust, warranted or unwarranted. Luckily for us, this has been debated for thousands of years. Hang on tight, our dropship is about to bounce back in time.

Over the past few thousand years in the west, philosophers have developed the just war tradition (JWT).[3] Cicero (106–44 BCE), Thomas Aquinas (1225–1274), Hugo Grotius (1583–1645), and many others have contributed to this line of thought over the centuries. We should consider the JWT as a series of compromises between different perspectives, including legal and theological concerns, deontological and utilitarian stances, and differences between the views of Thomas Hobbes (1599–1679) and John Locke (1632–1704) on the state of nature. This idea of ongoing compromises, especially those between followers of Hobbes and Locke, is really useful in highlighting an important, if invisible, assumption about humankind and the organized violence that is war. The assumption is that war generates an overriding need for survival, but it's not the natural state of human relations. As the price of existence, we may be engaged in constant struggle, but not all struggle is violence, and not all violence is war.

This line of thought suggests that we, as sentient beings, should seek to rise above this slide into violent conflict, but sometimes this violence occurs despite our best efforts. Sometimes we must even initiate that violence on behalf of others. If it must occur, then JWT claims to set limits so that a combatant's actions are right and just, even in the midst of violence. The hope is that the current war will not turn into the reason for the next conflict.

Keeping to just actions in war isn't all that hard to do by applying principles of JWT. There are two sets of criteria: one set that, if held to, ensures that a state enters a war justly, and the other set that can ensure that a state conducts themselves justly in a war.[4] It's this second set that's important to our warring states of Engineers, Xenos, and humans. It consists of a handful of sub-criteria about how military actions should (a) distinguish between combatants and noncombatants, (b) be militarily necessary for achieving your goals, and (c) be proportional in the sense of measuring the harm and damage from fighting against the military advantage generated by the action. In short, this set of criteria with the fancy name of *jus in bello* is about fighting well, which often means that combatants restrain themselves from fighting in certain ways. Let's flesh this out a bit more by examining these sub-criteria in greater detail.

A good place to start is with discrimination, distinguishing between combatants and noncombatants. We can boil it down to a simple question: is the person (or persons) on the business end of that gun, extending inner jaw, or flamethrower, an armed belligerent, otherwise known as a combatant? This matters because unarmed civilians, noncombatants, have a right to not be attacked. Of course it's not all fancy free for noncombatants. They have a corresponding duty to refrain from taking up arms unless in direct, immediate self-defense. Outside of self-defense, they lose this right if they take up arms. Combatants don't have that option; they can be attacked at any time.[5] So a belligerent must discern between combatants and noncombatants and make the appropriate choice to pull the literal or figurative trigger. You might be thinking, "hang on a tic, what if combatants and noncombatants are mixed, like a bunch of cocooned colonists surrounded by Xenos? Does this mean that a combatant can't act?" Not exactly. We still have two other sub-criteria to consider, and we have to see how they interact.

The two remaining sub-criteria of proportionality and military necessity are heavily intertwined, and it makes sense to look at them at the same time rather than independently. Proportionality speaks to using the right amount of force for the situation. A Marine doesn't use an M41 Pulse Rifle to take out a pesky mosquito. Sure you'll get the mosquito, but the damage to your walls will be much more than was bargained for. Maybe you convert your spaceship into a nuclear-powered flying bomb to take down another spaceship that is headed to Earth. As that's the only thing that can reasonably bring success, that's probably the right amount of force. Military necessity speaks to ensuring that the effects of this action further your own goals. The closer you can get to your goals, the sooner the conflict can be resolved in your favor. Does bombing part of the colony allow you to delay the Xenos trying to munch on colonists so that some can be evacuated? Or are the dropship pilots just bored? Do they just want to watch something explode? Both of these sub-criteria arrive at a common point, albeit from slightly different directions: don't do something that in itself is evil or can't be justified. Think in terms of torture, genocide, or using a weapon simply to cause excess pain and suffering rather than achieving your goal.

Back to the issue of combatants and noncombatants in close proximity: even though noncombatants can be distinguished, an action may also be necessary and proportional. That means it is likely some noncombatants will be killed. In modern parlance, this is "collateral damage." If these deaths and damages are foreseeable, how is discrimination not violated? The sub-criteria are now intertwined and what matters is how the combatant seeks to mitigate and satisfy each as much as possible. Let's say there's a key bridge that would prevent an opponent from resupplying its armed forces, but civilians also use the bridge for food and trade. The ability to prevent the opponent's armed forces from resupplying would bring the war to a swift end with fewer deaths of both combatants and noncombatants. Thus military necessity and proportionality are satisfied. Using a precision weapon would make sure that civilian casualties are minimal, which speaks to proportionality and discrimination. Attacking when civilian traffic tends to not be on the bridge, say midnight as opposed to rush hour, would also help for both proportionality and discrimination. Good faith efforts are made to satisfy each sub-criterion as much as possible. On the opposite side of the coin, when a combatant doesn't seek to address a sub-criterion, all sub-criteria tend to become unfulfilled. A real-world example is probably in order.

From Vietnam to Space

When a combatant starts to lose sight of these *jus in bello* criteria, like Ripley and the Marine survivors in the APC, the overall justness of their effort can start to unwind in a less than productive way. Let's take a dropship hop to the twentieth century: in 1968, the United States was involved in a conflict in Vietnam. That year saw a major event, the Tet Offensive, conducted by the Viet Cong and North Vietnamese Army. Many cities, towns, and villages became battlegrounds as the various combatants sought to gain or retain control of these population centers. Ben Tre was one of those towns. American forces retaking the town basically flattened it by using heavy artillery and aerial bombing. In a press conference about this action, a United States Army representative stated that "it became necessary to destroy the town to save it."[6] Was this a poor choice of words? Undoubtedly. Flawed logic? Without a doubt. Unjust behavior in the just war tradition? If you answered yes, you win a prize.

Let's highlight just military necessity and proportionality right now. How does the destruction of the town, in terms of both lives and property, lead to achieving US goals in Vietnam? Was the widespread bombardment of the town by artillery and aircraft necessary to regain control? It's hard to find a logical path that can justify the actions as they occurred in terms of either sub-criterion. The lack of attention to either unravels both, and it was likely, although we aren't going to look at it here, that discrimination wasn't satisfied either.

This leads to a key point about JWT: a combatant must satisfy all the sub-criteria, all the time, if their presence in the conflict is to be considered just. When you lose the bubble on a single sub-criterion, odds are you'll start to lose the bubble on others. But more significantly, the justness of your entire position comes into question. JWT generally and *jus in bello* specifically are "all or nothing" propositions. If a combatant cannot conduct a war justly, the combatant's presence in the war becomes unjustified and the likelihood of justly achieving goals drops drastically.

If you can't establish a logical pathway to explain how an action is necessary to get you closer to your own goals, and would be done in a proportional manner, you probably shouldn't take the action. You compromise your justness by abandoning *jus in bello*, and this may actually hurt your chances of achieving your larger security goals. Think back to political realism where the logic for an action was to improve your security. It seems the tension between JWT and political realism is somewhat moot. They both reach the same conclusion: if an action does not further your security goals, or worse yet actually harms them, then neither realism nor JWT can back it up. Taking an action simply because you can, often doesn't turn out so well. Ask a fifth-century BCE Athenian or the US Army in Vietnam for their experiences with that (spoiler alert: not so great).

There were a lot of issues souring domestic opinion in the United States about Vietnam. We can't say Ben Tre was the straw that broke the camel's back, but it certainly didn't help matters. Instances like these make citizens of states start to ask things like, "Is this the type of thing we want done in our name? Is this what we, as a society, value?" There are implications that stem from how those questions get answered. Strap in, we're bouncing back to LV-426!

Easing Back on the APC's Throttle

The American political theorist Michael Walzer asks us to consider a "supreme emergency," such as an existential danger of unusual and horrifying depths. This is the kind of danger that might let the survivors in the APC slide a bit on *jus in bello* principles. Almost everyone in the APC considers themselves to be in existential danger. Seven-foot-tall creatures that don't show up on infrared, have acid for blood, and seemingly pop out of the walls? Let's put a big check mark next to unusual and horrifying. But Walzer specifies that a supreme emergency needs to be both dangerous *and* imminent. The danger has to be in the here and now.

In most cases, danger and imminence are distinct characteristics of a situation. You can have danger without imminence and, conversely, you can have imminence without real danger. But not so when talking about Xenos. The Xenos are an interesting case because the immediacy of the danger is directly related to their proximity. A human needs to be within scaly armed reach, or at least leaping range. When they are close, imminence is high and danger goes through the roof. When the Xeno threat is distant, imminence is low, and danger drops close to nil.

Many of the ideas being tossed around in the APC (even slimy Burke's) keep the Xenos distant and so actually reduce the threat, backing the humans away from the need to make decisions in a "supreme emergency." What would Vasquez's nerve gas or Ripley's proposal to nuke the colony really accomplish? A little vengeance, a cathartic release, sure, but no real benefit to ensuring their survival. These direct engagements don't make the humans any stronger out in the universe, so Ripley's and Vasquez's plans can't claim a lineage to realism. They are born out of fear and are an attempt to mimic a realist position, but they don't quite hit the mark. They go beyond what realism, much less JWT, would call for once the danger is no longer clear and present. The humans are mistakenly conflating survival with destruction for destruction's sake.

If the humans wanted to be realists, they'd just leave. If the humans wanted to consider themselves better than merely being survivors, they'd simply leave. The folks in the APC might need to take a step back from the breathless considerations. Hudson and Burke, though stumbling ass-over-butt into it, actually come up with a solution that fits both realism and JWT. It's very tempting to use whatever strength you have in a situation to strike out at what you perceive to be a threat, especially when you're weak. Advocates of actions like these may claim the mantle of realism, but realism doesn't support absolutely *anything*. Though it may seem like realism and JWT would have significant tensions and reach different conclusions, this isn't always the case. There are times when they can be quite complementary and can help steer us away from just lashing out. A little something to consider the next time you're walking around on the surface of LV-426.

Notes

1. Thucydides, *The Peloponnesian War*, trans. Richard Crawley (Modern Library, 1982), 351.
2. Scott Camazine et al., *Self-Organization in Biological Systems* (Princeton University Press, 2001), 16–18.
3. Or just war theory if you're wearing a lab coat. Jokes aside, either label is considered acceptable.
4. There's a third criteria, *jus post bellum*, currently being debated about ensuring states end wars justly, but that's a relatively new development, spearheaded by Brian Orend. Orend's *The Morality of War* (Broadview Press, 2006) is the perfect place to begin exploring this debate.
5. There are exceptions, of course, such as combatants who are wounded, or surrendering, etc. But we're painting with broad strokes here.
6. "Major Describes Move," *The New York Times*, February 8, 1968, 14.

Xenomorphs and the Benefits of Exposure to Violence as Education

Adam Barkman and Sabina Tokbergenova

What parent doesn't want the best for their children? Parents try to get the best clothes, food, toys, education, and other essentials for them. Everyone agrees that it is important to meet children's needs. However, when it comes to the question of the proper way of raising a child, people often have very different opinions. In particular, it is important to know whether or not children should be exposed to violent media. Nowadays, many parents want to limit their children's exposure to violence, believing it is harmful to them. As we'll see, though, violence in video games and movies can be beneficial for children, making them mentally tougher and preparing them for a difficult life with stressful situations.

The Greek philosopher Plato (*c.349–c.*327 BCE) would have agreed that violent media should not be completely avoided. In the *Republic*, he depicts Socrates as arguing that men and women should take children to war so that they can observe and act as their apprentices.[1] *Aliens* validates Socrates in its depiction of Newt, a perfect example of how violence can shape a child into a strong and rational person.

Hadley's Hope and Plato's Republic

Before going into the details of how violence was beneficial to Newt, it's essential to note that the colony in *Aliens*, Hadley's Hope, resembles in *some* ways Socrates' ideal state. In *Republic*, Socrates proposes

Alien and Philosophy: I Infest, Therefore I Am, First Edition.
Edited by Jeffrey Ewing and Kevin S. Decker.
© 2017 John Wiley & Sons Ltd. Published 2017 by John Wiley & Sons Ltd.

to sketch out an ideal republic, so he can determine what role justice plays in the lives of people. Socrates divides his just society into three classes: the producers, the auxiliaries, and the guardians. The producing class is the largest class in society; it includes all professions other than warriors and rulers. The auxiliaries are warriors, and they are responsible for defending the city from invaders. The guardians are responsible for ruling the city. They are chosen from among the ranks of the auxiliaries, and raised according to a strict program of education that emphasizes physical fitness, honor, and wisdom.

When Socrates imagines his ideal society, the Republic appears isolated, away from the other people who do not belong in the community. In *Aliens*, Hadley's Hope colony is on the lonely planet Acheron, isolated from other civilization. Hadley's Hope colony was fairly small; it consisted of 158 workers (60–70 families) and focused on research and mining. The colony's main function was ensuring the continued operation and maintenance of the nearby atmosphere processing plant, which made the planetoid's atmosphere breathable. By processing the planetoid's atmosphere, they were trying to create a suitable environment for large-scale human habitation. Sadly, the planet's surface was an unpleasant place, racked by savage winds and severe storms. The surrounding atmosphere of Acheron was dreary— no trees or flowers to please the eye, only sharp rocks. Although Socrates' state is not as dispirited as this planet, it still appears to be an unpleasant place to live due to its strict rules. The colonists' children do not know any other way of living because they were born in the harsh conditions of the planet, just as Socrates' citizens only know one way of existence according to their class structures. Similar to the citizens of Socrates' society, the people of Hadley's Hope have particular roles to play in order to coexist on the bitter planet. Most importantly, in many ways, Newt might represent a child of the guardian class.

Newt the Apprentice Guardian

Socrates says that male and female auxiliaries should take sturdy children with them to war. These children will be young apprentice guardians; they have to observe and participate in warfare as much as possible.[2] Newt resembles an apprentice guardian and Ripley is like her auxiliary supervisor during the battle with the Xenomorphs. Newt always keeps close to Ripley, even when the aliens attack them, and in this way she observes the war like an apprentice guardian. Newt assists the Colonial Marines in fortifying the administration building where she can, helping them carry equipment and move supplies. Although the little girl does not wield a weapon, she manages to stay alive, unlike many of the armed soldiers. Newt is brave enough to face the Xenomorphs and the violence around her when Ripley and the other soldiers are fighting them.

Additionally, Newt is a kind of combatant in the battle. When Ripley and Newt are sleeping inside the colony's med lab, Carter Burke releases the live Facehuggers before sealing the door to the room. Burke hopes to impregnate the two females to smuggle live Xenomorphs through quarantine and back to Earth. In this terrifying situation, Newt was capable of protecting herself. She was wise to hide under the bed, and when a Facehugger attacked her she was not helpless. She fought it bravely, keeping it at arm's length. Newt also participates when observing the challenging map of the colony complex along with Ripley and Corporal Hicks. She does not solely depend on adults the way most children do. Rather, she strives to learn the useful information herself, so she can rely on her own knowledge as well.

Part of what makes Newt an excellent apprentice guardian is that she displays reason and intelligence in all of these situations. For example, when Ripley and the soldiers first find her, Newt understands that she's not safe with them. Most children would have felt safer if they were in the presence of the adults, but Newt wisely realizes that she should not immediately trust them and their ability to protect her. Indeed, Newt's smarts enable her to not just keep herself alive, but also to protect others. In the final scenes of the movie, she and Ripley are trying to escape the hive after finding the Xenomorph Queen. During this event, Newt warns Ripley of the Xenomorph behind her, saving Ripley's life. A courageous—indeed, guardian-like—act, to be sure.

For her part, Ripley is a good guide and attendant for her little apprentice guardian. In *Republic*, Socrates admits that it can be dangerous for children to observe and participate in war because something could go wrong and they could be hurt or killed. Consequently, these children need auxiliary supervisors. The auxiliary supervisors, in their responsibility for the safety of their children, should know all that can humanly be known about warfare, and they should be able to distinguish risky military ventures from safe ones.[3] Ripley qualifies as a great supervisor for these two reasons. She knows a lot about the war with the Xenomorphs, which is why she was taken to Acheron in the first place. She also knows when the military venture is too risky. When the rest of the colonists are tracked to the atmosphere processing plant, Ripley and Newt accompany the Colonial Marines to investigate, remaining inside their APC while the troops move into the building. Ripley observes the HUDs of the troops on the computer inside the APC, and, anticipating something horrible, asks Newt not to look because she anticipates a horrifying view of the cocooned people impregnated with the Chestbursters. Newt's father was impregnated with a Chestburster and died because of it, so Newt would have reexperienced agonizing memories of her father's death if she had not looked away. Thus, Ripley recognizes when Newt can handle the situation and when she might be too traumatized by it.

In these situations and others, Ripley protects her young apprentice guardian, thus demonstrating what Socrates would describe as her responsibility for Newt. Yet in so doing, Ripley never disregards Newt as someone who is too small or insignificant, or someone who simply needs to be protected. Ripley—not to mention Corporal Hicks—is aware of Newt's great survival skills and strength.

Still, Socrates realizes that auxiliary supervisors might not be enough for children's safety. He suggests that young apprentice guardians should be equipped with the fastest horses so that they could escape if they had to. Even though Newt did not have a horse, she expertly used the ventilation ducts to quickly hide and run away.

Newt is Hardened Like an Egg

Now it's time to investigate how violence has made Newt mentally tough. It is clear that Newt has gone through a lot on the planet Acheron. She has lost her family and has surreptitiously observed the Xenomorphs by hiding in the extensive ventilation system, building a den near the operation center. By enduring all this violence, Newt has become less sensitive to frightening situations. In fact, she is much calmer than the soldiers around her, and by remaining calm Newt is capable of using her reason to save herself and the others. She was the only one who remained calm in the APC during the Xenomorph attack. After the creatures ambushed the Marines inside the hive, Newt and the survivors escaped the area and planned to evacuate. However, their dropship was destroyed by the Xenomorphs and its crew was killed, stranding the survivors on the dangerous planet. In the aftermath of the crash, everyone panicked except for the little girl. While the adults were screaming in despair, unsure what to do next, Newt was the only one who remained calm and did not give up, telling the survivors that the Xenomorphs mostly came out at night and that they should return to the relative safety of the operations building.

This scene reveals that Newt was the only rationally-in-control person during the dreadful situation. When everyone followed Newt's advice and came back to the operations building, Ripley asked Corporal Hicks how much time they would have to wait until they would get rescued. Upon finding out that they would have to wait seventeen days on Acheron, Private Hudson starts to panic, complaining that they won't last that long. While Hudson hysterically wastes his time on useless griping and regret, Newt remains composed. This scene proves that mental instability and inability to calm down can be fatal. It is pathetic to see a strong man instantly giving up and breaking down while a little girl sits calmly and tries to think of possible ways to survive. Indeed, Ripley points out that it's foolish to think that they cannot survive seventeen hours when little Newt survived for many days alone and unarmed.

In real life, many people behave like Hudson when they are faced with stressful situations. Their inability to remain calm and try to solve the problem at hand shows not merely a moment of weakness, but a character framed by mental weakness. This is why it's important, Plato stresses, to start preparing people for a challenging life from an early age. There is an old folk saying with which Plato would likely agree: "The same boiling water that softens potatoes, hardens eggs. It is all about what you are made of, not your circumstances." Parents should help their children become strong, so they can face any circumstance in life, as in *Aliens* when Newt was able to save Ripley and Corporal Hicks by leading them out through the ventilation ducts during a Xenomorph attack at the operations center. Without Newt's help, Ripley and Hicks would've been killed by the Xenomorphs or lost in the ventilation ducts. If Newt did not have the ability to remain calm in desperate and dangerous situations, she could not have found the correct way in the ventilation system—people are rarely capable of thinking rationally when they panic. Indeed, even when the little girl herself is knocked down a shaft by an explosion into the colony's sewers, she doesn't panic, but bravely waits for Ripley to save her.

Another benefit of Newt's experience of horror and violence is that she is not ashamed to admit when she feels scared. She expresses her fears to Ripley in the scene where they are trapped in the medical facility with the Facehuggers. She still remains calm and reasonable when she's scared, for being afraid is one thing and being *controlled by fear* is another. Plato would have been proud of Newt because he says that courage does not simply mean fearlessness. Rather, courage is a sort of retention of what reason dictates. To put it another way, courage is the ability to "retain under all circumstances a true and lawful notion about what is and is not to be feared."[4] For example, it is better not to fear death as much as one fears being a coward. Courage involves keeping this disposition intact and not losing it whether one is experiencing pain or pleasure. Newt is under the influence of pain (danger) in this particular scene; however, she keeps intact her knowledge of what she must really fear, thus remaining calm and reasonable. She likely understands that she must really be afraid of panicking because panic often causes wildly unthinking behavior, which is never helpful. Consequently, courage helps Newt endure obstacles and not fear death. Newt admits her fear, but she is still courageous because she is confident in the face of fear.

Furthermore, exposure to violence has gifted Newt with quick reactions. When Ripley orders her to run, fight, or hide, Newt is quick to obey. For example, in the scene where the second dropship (with Newt, Ripley, Hicks, and Bishop) lands back aboard the *Sulaco*, the Xenomorph Queen is revealed to have stowed away in the dropship's landing gear and moves towards Newt to attack her. Ripley orders Newt to run, and she quickly follows her command by hiding beneath the floor grating in the *Sulaco*'s hangar bay. Had Newt frozen in horror, she would have died. It is vital for children to have quick reactions like Newt because it is possible that they may find themselves one day in a life-threatening situation. For example, if there is a fire in the child's house, or an angry dog gives them chase, it's important that the child listen to their parents' orders and act quickly. Otherwise, it could be fatal for them. It is conceivable, then, that violent movies and video games make children less prone to be scared in dangerous circumstances, and, if this is true, they would more likely survive the threat instead of freezing in terror.

Should Your Child Watch *Aliens*?

Of course, there are many parents who prohibit all forms of violent media for their children. They might claim that they fear their child might imitate cartoon or movie violence and behave aggressively. While it is true that children can learn aggressive behavior from television, many psychologists would agree with Plato that parents (or the child's guardians) have tremendous power to moderate that influence. Parents should play games and watch movies and the news with their children. For school-age kids and teenagers, parents should use these times as an opportunity to talk with them about their reactions to what they see on TV, the impact on them, and whether they get scared after playing or watching media. It's good to start such discussions early in a child's life and keep an ongoing, open dialogue about these issues. People shouldn't be afraid of on-screen violence, but rather of not talking about it with their children. The key to preventing children from imitating a violent behavior is to teach them about the meaning of the messages put out by the media: that is, parents should define the difference between violence in reality and violence in video games or films. As long as children can differentiate the violence portrayed in media from violence in real life, they are less likely to imitate negative, aggressive behavior. Indeed, sooner or later a child will be exposed to violent media anyway, because nearly all contemporary movies and many TV shows depict violence of some sort. Thus, it's better to talk with children about it from an early age, before they draw poor interpretations of the violence.

In response, however, critics of exposure to violence may argue that violence in movies or video games can be traumatizing for children, who may become fearful of the world around them. The solution to this problem is for parents and guardians to act like the auxiliary supervisors in Plato's *Republic*. Just as auxiliary or guardian supervisors are able to distinguish risky military ventures from safe ones, parents should know when the game or movie is too violent or scary for their child's age. And this leads to our final question, namely, whether or not you should allow your child to watch *Aliens*.

We think that a reasonable amount of screen violence, including watching *Aliens*, can cause children to become mentally tougher and so make it easier for them to deal with stressful situations. It is not right to completely shelter a child, even a relatively young child, from media violence. If we live in dangerous situations, then we should want our children to be like the brave and temperate girl Newt. Yes, Newt eventually dies when her ship crashes into the sea and her cryo-chamber is flooded. Yet Newt, and our children and their children as well, will certainly survive longer and enjoy a more rational life with some training in, and exposure to, violence rather than a policy of total protection. In this way, Plato's argument from two and a half millennia ago is still valid today.

Notes

1. Plato, *Republic*, trans. Robin Waterfield (Oxford University Press, 2008), 183.
2. Ibid., 182.
3. Ibid., 184.
4. Ibid., 136.

10

Alien, Alienation, and Alien Nation

Daniel Conway

Long before the viewers of Ridley Scott's *Alien* catch their first, fleeting glimpse of the terrifying alien, they have already made the acquaintance of the alienated human beings aboard the USCSS *Nostromo*. Alternately distracted, detached, and disaffected, the members of the crew squabble over pay, gripe about working conditions, joylessly perform their assigned tasks, and demean themselves by meekly taking orders from a central command unit whom they address, without a trace of irony, as Mother.

In fact, the human members of the crew of the *Nostromo* exhibit "alienation," a condition identified by Karl Marx (1818–1883) in the "Estranged Labor" section of his *Economic and Philosophic Manuscripts of 1844*.[1] In this section, Marx developed a distinctly moral indictment of the capitalist mode of production, insisting that it strips workers of their basic humanity and dignity. In particular, Marx claimed, capitalism entails the alienation of workers in four identifiable forms: from the products (or fruits) of their labor; from the labor process itself; from what he called their "species-being"; and from one another.[2] In *Alien*, each of these forms of alienation is on display in the build-up to the startling debut of the chestbursting Xenomorph. By then, of course, we know (or at least sense) that the alienated members of the crew are doomed. Ripley alone refuses to accept without challenge the status quo and its enabling ideology, which perpetuates the fiction that the crew is in good hands with the Company. Personally victimized by Ash, the passing android aboard

Alien and Philosophy: I Infest, Therefore I Am, First Edition.
Edited by Jeffrey Ewing and Kevin S. Decker.
© 2017 John Wiley & Sons Ltd. Published 2017 by John Wiley & Sons Ltd.

the *Nostromo*, Ripley finally understands that she must destroy the Company's property, i.e., its means of production, which allows it to extract and profit from the crew's labor, if she is to survive with her humanity and dignity intact.

Alien

The plot of Ridley Scott's *Alien* is well known to science fiction buffs and film enthusiasts more generally. In the film's first act, we witness the premature awakening of the crew of the *Nostromo* as the ship's central command unit, MU/TH/R (pronounced "Mother"), receives a signal emanating from an unidentified acoustic beacon in space.[3] Contractually bound to investigate the source of any signal suggestive of intelligent life, the crew dutifully sets a course for an uninhabited moon, LV-426. Our initial impressions of the crew are formed as we observe their reactions to this unexpected change of plans. Needless to say, these impressions are neither obviously nor consistently positive. Understandably disinclined to prolong their time in space, they only grudgingly accept their new mission from Mother. They are introduced to us, that is, neither as heroic adventurers nor as admirable altruists, but as weary long-haul transporters who resent the postponement of their return home.

And what awaits them at home? We don't really know. There is very little small talk among them, except for the predictable complaints about the ship's food, and precious few references to interests and concerns beyond what immediately pertains to their work. While the girlie pin-ups that clutter Ash's workstation may suggest an improbably zesty interest in women, we know he means to disguise his true identity, even before we know why he might need to do so. Ripley apparently has a daughter at home, whose birthday party she needs to plan and attend, but this we learn only from another director (James Cameron of *Aliens*), who invests Ripley with a very different character and psyche. For his part, Ridley Scott wishes for us to know as little as possible about the crew of the *Nostromo*. His realization of this wish not only heightens the tension of his slowly advancing plot, but also reinforces our sense of the crew as disconnected, disengaged, and sorely lacking in passion and vitality.

In the film's second act, we learn more about the crew as they grapple with the unexpected consequences of their contact with the alien life-form on LV-426. Most notably, we learn that they don't work well together, don't follow well-designed regulations and procedures, and don't display good judgment. While the machinations of Ash complicate the situation in ways not yet apparent to the human members of the crew, his alternative agenda is sufficiently overt as to place their alienation in sharper relief. Despite being the ship's science officer, for example, Ash disobeys Ripley's direct order and violates the Company's established quarantine procedure. Had his crewmates not been so thoroughly disengaged from what turn out to be matters of life and death, they might have discovered his secret and, perhaps, collectively thwarted his plan to capture the alien life-form.

The third act of the film pits the crew against the alien they have unwisely brought aboard the *Nostromo*. Finding the Facehugger detached from Kane, they foolishly believe that the threat has passed and settle in for a celebratory (and now iconic) last supper. One by one they are captured or killed, until only Ripley and the cat, Jones, remain. After initiating the ship's self-destruct sequence, Ripley escapes (along with Jones) in the shuttle *Narcissus*, where she discovers to her chagrin that the alien too is aboard. Establishing what would become the go-to plan for eliminating the alien threat, she cleverly ejects the unsuspecting Xenomorph from the *Narcissus*. Once expelled into space—and yes, we do hear its scream—the Xenomorph is incinerated in the super-heated exhaust from the shuttle's thrusters. Ripley and Jones settle down for a well-deserved (and longer than expected) nap.

Yet the film's potent backstory remains largely underexplored and underappreciated. Our attention to this backstory will not only reveal the larger forces at work in determining the fate of the crew, but also explain why they underperform so stunningly in response to the threat posed by the rapidly maturing alien. As it turns out, the members of the crew were alienated from one another, and doomed in that respect, long before they encountered the terrifying Xenomorph. *Alien*, in short, is a film about *alienation*, which is the debilitating condition in which we (along with the Xenomorph) find the unfortunate crew of the *Nostromo*.

The backstory of *Alien* rests on a dystopic vision of the near future, in which an advanced form of industrial capitalism has spread its dominion across the known cosmos. An unspecified period of rampant interstellar colonization has spawned trans-planetary corporations of unprecedented reach and ambition. One such entity, the cartoonishly nefarious Weyland-Yutani Corporation, oversees a far-flung colonial mining empire and aims very soon to enter (and perhaps dominate) the lucrative field of bioweapons research. If this new era of corporate proliferation boasts high-functioning governmental alliances or planetary labor federations that are empowered to check the expansionary designs of Weyland-Yutani, there is no sign of them in *Alien*. One gets the impression that ordinary individuals, working stiffs like the human members of the crew of the *Nostromo*, have neither rights nor recourse against the mighty Company. Even the captain of the *Nostromo* pleads deferential impotence: he simply does whatever the Company directs him to do, and he asks no questions.

The neocolonial backdrop of *Alien* thus imbues the film with a dark ethos of capitalist greed, cynicism, and exploitation. By the time we realize that the parasitoid alien species seizes other creatures to host its multi-stage reproductive cycle, we are already well aware that, even in the twenty-second century, human beings continue to treat one another with a similarly proprietary violence.[4] Despite the technological progress on display in Ridley Scott's dystopia, we don't see any advances in the nontechnical, spiritual domains of human experience. In particular, moral progress continues to elude humanity. While it may be true that "in space, no one can hear you scream," the isolation this tagline suggests is surely amplified by the neocolonial, capitalist ethos of the film.

Alienation

One of our earliest encounters with the crew of the *Nostromo* centers on a dispute about wages. Brett and Parker lobby their shipmates for full shares of the anticipated bonus, but Dallas and Ash contend that there is nothing to discuss. Instead of siding with the engineers, who are indispensible to the success of the mission, Dallas promotes the interests of the Company, despite its disregard for him. The irony here is that the very contract he cites as the basis for a "fair" distribution of bonus shares *also* obliges the crew to respond to any potential distress signal the ship might receive. Dallas is thus exposed as serving, simultaneously, as a spineless shill for the Company *and* as a disposable asset in its covert bioweapons research program.

We shouldn't be surprised by any of this, Karl Marx would claim. So long as the capitalist mode of production remains viable and authoritative, Marx insists, workers will suffer the indignities associated with alienated labor. According to him, the true aim of labor isn't limited to the immediate satisfaction of the basic needs of particular human beings. In a passage that speaks both to the supposed "purity" of the Xenomorph and to the potentially burdensome complexity of human beings, Marx explains, "[A]n animal only produces what it immediately needs for itself or its young. It produces one-sidedly, whilst man produces universally...even when he is free from physical need and only truly produces in freedom therefrom."[5] To be fully human, Marx believes, is to be involved with others in the free, creative transformation of the natural world and, then, to see oneself reflected in the fruits of one's labor. This positive reflection activates a self-sustaining feedback loop, inspiring all workers to continue to improve themselves and the fruits of their labor.[6] According to Marx, that is, labor is the activity through which human beings may attain *self-knowledge*, which includes the recognition of themselves as representative members of humanity as a whole.[7]

Let's begin by considering the first of these forms: *alienation from the product(s) of one's labor*. As Marx explains,

> [T]he object which labor produces—labor's product—confronts it as *something alien*, as a *power independent* of the producer...Labor's realization is its objectification. In the conditions dealt with by political economy this realization of labor appears as *loss of reality* for the workers; objectification as *loss of the object* and *object-bondage*; appropriation as *estrangement*, as *alienation*.[8]

Marx tends to emphasize two aspects of this initial form of alienation. First, the product of labor under the capitalist mode of production is not for the worker's use and enjoyment. The alienated workers do not recognize themselves in the product of their labor, and the product of their labor does not honor them as its creators. Second, the product of labor eventually is mobilized, either directly or indirectly, *against* the workers who produced it, adding to their misery.[9] As a result, the world shaped by alienated labor never becomes a *home* to the workers who labor to improve it. Ridley Scott makes a similar point by presenting the Xenomorph as both a product of the crew's contractual labor—unwittingly extracted by them from the derelict spacecraft—and, with the exception of Ripley, the occasion of their demise. A similar cruelty obtains when an assembly line worker is struck and killed by one of the automobiles he has produced but cannot afford to own.

The second form of alienation identified by Marx is *alienation from the labor process*. Rather than find their work to be satisfying, enriching, and conducive to their self-respect, alienated workers see themselves as squandering their life activity in exchange for a mere subsistence wage. As Marx explains,

> The relation of labor to the *act of production* within the *labor* process... is the relation of the worker to his own activity as an alien activity not belonging to him; it is activity as suffering, strength as weakness, begetting as emasculating...Here we have *self-estrangement*, as we had previously the estrangement of the *thing*.[10]

If, as Marx believes, one's labor is integral to one's sense of identity and self-worth, then workers who are alienated from the labor process have no means of securing a stable, positive sense of self.[11] Under these conditions, the workers can't help but experience the labor process as burdensome and disagreeable.

Few ventures evoke the rapacity of capitalism like that of colonial mining. Valuable resources are claimed and extracted, typically by force and fiat, to be transported from one locale for use and enjoyment in another. The native inhabitants of the colony may be displaced or disinherited by the mining operation. Alternately, they may be enslaved, conscripted, or employed at subsistence wages by the colonizers. Moreover, colonial mining is widely understood to be a rough, dirty, exploitative, and unhealthy business, resting on an unbalanced, inequitable relationship between the colonizers and the indigenous peoples they have colonized.

To date, the reach of real-world colonial mining ventures has been limited by the Earth's resources and the technologies available for the extraction, transport, and refinement of ore, oil, and gems.[12] But what if there were no such limitations? Would the psychology of empire dictate an interstellar expansion of colonial mining operations and their attendant evils? Would human greed swell to fill (and pollute) the known cosmos? In *Alien*, Ridley Scott unsentimentally answers, "yes." Despite the scientific and technological wonders at its disposal, which might have been employed to heal the Earth and project good will across the cosmos, Weyland-Yutani displays no greater moral capacity than the nineteenth-century factory owners described (and reviled) by Marx.[13]

As we learn in James Cameron's sequel, the Company's colonial mining empire is but a gateway venture to the far more lucrative (and far more exploitative) business of *terraforming*. Not content simply to appropriate and extract gem and mineral resources, the Company is determined to seize entire worlds with the aim of furnishing them with an Earth-like climate, topography, and atmosphere. In *Aliens*, when Ripley returns to LV-426, the emergency to which the USCSS *Sulaco* responds is directly linked to the Company's terraforming efforts. In order to further its aim of mapping and domesticating LV-426, the Company has established a "shake-and-bake" colony of technicians, engineers, support staff, and their families. Of course, the colony also includes the kind of freelance prospectors and wild card adventurers who might be expected to stray from the compound and stumble upon the derelict spacecraft and its cargo. Inasmuch as the Company is aware of the alien presence on LV-426, its actual business plan thus involves producing a habitable, Earth-like world while *also* gulling some of the colonists into hosting alien life-forms for its bioweapons research program. According to Marx, the high-risk complexity of the Company's full business plan is no aberration. The expansionist logic of capitalism enjoins the pursuit of profit even, as in the case of Weyland-Yutani, at the expense of the Company's long-term financial interests.

Let's turn now to examine the third form of alienation identified by Marx. As he explains,

> In estranging from man (1) nature, and (2) himself, his own active functions, his life-activity, estranged labor estranges the *species* from man. It turns for him the *life of the species* into a means of individual life. First it estranges the life of the species and individual life, and secondly it makes individual life in its abstract form the purpose of the life of the species, likewise in its abstract and estranged form.[14]

These ideas may require further elaboration. In particular, the notion of *species-being* may be either obscure or unfamiliar. Let's consider how Marx explains what he has in mind:

> Man is a species being, not only because in practice and in theory he adopts the species as his object (his own as well as those of other things), but—and this is only another way of expressing it—but also because he treats himself as the actual living species; because he treats himself as a *universal* and therefore a free being.[15]

The key terms here are *universality* and *freedom*. Unable to summon the collective virtues and achievements of humanity as a whole, workers estranged from their species-being are doomed to unfree lives of narrow scope and limited ambition. Because the "objective world" only reflects back to them their individual limitations,[16] they don't feel encouraged or entitled to produce freely and creatively.

The crucial point is this: labor becomes and remains meaningful only for workers who can avail themselves of the universality and freedom of their species-being. Whereas alienated labor can aspire to nothing more or higher than the satisfaction of an individual's basic needs, free labor aspires to the enhancement of humanity itself. So long as workers remain alienated from their species-being, they will form no reasonable expectation of finding their work to be meaningful, fulfilling, or conducive to greater connectivity to the species as a whole.

A telltale sign that the human members of the crew of the *Nostromo* are alienated from their species-being is their unquestioned (and undignified) reliance on Mother. With a single, well-placed acronym, Ridley Scott conveys the infantilization of the crew of the *Nostromo*. Like dependent children in a dysfunctional family, the human members of the crew cede their autonomy to a distant, emotionally unavailable authority figure, whom they have no reason to trust and good reason to fear. Mother puts them to bed, inconsiderately changes her mind about their route and destination, rouses them to run her risky errand on LV 426, prepares their (bad) food, empowers the rogue agent in their midst, and, ultimately, deems them expendable in pursuit of the alien "child" she genuinely favors.[17] This strict regimen of dependency ultimately emboldens Mother not only to dispense the bitter milk of Special Order 937, but also to admit to having done so, as if to humiliate the crew with her callous subordination of their welfare.

Let's take this a step further. Marx also positions us to understand that Special Order 937 is in fact superfluous, and chillingly so. Alienated from their species-being, the human members of the crew *already* live as if they were expendable. Despite their polite grumbling, for example, no one questions the validity (or the safety) of their prescribed change of course in response to the supposed distress signal. Aside from Ripley, moreover, no one complains that an unidentified alien creature, known by its facehugging of Kane to be potentially harmful, is allowed on the ship. Other than Ripley, no one, including the captain, rebukes Ash for his reckless act of insubordination.

Despite their advantage in numbers, intelligence, firepower, and, supposedly, familiarity with the *Nostromo*, they are no match for the stealthy Xenomorph, which effortlessly turns the hunters into the hunted. Although Ash impairs the crew's efforts to track and flush the Xenomorph, they have ample reason to question his judgment and loyalties. That they continue to rely on his scientific expertise, entrusting their very lives to the dubious tracking devices he rigs for them,[18] is symptomatic of their estrangement from their species-being. Rather than pursue their collective interests, seizing control of a situation gone horribly awry, they continue to entrust their lives to the guidance and supposed good will of the Company and its agents.[19] Only Ripley determines to take full responsibility for her own life, and she does so only after being attacked and nearly killed by Ash.

Estrangement from one's species-being leads to the fourth, and perhaps most obvious, form of alienation: *alienation from one's fellow workers*. Reduced to lives of lonely isolation, alienated workers are unable to appreciate themselves and their fellow laborers as constituting a universal socioeconomic class. As such, alienated workers are generally unable to work together to further their class-based interests, which they tend to ignore, misidentify, or repudiate.

Rather than band together against a common foe, alienated workers readily direct their enmity and mistrust toward *one another*. In some cases, they may turn on each other in a self-destructive effort to protect or further the interests of the property-owning class, which, in their confusion, they may hope one day to join. Marx explains:

> An immediate consequence of the fact that man is estranged from the product of his labor, from his life-activity, from his species being, is the *estrangement of man* from *man*…Hence within the relationship of estranged labor each man views the other in accordance with the standard and the position in which he finds himself as a worker.[20]

Marx is concerned here to make two related points. First, he identifies alienation (or estrangement) as a product of the division between socioeconomic classes, e.g., between owners and workers, between bourgeoisie and proletariat, and between the Company and the human crew of the ship. As shocking as it may be to learn in the film that the Company deems the crew of the *Nostromo* "expendable," this revelation really shouldn't surprise anyone. According to Marx, it's inevitable that an expansionist, capitalist enterprise like Weyland-Yutani would come to assign "secondary" importance to the welfare of its "expendable" workers. Although most corporations are careful not to say so in public, all such ventures are obliged at some point to consider the depreciation and loss of "human capital" in their all-important cost–benefit analyses.

Second, this division between socioeconomic classes is reproduced *within* the working class itself. Stipulating from the outset the class-based antagonisms disclosed by Marx, Ridley Scott is far more concerned to depict the estrangement of members of a single socioeconomic class—the workers—from one another. Seemingly content with relationships stalled out on a last-name basis, the human members of the crew fail to see themselves and their mates as belonging to a universal class of laborers. Understanding themselves as *competitors*—initially, for wages, and subsequently, for survival—they regard their fellow crew members as potential obstacles to their enrichment and welfare. As a result, their responses to the Xenomorph take shape and find direction only within the narrow scope of the alien-friendly tactics prescribed for them by Mother and the Company. Rather than arrive freely at mutually beneficial and collectively determined choices, the human members of the crew address the alien threat by relying on Company-approved measures that exacerbate their alienation from one another. The irony, of course, is that the one member of the crew the others *ought* to mistrust is shielded from their suspicions by the undeserved, corporation-awarded halo of "ship's science officer."

Alien Nation

Marx's analysis of alienation is also useful in appreciating the outcome of the battle that slowly unfolds and quickly deteriorates in James Cameron's *Aliens*. In a development that fairly mocks Eisenhower's famous warning about the unchecked growth of the "military–industrial complex," Weyland-Yutani is not only back in business, but also in command of its very own paramilitary assault force, which it deploys as needed to protect its terraforming assets and operations. War may be good for business, as the saying goes, but business can be bad for war, especially when military and corporate interests diverge or clash.

Representing the grim, cynical union of military and corporate interests in very late industrial capitalism, the Colonial Marines are loud, cocky, disrespectful, homophobic, and armed to the teeth with state-of-the-art, genocide-grade weaponry. When Ripley attempts to brief them on the threat presented by the Xenomorphs, the Marines refuse to listen. Confident that their weapons and bravado will carry them to victory, they prove to be undisciplined, impetuous, unprepared, and, in some cases, craven. What we soon learn, in fact, is that they're not even real soldiers; indeed, they never coalesce into a disciplined fighting unit. Alienated from their (admittedly clueless) leadership, their cloudy mission objectives, and one another, and overly dependent on their military hardware, the Colonial Marines are no match for the coordinated attack of the alien species.

In the transition from *Alien* to *Aliens*, the added *s* makes a huge difference. Plurality implies reproduction; reproduction implies motherhood, and, in this case, queen-hood.[21] As we learn, moreover, plurality also implies community. On our return visit to LV-426, we finally have the chance to observe the aliens in their social existence, as a smoothly running and prosperous collective, perhaps also as a nation. They're still lethal, to be sure, but we now understand their lethality to serve a recognizable end, even if we don't condone the cost in human lives of its pursuit. In any event, we are finally in a position to consider the aliens as intelligent, resourceful, team-oriented, and goal-directed creatures.

The single alien creature we encountered in *Alien* may have been an easy target for demonization. Under Ridley Scott's direction, we may have applauded without question the crew's ambition to hunt the alien and flush it from the ship. But now that we encounter an entire society or nation of Xenomorphs, ruled by a hard-working queen, our impressions may shift, perhaps even dramatically so. If James Cameron has succeeded in realizing his artistic aims, we viewers may have grown sympathetic to the plight of the alien nation. (As we learn in *Prometheus*, the aliens marooned on LV-426 may be considered victims and refugees in their own right, transported to that planet by the Engineers in a failed attempt to destroy the hominid population of Earth or some other distant planet.)[22] Whereas Ripley and Hicks are understandably keen to "nuke the planet," we may be less enthusiastic to promote what Stephen Mulhall, in his treatment of the film, correctly identifies as *genocide*.[23]

In guiding the viewer's transition from *Alien* to *Aliens*, James Cameron succeeds in complicating the moral terrain that was introduced and traversed by Ridley Scott. Especially when compared to the nasty, thuggish, not-ready-for-prime-time Colonial Marines, the alien nation may begin to grow on us. In particular, we may be inclined to acknowledge its superior capacity for coordination, cooperation, and mutual defense. As the unambiguous outcome of the battle suggests, in fact, we alienated humans may stand to learn something from this supposedly primitive species. If nothing else, we may be persuaded to revisit the cogency of our well-worn claims to evolutionary superiority and biological exceptionalism. As the direction provided by Scott and Cameron suggests, we humans may not strike an unbiased observer as the superior species, even though, according to Marx, that's precisely what a very different mode of production, or way of laboring, might allow us to become.[24]

Notes

1. Karl Marx, *Economic and Philosophic Manuscripts of 1844*, in *The Marx–Engels Reader*, second edition, ed. Robert C. Tucker (W.W. Norton, 1978), 77.
2. For similar treatments of the theme of alienation, see Amy E. Wendling, *Karl Marx on Technology and Alienation* (Palgrave Macmillan, 2009), 37–49; and Jonathan Woolf, "Karl Marx," in *The Stanford Encyclopedia of Philosophy* (Winter 2015 Edition), ed. Edward N. Zalta, http://plato. stanford.edu/archives/win2015/entries/marx/. On the reception of the "early" Marx and the construction of a "theory" of alienation, see Terrell Carver, "Marx and Marxism," in *The History of Continental Philosophy*, vol. 2, eds. Alan D. Schrift and Daniel Conway (Acumen, 2010), 51–54.
3. See the excellent discussion by Stephen Mulhall in *On Film*, third edition (Routledge, 2016), 9–11.
4. As Ripley bluntly explains to Burke in *Aliens*, "at least you don't see [the aliens] fucking one another over for a percentage."
5. Marx, *Economic and Philosophic Manuscripts of 1844*, 76.
6. As Marx elaborates, "Let us suppose that we had carried out production as human beings…In the individual expression of my life I would have directly created your expression of your life, and therefore in my individual activity I would have directly *confirmed* and *realized* my true nature, my *human* nature, my *communal nature*"; "Comments on James Mill, *Éléments d'Économie Politique*," https://www.marxists. org/archive/marx/works/1844/james-mill/.
7. For an account of the residual influence of Hegelian philosophy on Marx's discussion of alienation, see Wendling, *Karl Marx on Technology and Alienation*, 14–24.
8. Marx, *Economic and Philosophic Manuscripts of 1844*, 71–72.
9. See Wendling, *Karl Marx on Technology and Alienation*, 49–51.
10. Marx, *Economic and Philosophic Manuscripts of 1844*, 74–75.
11. Marx thus observes that "My labor can appear in my object only as what it is. It cannot appear as something which by its nature it is *not*. Hence it appears only as the expression of my *loss of self* and of my *powerlessness* that is objective, sensuously perceptible, obvious and therefore put beyond all doubt"; "Comments on James Mill, *Éléments d'Économie Politique*."

12. Even as I write, there is news from Luxembourg of a major investment in "asteroid mining."

13. On the development within advanced capitalism of "technological alienation" and "machine fetishism," see Wendling, *Karl Marx on Technology and Alienation*, 55–60.

14. Marx, *Economic and Philosophic Manuscripts of 1844*, 75.

15. Ibid.

16. Ibid., 76. Mulhall may have this form of alienation in mind when he attributes to Ripley a "sense of alienation from life, nature, and the cosmos, and from everything in herself that participates in—that binds her ineluctably to—that which she hates so purely"; *On Film*, 19.

17. Here I follow Mulhall, *On Film*, 15–19.

18. This point is made in ibid., 17.

19. An interesting example here is the case of Parker, who springs into action to save Ripley from Ash. A largely benign presence in the drama thus far, Parker resorts to violence and, in an obvious departure from his thankless role as ship's steward, wantonly destroys Company property (Ash) in the process. What is most remarkable about this scene, however, is that Parker reacts to Ripley's plight with a ferocity that he cannot muster to save himself. Later, as he endeavors in vain to protect Lambert from the Xenomorph, it becomes clear that he can save others (= women) but cannot show himself a similar level of concern.

20. Marx, *Economic and Philosophic Manuscripts of 1844*, 77.

21. Here I follow Mulhall, *On Film*, 40–42.

22. See Daniel Conway, "No Planet for Old Men: Idealism and Sexual Difference in Ridley Scott's *Prometheus*," *Per la Filosofia* 93–94 (2015): 47–62.

23. Mulhall, *On Film*, 42.

24. I am grateful to the editors for their instructive comments on earlier drafts of this chapter.

Part IV

HORROR: "THEY MOSTLY COME AT NIGHT"

11

Terror from the Stars: *Alien* as Lovecraftian Horror

Greg Littmann

Alien is the best science fiction horror film ever made—in my opinion.[1] Nothing has ever been quite as chilling as the tale of six space-truckers trapped with a shape-changing predator in a tiny starship sailing through an endless void.

One reason why the power of *Alien* is philosophically interesting is that it supports the theories of seminal American horror writer H.P. Lovecraft (1890–1937) about what makes good science fiction horror. Lovecraft, in case you don't know, is the greatest science fiction horror *writer* ever, and arguably the greatest horror writer period. Most of Lovecraft's stories were set in a common fictional universe, with recurring characters and alien races.

Lovecraft never directly offers a philosophy of science fiction horror. However, at different points in his essays and letters, he addresses the genres he calls "interplanetary fiction," "horror," "supernatural horror," and "weird fiction," the last being a broad heading covering both supernatural fiction and science fiction. Taken together, a philosophy of science fiction horror emerges.

Dan O'Bannon, author of the original *Alien* script, was a lifelong Lovecraft fan and was directly influenced by him in writing *Alien* and other scripts. Strikingly, *Alien* shares its basic plot with numerous Lovecraft stories: an individual or small group, alone in an immense barren nowhere, explores bizarre and mysterious ancient ruins, leading to a hideous and deadly encounter with one or more alien monsters, usually leaving a sole survivor to tell the tale.[2] More importantly though, the effectiveness of the film *Alien* provides support for

Alien and Philosophy: I Infest, Therefore I Am, First Edition.
Edited by Jeffrey Ewing and Kevin S. Decker.
© 2017 John Wiley & Sons Ltd. Published 2017 by John Wiley & Sons Ltd.

Lovecraft's *philosophy* of science fiction horror. That isn't to say that the *Alien* production team were thinking about Lovecraft, but rather that the film happens to do what he recommends, to unnerving effect!

How to Frighten People

Lovecraft believes that the scariest threats are mysterious ones. He writes: "The oldest and strongest emotion of mankind is fear, and the oldest and strongest kind of fear is fear of the unknown."[3] The power of mystery extends to location, and especially unknown worlds: "Uncertainty and danger are always closely allied, thus making any kind of an unknown world a world of peril and evil possibilities."[4]

But mystery isn't enough. He writes: "The essence of the horrible is the *unnatural*."[5] The most powerful horror fiction, in his view, relies on an emotion he calls "cosmic fear," caused by violations of nature by mysterious and foreign entities: "A certain atmosphere of breathless and unexplainable dread of outer, unknown forces must be present; and there must be a hint, expressed with a seriousness and portentousness becoming its subject, of…a malign and particular suspension or defeat of those fixed laws of Nature which are our only safeguard against the assaults of chaos and the daemons of unplumbed space."[6]

In *Alien*, the planetoid visited by *Nostromo* is an unknown world, as—in a sense—is the alien shipwreck. The alien predator is an entirely mysterious and unpredictable threat. As Ash notes, "This is the first time we've encountered a species like this." The crew are constantly being surprised by its abilities, as it pulls tricks like attacking straight out of the egg, keeping Kane paralyzed but alive even though he's biologically unrelated to its natural prey, defending itself with acidic blood, reproducing by bursting out of Kane's chest, and suddenly growing from the size of a small cat into a hulking horror. The importance of generating mystery in cultivating fear explains, in part, why each film set in the *Alien* universe has been less frightening than the one before, up until *Prometheus* broke the curse by not having the familiar alien predator appear at all.

The alien's abilities are so surprising because they break our Earthling rules about what animals should be able to do. They seem like unnatural abilities because nothing in nature as we know it can do what the alien can. The crew of *Nostromo* could have been placed in just as much danger by a pride of lions getting loose on the ship, but the film would be much less frightening. Lions are lethal, but not…*alien*.

Keeping it Real as Aliens Attack

Lovecraft stands out among contemporary weird writers for his efforts to be realistic. Regarding spaceship-based fiction, he writes, "Inconceivable events and conditions form a class apart from all other story elements, and cannot be made convincing by any mere process of casual narration. They have the handicap of incredibility to overcome; and this can be accomplished only through a careful realism in every *other* phase of the story."[7] He's unknowingly echoing the advice given by Aristotle (384–322 BCE) in his *Poetics* for good serious theater: "Any impossibilities there are in [the author's] descriptions of things are faults. But from another point of view they are justifiable, if they serve the end of poetry—if...they make the effect of...the work...more astounding."[8] In other words, Aristotle thinks it's alright to include amazing elements in order to tell an amazing story, but that even an amazing story should default to realism. Even if the work is based on astounding premises, "There should be nothing improbable among the actual incidents."[9]

Lovecraft claims that realism in science fiction requires scientific accuracy. He writes of spaceship stories: "[A] strict following of scientific fact in representing the mechanical, astronomical, and other aspects of the trip is absolutely essential."[10] Likewise, alien planets must be scientifically plausible.

Alien isn't a scientifically realistic film. Even the existence of starships like *Nostromo* is scientifically absurd: *Nostromo* flies faster than light, a feat that requires *more than* infinite energy! However, as Lovecraft *should* have noted, and as is demonstrated by both *Alien* and his own work, there are ways of cultivating the necessary *atmosphere* of scientific realism other than being scientifically realistic. *Alien* is rich in suggested "scientific" detail. As the *Nostromo* crew considers exploring the planetoid on foot, Ash analyzes the environment: "There's inert nitrogen, high concentration of carbon dioxide crystals, methane...I'm working on the trace elements." Having studied the alien, he explains, "he's got an outer layer of protein polysaccharides. He has a funny habit of shedding his cells and replacing them with polarized silicone, which gives him a prolonged resistance to adverse environmental conditions." When he invents an alien-tracking device, he can explain how it works; when Ripley asks, "What's it key off?," he answers, "Microchanges in air density." Most elegantly, when we first see the *Nostromo* computers wake up, numbers and words stream across the screens in green and blue, their glare reflected in the faceplate of an empty helmet. It's all meaningless to the viewer, but assures us that complicated technical reports are being prepared, taking account of all the facts.

Technology is made to seem more plausible by being imperfect. Even though *Alien* violates physics by having the *Nostromo* travel faster than light, the film cultivates an air of realism by having the crew "frozen" in suspended animation for interstellar trips, in acknowledgment of the vastness of space and the difficulty of crossing it. Being frozen is an unpleasant process, leaving Lambert feeling chilled and Kane feeling "dead." Maneuvering the ship is laborious, requiring painstaking calculations, and just landing on the planetoid is so dangerous that the ship is badly damaged. Workstations are cramped and cluttered; there are bewildering masses of displays, lights, controls, and mysterious tubing and wires. Lighting is deficient and the rations tasteless. "The first thing I'm going to do when I get back is get some decent food," smiles Kane as he spoons up space-noodles. One of the crew has even put up a photograph of a fried egg on the wall, alongside pornographic centerfolds.

Truck Drivers in Space

Alien further fosters an atmosphere of realism by emphasizing the mundanity of the characters. *Nostromo* is a commercial towing vehicle belonging to a large corporation, a ship full of ordinary people doing ordinary jobs. The crew members are expected to show complete obedience. As Dallas notes, "Standard procedure is to do whatever the hell they tell you to do." Working spaces look lived in, with battered surfaces and scattered coffee cups, beer cans, and cigarette packets.

The actors' appearances are carefully tailored to emphasize ordinariness. Clothes are utilitarian and unflattering, hair is messy, and nobody bothers wearing makeup to work. Clothing styles are almost identical to what we wear today, complete with t-shirts, overalls, button-up jackets, and lace-up sneakers. It isn't actually realistic for clothes to have changed so little from today when technology has had time to advance so far, but it makes the film *feel* realistic because their clothes are familiar from life.

Lovecraft should appreciate the realistically mundane nature of the crew. He wrote: "We must select only such characters (not necessarily stalwart or dashing or youthful or beautiful or picturesque characters) as would naturally be involved in the events to be depicted."[11] However, he himself didn't tell stories about ordinary folk. He notes: "I do not write about 'ordinary people' because I am not in the least interested in them."[12] A loner, Lovecraft had no idea how ordinary people talked, and his stories contain remarkably little dialogue. Lovecraft's protagonists are almost always thinly disguised versions of himself, or some idealized version of himself: richer, better educated, and more respected. The independently wealthy antiquarian Jervas Dudley who explores his family vault in "The Tomb" (1917) is interchangeable with the independently wealthy antiquarian Randolph Carter who goes hunting for the gods in "The Dream-Quest of Unknown Kadath" (1927) as well as the independently wealthy antiquarian and author of weird fiction Robert Blake, who explores the ruins of an old church in "The Haunter of the Dark" (1935), and most other Lovecraft protagonists.

How to Build an Alien

The alien predator in *Alien*, like the *Nostromo* itself, is scientifically absurd. Even leaving aside its improbable molecular acid for blood, the thing has the ability to grow to the size of a large human without eating anything to use as new mass. Perhaps most impressively, it is able to paralyze, sustain, and utilize a human for breeding purposes, despite humans being biologically unrelated to its natural prey. Realistically, the Facehugger should have just spat Kane out, as you would spit out food fit for a spider, a crab, or a plant—all forms of life much more closely related to humans than the alien is. However, Lovecraft encouraged the breaking by alien creatures of what we humans foolishly take to be natural laws. This is the source of "cosmic fear" after all!

His alien visitors are happy to consume humans, like the sentient iridescence that drains the life from the Gardner family after moving into the well on their farm in "The Colour Out of Space" (1927), and the shape-changing colossus that preys on generations in suburban Providence and is buried under "The Shunned House" (1924). More remarkably, when Lovecraft's aliens decide to traverse space, they break the laws of physics in ways that make *Nostromo* look realistic. Generally, they fly through the "aether" by flapping their wings. Otherwise, they might travel by telekinesis, take over a human body remotely, or cross dimensions by walking, burrowing, or swimming.

For all that, Lovecraft thinks it essential that aliens be realistic in their *alienness*. That is, they must be genuinely alien rather than being essentially like humans. He wrote that aliens "must be definitely non-human in aspect, mentality, emotions, and nomenclature…It must be remembered that non-human beings would be wholly apart from human motives and perspectives."[13]

Appropriately, the wrecked alien ship found by the *Nostromo* crew looks nothing like what we expect a spaceship to be. The outside is weirdly asymmetrical and has no obvious rockets. Entering through a vaginal doorway, the exploration team find themselves in what seems to be the interior of a massive organic body, the glistening black corridors lined with ribs. The corpse of the alien navigator is like no form of life on Earth, apparently half-biological and half-mechanical, with a body that is one with the chair it reclines in. Judging from its desiccated bones, it wasn't only unable to leave its seat, but couldn't even turn its head away from staring into its massive telescope. According to *Prometheus*, the "corpse" we see is actually a suit, containing a humanoid being. Taken by itself, though, *Alien* offers the more Lovecraftian, and much more disturbing, possibility that the navigator's race are just as unlike us as they first seem. The corpse suggests that they are not just physically alien, but psychologically alien as well. For us, the life of the immobile navigator would be a special hell. It presumably suited the navigator just fine.

As for the alien predator, it has not one but three completely unfamiliar forms, used at different stages of its bizarre life cycle. The inspiration for the look of the predator came from artwork in Swiss artist H.R. Giger's book *Necronomicon*. Giger, a Lovecraft fan, took the name "Necronomicon" from his work. Lovecraft's fictional *Necronomicon* is a magical grimoire and a store of terrible secrets about the true nature of the universe.

Darwin's Nightmare

What we see as "realism" in fiction will depend on what our view of reality is. For Lovecraft, humanity is insignificant and the universe is indifferent to us. He writes: "All my tales are based on the fundamental premise that common human laws and interests and emotions have no validity or significance in the vast cosmos-at-large."[14] Lovecraft accepted Darwin's theory of evolution and was passionately atheist, writing that, "I have never been able to soothe myself with the sugary delusions of religion; for these things stand convinced of the utmost absurdity in light of modern scientific knowledge."[15]

Appropriately, the background assumptions in *Alien* are not religious but Darwinian. In place of the ghosts and demons of traditional horror, the alien navigator and the predator alike spring from evolution, making them seem more plausible, and so more threatening. Even if one or both were engineered, whatever engineered them was presumably a product of nature rather than a supernatural force.

Along with religion, Lovecraft dismissed morality as mere human convention. He writes, "good and evil are local expedients—or their lack—and not in any sense cosmic truths or laws."[16] His alien creatures generally do without moral rules. A Lovecraftian alien is, as Ash describes the alien on *Nostromo*, "A survivor, unclouded by conscience, remorse, or delusions of morality."

Real Men Cry in Terror (and So Do Real Women)

Maintaining realism requires maintaining realistic characters. Lovecraft says of weird fiction, "the characters and events must be consistent and natural except where they touch the single marvel."[17] Again, he's unknowingly echoing Aristotle's advice for serious theater: "The right thing…is in the characters just as in the incidents of the play to seek after the necessary or the probable; so that whenever such-and-such a personage says or does such-and-such a thing, it shall be the necessary or probable outcome of his character."[18]

Lovecraft is particularly critical of the artificiality of characterization in the science fiction of his day. He writes, "Insincerity, conventionality, triteness, artificiality, false emotion, and puerile extravagance reign triumphant,"[19] while "a good interplanetary story must have realistic human characters; not the stock scientists, villainous assistants, invincible heroes, and lovely scientist's-daughter heroines of the usual trash of this sort."[20]

Appropriately, the crew of *Nostromo* act more like real coworkers than any starship crew previously appearing on film or TV. They genuinely get on each other's nerves. "Quit griping," Kane snarls at Lambert. "I like griping," she retorts. "Knock it off!" snaps Captain Dallas at them both. Parker and Brett deliberately annoy Ripley to amuse themselves, turning up the steam while she's trying to talk. Even more impressively, they get away with it, without Ripley ever getting the last laugh. Later, Ripley can only get Parker to listen to her plan by shouting at him to shut up. The crew speak like ordinary people. Ripley's plan to deal with the alien is to "blow it the fuck out into space."

The crew are bound together only by professional obligation. When they expel Kane's corpse into space, Dallas asks, "Anyone want to say anything?," but nobody does and they eject him in silence. When Ripley tells Dallas that she doesn't trust Ash, he replies, "I don't trust anybody." When Dallas is trying to gain advice from Mother, he doesn't even type "WHAT ARE OUR CHANCES?" but "WHAT ARE MY CHANCES?"

Even a heroic character like Ripley isn't morally simplistic, because the universe she lives in, like the real universe, doesn't permit it. Ripley is brave enough to volunteer to go after the exploration team when she thinks they may be in danger and even brave enough to risk her life to save Jones the cat, leaving the shuttle and returning to an alien-infested *Nostromo* set to self-destruct. But she refuses to let the infected Kane back inside until he's gone through quarantine: "You know the quarantine procedure. Twenty-four hours for decontamination." When Dallas orders, "He could die. Open the hatch," she reasons, "Listen to me. If we break quarantine, we could all die." In most films, such an objection can come only from a cowardly character who gets shown up by the courage of the protagonists.

Characters in *Alien* act as though they feel real emotions. After Ripley refuses to let the infected Kane back onto the ship, Lambert slaps her. When Mother won't stop the self-destruct countdown, Ripley screams, "You bitch!" and hits the computer with a piece of equipment. Most importantly, the characters behave as if they feel real fear. The actors' faces show shock and horror as the alien bursts out of Kane, splattering them with his blood. As the adult alien moves in on Dallas in the air vents, Lambert starts weeping, "Move Dallas! Get out of there!" She cries again at the strategy meeting following Dallas's death, so afraid that she suggests they draw straws for the seats in the shuttle. Even Ripley sobs after learning from Mother that the crew are expendable and from Ash that he knew this all along. Indeed, it is Ripley's evident terror that drives the film's tensest moments, as she crawls on the floor to escape Ash's attack, runs through the corridors as the self-destruct counts down, and creeps around the shuttle in her undies, three feet from the monster. Tellingly, her last verbalization before triggering the rocket booster and finally killing the alien isn't a triumphant one-liner, but a scream of fear.

Lovecraft claims that to keep emotions in a weird story realistic, the characters must remain focused on the weird element itself. In spaceship-based fiction, "The emphasis, too, must be kept right—hovering always over *the wonder of the central abnormality itself*. It must be remembered that any violation of what we know as natural law is *in itself* a far more tremendous thing than any other event or feeling which could possibly affect a human being."[21] Lovecraft characters, even the heroic ones, frequently respond to the alien by fainting, screaming hysterically, or panicking and running, and they routinely suffer memory loss, chronic insomnia, or temporary or permanent insanity from their experience.

Alien achieves mixed results by this standard. While the crew are appropriately terrified of the alien, Lovecraft would find them insufficiently astonished by it, and by the wrecked starship they found it in. Evaluating exactly *how* astonished they should be depends on how much contact with alien life, and especially intelligent alien life, humanity has had so far. Still, discovering two new forms of life, one of which is intelligent and the other of which invades a colleague's body for reasons unknown, should be enough to blow anyone's mind. Lovecraft would find it unrealistic that when the crew sits down to what is supposed to be their final meal before returning to Earth, they discuss the food and the journey, rather than the alien starship they found and the mysterious creature that attached itself to Kane's face.

How to Tell a Horror Story

Lovecraft recognized that atmosphere relies as much on how the events of the story are related as on what those events are. Engaging the audience with an improbable story requires slowly building the mood to make them receptive. He writes of science fiction: "the handicap of incredibility can only be overcome if there is a gradual atmospheric or emotional building-up of the utmost subtlety."[22]

Appropriately, *Alien* moves very slowly, right from the moment we first see *Nostromo* gliding leisurely through space. It's about twelve minutes into the film before the first mention of aliens, twenty-five before the first glimpse of alien technology, thirty until the first alien corpse, thirty-five before the first living alien, and over an *hour* before the first full-grown specimen emerges.

Lovecraft believed that emphasizing suggestion over explicit detail is essential for building atmosphere. He writes: "Prime emphasis should be given to *subtle suggestion*—imperceptible hints and touches of selective associative detail which express shadings of moods and build up a vague illusion of the strange reality of the unreal." He committed himself early to refraining from clearly describing horrific entities. Given his belief that fear stems from the unknown, this is hardly surprising. Sometimes, he didn't describe his monsters at all, while at other times he went to considerable trouble to convey a vague but horrible impression. In "The Festival" (1923), the protagonist enters ancient catacombs and encounters "hybrid winged things that no sound eye could ever wholly grasp, or sound brain ever wholly remember. They were not altogether crows, nor moles, nor buzzards, nor ants, nor vampire bats, nor decomposed human beings; but something I cannot and must not recall."[23] In "The Unnameable" (1923), a writer of weird fiction argues that the truly alien would be impossible to describe, and then proves it to the horror of his skeptical friend.

Alien is a masterpiece of suggestion, reminiscent of the work of director Alfred Hitchcock and his seminal horror films *Psycho* (1960) and *The Birds* (1963). The details of the *Alien* sets are kept obscured to give our imaginations free play. The planetoid's surface is dark, misty, and scoured by howling winds. Lambert rightly keeps complaining that she "can't see a goddamn thing." When we watch events play out on Ash's video screen, the image is further blurred. When the crew hunts the alien in the cargo bay, the bay is dark and steamy. We see the full-grown alien gradually, with a little more detail revealed each time it strikes. We're never given a display of exactly *what* it does to people. It bites Brett in the throat and hauls him off-screen, with the camera inviting us to speculate by lingering on the face of Jones the cat as he watches the carnage. Later kills are no more illuminating. The alien makes jazz hands at Dallas and his camera goes dead. It bites Parker's throat and hauls him off-screen like Brett, then snakes its tail suggestively up Lambert's leg until we cut to Ripley listening to her screams.

Late in his career, Lovecraft changed his mind about refusing to offer clear descriptions. One of the highlights of *At the Mountains of Madness* (1931) is a detailed account of the dissection of an Elder Thing, as the arctic explorers who found the corpse strive to make sense of its weird biology. Likewise, *Alien* sometimes leaves suggestion behind in favor of explicit shocking weirdness. The Elder Thing dissection in Lovecraft is echoed by the wonderful dissection scene in *Alien* and subsequent discussions about the creature's biology. These scenes not only heighten the sense of realism by making the alien the subject of scientific study, but serve to showcase the horrific creature that the audience were hoping to see when they sat down to watch a movie named "*Alien*."

In Space, No One Can Hear You Scream

Lovecraft emphasizes the vulnerability of humans by contrasting our small size and brief existence with the vastness and age of the universe. His simplest technique for this is to place characters against an immense backdrop. He writes: "Probably the worst thing is *solitude in barren immensity.*"[24] His principle is borne out in *Alien* by the tension when the exploration team is alone on the lifeless planetoid, when the crew must face the alien in the emptiness of space, and especially when Ripley is left to face the alien alone. Vast distances are suggested by *Nostromo* drifting slowly across the screen although it is traveling at tremendous speeds.

Just as we are dwarfed by space, our little lives and civilizations are dwarfed by time. Lovecraft writes: "The reason why *time* plays a great part in so many of my tales is that this element looms up in my mind as the most profoundly dramatic and grimly terrible thing in the universe. *Conflict with time* seems to me the most potent and fruitful theme in all human expression."[25]

The inevitable extinction of humanity is a recurring theme in Lovecraft's work. In his mythos, time will run out for us when our civilization is destroyed by aliens, a possibility also threatened by *Alien* in the form of the corporation's plan to keep live specimens. However, Lovecraft isn't content to have us crushed by just one type of alien. Instead, when the right alignment of the stars finally arrives, many different sorts will be free to attack at once, in an orgy of destruction.

Lovecraft likewise depicts civilized alien species being wiped out by *other* alien species, generally leaving only ruins behind, like the ruined starship in *Alien*. The Earth was once ruled by vegetable Elder Things, but they were exterminated by shoggoths, creatures they had created to be their slaves. Likewise, the conical Yithians also once ruled Earth, but were overthrown by "polyps" from yet deeper reaches of space, while the snouted Yaddithians, who live too far away to bother us, are doomed to be annihilated by dholes, gigantic worms.

The predator from *Alien* that threatens humanity resembles Lovecraft's civilization-destroying aliens in two major ways. Firstly, it keeps changing form, leaving the crew guessing about what horror they will face next. The shoggoths and polyps have no form at all, being amoeba-like and taking whatever shape suits their fancy. The same is true of the sentient black slimes that live beneath the subterranean human civilization of K'n-Yan and will one day ooze up and obliterate it. The formlessness of the destroying races expresses the chaos and directionlessness of evolution.

Secondly, the predator alien in *Alien* shows no sign of being as intelligent as its prey, whether biomechanical or human, and relies less on technology. It hunts like an animal, attacking from ambush and striking with its teeth. Similarly, the ape-like creatures that overthrow the ancient human city of Olathoë in "Polaris" (1918) are brutes with basic tools, the dholes are mindless, and the shoggoths and polyps, who have no known technology, are vastly intellectually inferior to the species they wipe out. The way that mindless or mentally limited forces destroy more advanced societies expresses both the mindlessness of evolution, and the recognition that superior intelligence is only one way to outcompete a rival species, and not necessarily the most effective.

In Lovecraft's Taloned Footsteps

There are three more ways in which *Alien* echoes Lovecraft's work. Firstly, Lovecraft cultivated claustrophobia by setting his tales in confined spaces. In *Alien*, claustrophobia is overwhelming as the crew are hunted through the cramped *Nostromo*. Lovecraft produces the same effect by setting events underground in too many tales to list, including all three of his novellas.

Secondly, Lovecraft cultivated an atmosphere of paranoia by having inhuman creatures walk amongst us in disguise, often while plotting against us. In *Alien*, the robot Ash pretends to be a human as he schemes to return the predator to Earth even at the cost of the crew. In Lovecraft, Yithians pass as human by taking over human bodies, while fungoid Mi-Go prefer disguising themselves with wax masks, and froglike Deep Ones just hide in enormous coats. In *Alien*, paranoia is stoked by having the crew betrayed by other humans: the corporation. In Lovecraft, myriad secret human cults, like the Order of Dagon and Church of Starry Wisdom, work with the alien forces that would harm us.

Thirdly, Lovecraft violates the human body in horrific ways. In *Alien*, such violation is central to the horror. Most dramatically, the alien occupies Kane's face and metaphorically rapes him, laying its eggs in his stomach. Kane subsequently gives birth by being torn open from the inside. Further such abuses of biology are hinted at for Dallas, Brett, Parker, and Lambert. Likewise, in Lovecraft, things happen to human bodies that make simple butchery look mild. For example, when "The Colour Out of Space" preys on humans, it drains them until they are grey and brittle, crumbling to dust while still alive, while when the ancient creature buried beneath "The Shunned House" kills Dr. Whipple, it first blackens and decays his flesh, then melts him into a pool of faces of its previous victims. In *The Case of Charles Dexter Ward* (1927), botched resurrections from partial remains leave scores of people in hideously incomplete condition but unable to die, while "Cool Air" (1926) and "The Thing on the Doorstep" (1933) feature characters imprisoned in animate but decomposing corpses. Like *Alien*, Lovecraft is tastefully *nasty*. And what is horror fiction if it hasn't got a bit of nasty to it? The kiss of the Facehugger is one of the greatest kisses in cinematic history, and my personal favorite.

Final Transmission

The following, then, are the ultimate secrets for producing good science fiction horror, according to H.P. Lovecraft. The threat must be mysterious and, from our perspective, unnatural. Alien creatures must be genuinely alien, quite unlike humans both physically and psychologically. Everything else must be treated with absolute realism. Such realism requires that the characters react to the alien with extreme awe; their emotional response to alien encounters should be so strong that it overwhelms all of their other concerns. To inspire the audience's imagination, weird events should be conveyed by subtle suggestion.

Following Lovecraft's example, we might add any of the following: encourage claustrophobia by setting events in enclosed spaces; encourage paranoia by having nonhumans live amongst us unrecognized as they conspire against us; and keep in mind that the most horrible violations of nature, from our human perspective, are transformations and perversions of the human body.

Of course, no formula can be followed to guarantee good art. If it were possible to produce a film as excellent as *Alien* by consulting a simple checklist, then films as good as *Alien* would be a lot more common. On the other hand, given how rare films as good as *Alien* are, it makes sense to examine such examples of good science fiction horror in an effort to pick up useful tips and rules of thumb. It's been thirty-five years now since the crew of *Nostromo* walked out into the howling winds of a distant and hostile planetoid, to explore the forsaken ruins of an alien ship and discover its terrible secret. We haven't had a science fiction horror film as good since, and like a predator lurking in an abandoned starship, I am getting impatient.

Notes

1. I say that as someone with mad love for the genre of science fiction horror, and for wonderful films like *Frankenstein* (1931), *Invasion of the Body Snatchers* (1978), *The Thing* (1982), *Re-Animator* (1985), *Cube* (1997), and *Cabin Fever* (2002).
2. Lovecraft uses this plot in "Dagon" (1917), "The Nameless City" (1921), "Imprisoned with the Pharaohs" (1924), "The Call of Cthulhu" (1926), "In the Walls of Eryx" (with Kenneth J. Sterling, 1936), and in the novellas *At the Mountains of Madness* (1931) and *The Mound* (with Zealia Bishop, 1930), and variations on the formula appear in many more tales. All dates given for Lovecraft's works are dates of composition, not publication.
3. H.P. Lovecraft, *Supernatural Horror in Literature* (Dover, 1973), 12.
4. Ibid., 14.
5. H.P. Lovecraft, "In Defense of Dagon," in *Collected Essays of H.P. Lovecraft*, vol. 5, ed. S.T. Joshi (Hippocampus Press, 2008), 48.
6. Lovecraft, *Supernatural Horror in Literature*, 15.
7. H.P. Lovecraft, "Some Notes on Interplanetary Fiction," in *Collected Essays of H.P. Lovecraft*, vol. 2, 179.
8. Aristotle, *Poetics*, in *Aristotle: Complete Works*, ed. Jonathan Barnes (Princeton University Press, 1984), 2338.
9. Ibid., 2326.
10. Lovecraft, "Some Notes on Interplanetary Fiction," 180.
11. Ibid.
12. Lovecraft, "In Defense of Dagon," 11.
13. Lovecraft, "Some Notes on Interplanetary Fiction," 181.
14. H.P. Lovecraft, "Letter to Farnsworth Wright," July 5, 1927, in *Selected Letters of H.P. Lovecraft*, vol. 2, ed. A. Derleth (Arkham House, 1965), 201.
15. H.P. Lovecraft, "Letter to Reinhardt Kleiner," September 14, 1919, in *Selected Letters of H.P. Lovecraft*, vol. 1, 315.
16. H.P. Lovecraft, "Nietzscheism and Realism," in *Collected Essays of H.P. Lovecraft*, vol. 5, 69.
17. H.P. Lovecraft, "Notes on Writing Weird Fiction," *Collected Essays of H.P. Lovecraft*, vol. 2, 177.

18. Aristotle, *Poetics*, 2326.
19. H.P. Lovecraft, "Some Notes on Interplanetary Fiction," 178.
20. Ibid., 180.
21. Ibid., 179.
22. Lovecraft, "Notes on Writing Weird Fiction," 179.
23. H.P. Lovecraft, "The Festival," in *The Call of Cthulhu and Other Weird Stories* (Penguin Books, 1999), 116.
24. Lovecraft, "In Defense of Dagon," 48.
25. Lovecraft, "Notes on Writing Weird Fiction," 176.

12

Art-Horror Environments and the *Alien* Series

Martin Glick

Thanks to masterful set design by the Swiss artist H.R. Giger, the *Alien* films are memorably set in dark, wet, and slimy worlds where monsters bleed acid and terrorize humans with stealthy execution. The worlds he designed don't remain pristine, however. They are soon riddled with bullets fired by space Marines, blown apart by APCs, and adapted by the aliens so that they can breed in dark corridors. In all the *Alien* films, the environments are gloomy settings originally inspired by Gothic architecture, but it's the creature design—also dark, wet, and slimy—which leaves the most profound mark on us. Their otherworldly bodies remain in our minds as disturbing hybrids, these monsters with features of different kinds of animals: the movement of a reptile, the skin of a snake, the teeth of a crocodile, and so on. They are what Noël Carroll, in his book *The Philosophy of Horror, Or, Paradoxes of the Heart*, calls "fusion figures" or "art-horror objects,"[1] and they exemplify Carroll's theory about what fills us with fear and disgust when we watch horror films.

Nostromo Infected

The *interaction* between these art-horror monsters and the sterile-turned-grotesque environments of the *Alien* films can produce disgust or revulsion in the viewer. Carroll discusses the "fantastic biology" of

Alien and Philosophy: I Infest, Therefore I Am, First Edition.
Edited by Jeffrey Ewing and Kevin S. Decker.
© 2017 John Wiley & Sons Ltd. Published 2017 by John Wiley & Sons Ltd.

"art-horror" monsters, with a hybrid nature that makes them threatening and impure. What makes these monsters disgusting is often their relation to vermin we associate with being unclean, such as Dracula's ability to turn into a bat. Other times, these monsters tie in to our natural phobias and magnify them, for example the giant ants or bees in Cold War-era films. Elementary to Carroll's theory is the fusion of two opposing concepts in order to creep out the viewer who shares the "emotive assessment"[2] of the characters in the film when they witness the monsters. That is, when we watch horror films, we *know* that the monsters on the screen don't exist (because they're fictional, after all), but we still retain this sensation of fear because we empathize with the characters. It's the expression on the faces of the crew in *Alien* when a Chestburster emerges from Kane, for example, that increases our own sense of disgust at the scene.

Xenomorphs, however, don't merely fuse opposing elements of different species. They also "infect" the otherwise clean environment. As we can see with the characters' reactions to these changes in the environment, the aliens are not just predatory monsters. In fact, essential to their "alien" nature is the way they transform our recognizable environments into something extremely foreign.

In Gothic literature and the cinema based on it, the environment is merely a backdrop for the characters' actions. Even the most famous monsters of cinema, like Dracula or Frankenstein's monster, are civilized in their inhabitation of their surroundings. Rarely does their destructive rage result in more than the occasional broken window or ripped-off door. *Alien* breaks with the Gothic tradition by offering a destructible environment in which the creature is free to roam. In the sequel, *Aliens*, the viewer is witness to a mob of Xenomorphs adapting the environment to further their species' ability to breed. Ultimately, in *Alien: Resurrection*, Ripley is intertwined with the Queen alien in a complication of alien flesh and human flesh, wiping out the environment totally. Consequently, as Carroll analyzed the horror of a monster with features belonging to several different species, the *Alien* series shows the horror of the interaction of a repellent monster with a clean or spare environment. Let's call this an "art-horror environment." More than the interaction of monster and environment, art-horror environments suggest a sense of *accidental contamination*: the sense that something dreadful and corrosive has infected the previously "pure" or "sterile" environment but not as a direct result of a vicious predatory nature.

In the *Alien* series, we regularly witness contamination as the result of an interaction between monster and environment. In *Alien*, the acid blood of the Xenomorph drips on metal surfaces, corroding walls or floors. In *Aliens*, bound humans are found in organic webbing where they can serve as incubators for growing aliens. Another instance is found when Ellen Ripley is enveloped by the Xenomorph Queen near the end of *Alien: Resurrection*. Because these scenes occur without the alien itself, they don't fall under Carroll's definition of "art-horror objects." They also aren't the direct results of the art-horror object's predatory activity, but rather are *accidental* features of the alien's biology, which along with the accompanying perception of contamination, forms the heart of the "disgust" audiences feel when viewing these art-horror environments. Accidental events provoke the unsettling realization that *they could have been avoided*. It's an accident of genetics that the alien blood has enough acidic properties to melt the structures of humankind's vehicles of space travel. It is also an accident of technology that spaceships like the *Nostromo* weren't built with materials strong enough to withstand its corrosive nature. Accidents in the world are frustrating to contend with because they are by their very nature unpredictable. We may seek to individualize problems and attribute blame, hopefully making solutions easier to find. Accidents corrupt our ability to take control of, or responsibility for, the situation, like the "accidental" corrosive effects of the Xenomorphs on their environments.

Imagine that a parallel-universe-version of the alien creatures devour wood paneling and other housing materials like termites as a means to survive. There is nothing particularly gruesome about this kind of monster, and the destruction of its environment is a direct result of the principles by which a filmmaker has designed that monster. A central property of these parallel-universe creatures is that they are "environment-destroying," and that this activity is a known and expected result of encountering this kind of monster. But while these monsters would destroy the environment as their central goal, the way the Xenomorphs interact with the *Nostromo* and other environments is always simply an accidental side-effect of fragility in the equipment of Weyland-Yutani and the space Marines. In short, we expect the aliens to kill Marines; what we don't expect is the destruction of the environment in the process. *Alien* highlights how the extension of Carroll's theory about the source of our disgust can be extended to the destruction or modification of otherwise pristine, useful environments.

Corrosion

Environments in films typically place the viewer in a situation they're familiar with. In *Alien* a fair amount of time is spent on the relationships between the crew members. We get to know their places in the hierarchy of the ship along with their typical work duties. We become part of the gang, or at least the ship seems to us as a relatively safe place. This makes the acid blood of the aliens not only a corrosive agent, but a destroyer of *sanctuary*. Acid blood in the first film tunnels through the spaceship, and, deck after deck, the crew inspects the damage until, eventually, it stops. These holes also degrade the viewer's sense of safety as they devour the ship's material. The blood is not only an affront to the sterile and technical environments of the spaceship, achievements of humankind, but an attack on our sense of what is "home."

Key to Carroll's theory is the need for a fusion or fission of two creatures in order to creep out the viewer. We can extend these views by proposing that art-horror environments shake up the viewer in a different (but related) way. It's not just the disgusting quality of the monster foregrounded against a clean or technological environment that disturbs us. We're also made uneasy by a foreign entity's destruction or invasion of a space that serves as "home" (the AI computer is referred to as "Mother," after all). Early on in the first film, Ripley understands at least at a procedural level the importance of making sure there is no contamination on the ship. When Kane has a Facehugger attached to him after getting too close to an alien egg, Dallas insists that they let him on board. Ripley responds, "Wait a minute. If we let it in, the ship could be infected. You know the quarantine procedure. Twenty-four hours for decontamination."

Even worse, the violence of the acts becomes more horrific when our path to identifying with the perpetrator is cut off. Carroll's fusion-figures don't resemble humans closely enough to be properly classified or held accountable for what they've done. They act like animals, so they are beyond moral reproach, too. This strikes at the very heart of one of society's anxieties: these monsters have no regard for human life—or our "stuff"—and we have no recourse for retribution. Soldiers can at least get the satisfaction of revenge when their fellow crew members are killed, but the spoiling of personal property has no satisfying equivalent. The protagonists of the film series can't even "take back what is ours" to use a stereotypical line from action films, because nothing was stolen or lost. Instead, it was "accidentally harmed" or repurposed.

The accidental or arbitrary property of acid blood deserves a little more explanation as to why it so shakes us. Critical to accidental events is the unsettling realization that *they could have been avoided*. Humans are at fault for the space Marines' reliance on weapons that break alien skin, spaceships that are vulnerable to acid, and for disturbing the alien eggs in the first place. It is a genetic accident that Xenomorph blood is acidic enough to eat through human spaceships. Accidents in the world are frustrating to contend with because they are by their very nature unpredictable. The accident of encountering acid blood has no immediate solutions, and the viewer can recognize this, sympathizing with the mental frustration of the crew who must be placing the blame on themselves for their unfortunate situation. Expressed frustration regarding the alien encounters are peppered through the film *Aliens*. The space Marine Hudson, as the futility of the situation dawns on him, reminds the crew: "We're all gonna die, man!" and "Those things are gonna come in here just like they did before…and they're gonna come in here AND THEY'RE GONNA GET US!"

The Brood

In *Aliens* we get our first glimpse as to how these creatures transform environments and use humans to breed. Bodies trapped in a thick, slimy webbing are stuck on the wall while alien Chestbursters gestate inside them. One of the most horrific moments of the series is the cry of "kill me" that emerges from the half-conscious hosts as the space Marines explore the former colony of Hadley's Hope.

The humans' technological environment is contaminated by their presence as well. The atmosphere, once terraformed, has turned swampy on LV-426. Mist hovers where before there was clean air. The entire climate has shifted away from cold and machine-maintained, and has been replaced with heat, humidity, and the sights and smells of an organic interior. It's an excellent example of an art-horror environment, juxtaposing organic and hairy matter against cold steel plates. Central to Carroll's theory on art-horror is revulsion at the suggestion of physical contact with the fusion-figures. Mentioning imagined possibilities of contamination and disease, Carroll addresses the impact that the "impure"[3] nature of art-horror monsters has on us. While the infestation of art-horror environments certainly invokes the idea of contamination in the way that Carroll does, the interaction between aliens and the films' colony and spaceship environments doesn't need to resemble anything like the transmission of a disease. Instead, the Xenomorph's normal biological activities pose an affront to things and places we can envision as our own homes and property; this is enough to cause a feeling of revulsion.

The *accidental* quality of the breeding in *Aliens* is present on the screen. Just as acid blood couldn't be fought off because it was unpredictable, so too the Xenomorphs are seen by the audience in a new way: as an insurmountable force of numbers, to which there seems to be no end (at least until Ripley faces off against the Queen, the ultimate source of the eggs). When the Colonial Marines first land on LV-426, they find themselves up against hordes of aliens in numbers not seen in the first film, but before any alien contact is made, they first encounter a cocooned colonist. Carroll might claim that the implication of the fusion-figures' presence is enough to inspire disgust, but it is this modified environment that first does the work.

It is bad enough that their acid blood destroys our technology, but when the Xenomorphs propagate their species using human-kind's expensive and fragile technology—and *at the cost of human lives*—we have what Carroll labels one of the many "transgressions" they can put into practice. If their mere existence is horrifying, then for them to procreate their species could be considered a psychological transgression that art-horror monsters commit, the desire to "advance an alternative society."[4] Carroll writes that horror fiction relies on a three-part movement: from a normal state of affairs to a disruption of that state by the emergence of a monster, and finally to the defeat of the monster and a return to the previous cultural order. But when the aliens use and contaminate human technology, we're left with a sense in which this last step cannot be achieved. Contaminated ships, just like cocooned colonists, must simply be destroyed; there is nothing about the property "useful to aliens" that can be reversed or redeemed. This idea is expressed when Ripley says to the remaining crew, "I say we take off and nuke the entire site from orbit. It's the only way to be sure." The only way to be sure every trace of the repurposed environment is lost forever, even at the risk of human lives still on the surface.

The Melding

At the end of *Alien: Resurrection*, Ripley lies in the middle of the Queen's huge mass. It's the most striking image in an otherwise cartoonish film. The Queen essentially becomes an environment, of which Ripley is just a small part. We see in these ten minutes an idealized, if nightmarish, version of the paradigmatic *Alien* film art-horror environment, one that is dark and marked only by swirling limbs.

Whereas the aliens had previously exerted a corrosive effect on the human environment accidentally, adapting the surfaces of Hadley's Hope to reproduce, in this instance we see the environment *become* alien. All human-made visual cues have disappeared, subsumed in the Queen's need to further her species.

One of the paradoxes of horror and a central issue in Carroll's work is the question of how we can be horrified by monsters in situations that we know don't exist. Carroll remarks that cinema often achieves this goal by using cinematographic techniques to *overwhelm* the viewer. The existence and effect of art-horror environments go a long way towards our complete immersion in horror. Ripley, consumed by the dark Queen alien, is an image of the organic completely overtaking the human and its futurist technological aids to surviving in space. This signifies not only the appropriation of humankind's technology, but their complete absorption to an accidental, alien need. Our technology and the spaces that we require to live are more than stolen in this film; they are rendered unrecognizable, a total betrayal of human efforts. This image departs slightly from the other two cases where we had the fright of the characters spur our own revulsion. We saw on the faces of the crew how *gross* the dripping acid was, just as their shrinking back in fear at the pinioned, Facehugger-implanted colonists spurs us to do the same. In this case, the fear is totally our own. We stand both in awe and disturbed at Ripley's absorption into her new environment: assimilation with an alien body, part of the corrupting force that bleeds into the otherwise pristine environment.

Adding to Carroll's theory of art-horror objects these observations about art-horror environments help to explain why this final image is so striking. The viewer knows that this environment was once cold, sterile, reliable, and in a sense "home." It is not the hot, organic hive of reproduction from *Aliens*, but cold and sleek in a quite alien way. The Queen Xenomorph has taken our aesthetic principles of the design of machinery and technology and made them her own.

Notes

1. Noël Carroll, *The Philosophy of Horror, Or, Paradoxes of the Heart* (Routledge, 1990), 43.
2. Ibid., 53.
3. Ibid., 23.
4. Ibid., 43.

Contagion: Impurity, Mental Illness, and Suicide in *Alien³*

Kevin S. Decker

"If in heavy horrible dreams anxiety reaches its highest degree, it causes us to wake up, whereby all those monstrous horrors of the night vanish. The same thing happens in the dream of life when the highest degree of anxiety forces us to break it off."

—Arthur Schopenhauer[1]

During the twenty-second century, throughout our home arm of the galaxy, the Weyland-Yutani Corporation spreads like a plague of locusts, devouring the resources of worlds, moons, and even suns, and leaving devastated ecologies and burnt-out planetary husks in their wake. The latest of these is "grey, lifeless, alone in space… FIORINA 'FURY' 161/OUTER VEIL MINERAL ORE REFINERY/ MAXIMUM SECURITY WORK-CORRECTIONAL FACILITY/…a desolate industrial wasteland, black water in the distance." In addition to being a dark, sooty, abandoned industrial smelting facility, Fury 161 serves as a penal colony for maximum-risk male prisoners. They're scum, according to prison superintendent Andrews, but "scum that have taken on religion."

To call these prisoners "scum" or "dirt" is not merely to say they've broken laws or moral prohibitions, but that they've gone further than that, violating deeply rooted social taboos. Some of these taboos, like those against incest, make sense to us in a twenty-first-century context; we feel that the punishment for such a crime ought to be worse than for other, similar violations. Other taboos,

Alien and Philosophy: I Infest, Therefore I Am, First Edition.
Edited by Jeffrey Ewing and Kevin S. Decker.
© 2017 John Wiley & Sons Ltd. Published 2017 by John Wiley & Sons Ltd.

like religious dietary restrictions and not eating where you shit, can be validated through modern biological science. Still others, like fears about pollution from menstrual blood, have been influential in some times and cultures but seem unreasonable to us today. And the idea of "scum," "dirt," or the unhygienic in general isn't just a reference to biological impurity—it has deep roots in cultural symbolism and intellectual history. Dirt is "matter out of place," a "by-product of a systematic ordering and classification of matter, in so far as ordering involves rejecting inappropriate elements."[2] Hence confinement facilities like Fury 161: "out of sight, out of mind."

For Michel Foucault (1926–1984), in his *History of Madness*, the confinement of "the poor, the unemployed, the criminal, and the insane"[3] swept away certain social problems so that other issues of economic, political, and legal modernization could be addressed. "It is clear that confinement, in its primitive forms," Foucault writes, "worked as a social mechanism, and that the mechanism was extremely widespread, stretching from elementary economic regulation to the great bourgeois dream of a city where an authoritarian synthesis of nature and virtue reigned supreme."[4] The dystopian elements of the *Alien* films display the dark side of social mechanisms like these.

Modern philosophy is not exempt from the temptations of this "authoritarian synthesis." It also responds to the themes of impurity, whether through religious heresy, mental illness, or bodily invasion or corruption (as the *Alien* movies do such a great job of showing). Although Georg W.F. Hegel (1770–1831) has claimed that philosophy holds its time in thought, there may be some things (like Facehuggers) that we want to hold at more than an arm's distance. The horrors on Fury 161 represent the intersection of visceral and timeless fears about the evils of *contagion*—whether the infection is pathological, sexual, or even found in the realm of ideas, like religious blasphemy. This has led some to believe that contagion can only be purged by sacrificing the victim herself—a view Ripley shares in the dramatic conclusion of *Alien³*. In her history of philosophy that identifies *evil* as the core of our obsession since the eighteenth century, Susan Neiman writes that we seem to "lack the conceptual resources" to "seek understanding, explanation, catharsis, consolation" for the contagious nature of evil.[5] Can philosophy respond to these dark corners of reality? This chapter answers with an enthusiastic "yes!"

Infection

Alien³ allows us no time to get comfortable. It begins within the cramped, claustrophobic environment of the EEV and the survivors from the end of *Aliens*: three hypersleep tubes containing Ripley, Corporal Hicks, the young girl Newt, and what remains of the android Bishop. The opening credits are intercut with short bursts of action from within the escape pod: a Facehugger "finger" rising; a scan of its tendril reaching down a human throat; acid blood disintegrating the hull plating; crimson blood seeping through white fabric. The EEV lands explosively in the sea of Fury 161 and a lone survivor is washed up onto shore.

In the shooting script for *Alien³*, it's clear that Ripley has been "infected" by the Xenomorph Facehugger in the pod; on screen, that fact is held from us until much later in the film for dramatic effect. The fact that now Ripley is the carrier of the Xenomorph-in-embryo—a travesty of normal biological motherhood—is both tragic and ironic. Witness the following exchange between an edgy Ripley and the perplexed medico, Clemens:

RIPLEY: (*after looking at Newt's body*) We need an autopsy.
CLEMENS: You're joking.
RIPLEY: No way. We have to make sure how she died.
CLEMENS: I told you, she drowned. (*Clemens begins to slide the body back. Ripley stops him*)
RIPLEY: I'm not so sure—I want you to cut her open.
CLEMENS: Listen to me, I think you're disorientated—half your system's still in cryosleep.
RIPLEY: Look, I have a very good reason for asking this and I want you to do it—
CLEMENS: Would you care to share this reason?
RIPLEY: Possible contagion.
CLEMENS: What kind?
RIPLEY: I'm not the doctor—you are.
CLEMENS: You'll have to do better than that.
RIPLEY: Cholera.
CLEMENS: You can't be serious. There hasn't been a case reported in 200 years.
           (*Ripley simply stares at him*)
CLEMENS: As you wish.

Later, Ripley demands that Andrews cremate the bodies of Hicks and Newt, wary of a "public health issue." The comment is more than an occasion for the audience to enjoy Ripley's wry humor: the parasitoid Xenomorphs are a lot like macro-scale viruses, violently injecting their own DNA into unwilling host cells.

Ripley's fears about contagion actually fit together well with the thinking of the German Idealist philosophers of the late eighteenth and early nineteenth centuries, who were among the first philosophers of biology. These thinkers, among them the aforementioned Hegel and Friedrich Schelling (1775–1854), were wrestling with how to explain how the properties specific to living things—regeneration, self-reproduction, assimilation of the environment, irritation—had emerged from nonliving nature. Hegel may surprise us in that he's an early *ecological* thinker—for him, the "first organism" is "the Earth-body as the *universal system* of individual bodies."[6] Although the individual organism must be understood as existing "over against…non-organic nature," the connection between each living creature and inanimate nature is "absolute, indivisible, inner, and essential"; today, we would say that they are *interdependent.*[7] For Hegel, the living creature follows its instincts to assimilate things in its environment and make them part of itself through the activity of sensory perception, of passive "irritability" (these two are polar opposites), and digestion; in general, these are all forms of "assimilation." When assimilation goes wrong because, for example, a person eats a poisonous mushroom or has the larva of a huge, parasitoid Xenomorph pushed down her gullet, Hegel thinks that one of its systems or organs "establishes itself in isolation and persists in its particular activity against the activity of the whole, the fluidity and all-pervading process of which is thus obstructed."[8] Disease, for Hegel as it will be for Darwin later, cannot be understood as intrinsically evil, but only as one moment in much broader movements of nature; paradoxically, contagion, decline, and death are necessary for life.

For Schelling, a thinker who sees the universe as having its origin in the "duplicity" of conscious productive activity (God) and unconscious productive activity (Nature), assimilation always implies an assimilator and an assimilated. For nature to continue to exist, it must continue to reproduce "doubles" akin to its origin in God and Nature, and must do so ad infinitum. He often sees life as engaged in a life-or-death struggle with an inimical nature (and life, of course, doesn't always win). Schelling's view is that the main way in which life is touched by inorganic nature is through the process of "excitability"—a concept that can't be separated from sexual opposition.[9] So contagion can't be fully understood without examining its sexual aspects: "Infection is simultaneously assimilatory, sexual, pathological, and...eminently 'spiritual.'"[10] While we worry for Ripley's safety in the presence of serial murderers like Golic and rapists like Dillon, in fact this lone woman on Fury 161 is shunned—as if sexual desire were infectious—rather than ogled:

MORSE: I just want to say that I took a vow of celibacy. That also includes women. We all took the vow. Now let me say, that I for one, do not appreciate Company policy allowing her to freely intermingle...

DILLON: What brother means to say is...We view the presence of any outsider, woman, as a violation of the harmony, a potential break in the spiritual unity.

As Mary Douglas writes, moral and sexual attitudes are often chained to beliefs about dirt and pollution, leading to a staggering diversity of cultural attitudes about sexuality throughout the world.[11] Simultaneously, Dillon, the leader of the religious prisoners, nonetheless stands to represent our conventional moral view against rape, helping Ripley escape several lascivious prisoners at the colony's garbage dump while she is looking for the Bishop android.

Now, Ripley doesn't seem much interested in sex throughout the first two *Alien* films (though that does not stop her objectification by the male crew of the *Nostromo,* or Corporal Hicks's flirting), but she is interested in having a family, especially after Newt's death. In the climactic scene of *Alien³*, as Ripley faces the newly arrived Weyland-Yutani corporate thugs above the vat of molten lead, a man who claims to be the original Bishop knows exactly what to say:

BISHOP: We admit we made mistakes. We didn't know. But we can make it up to you. All the potential lost, all the time, you can still have children. We'll buy out your contract. Everything you deserve.

RIPLEY: You're not going to take it [the creature] back?

BISHOP: No. We realize now. You're right. But time is important. Let us deal with the malignancy. We've got a surgery room set up on the rescue ship, ready to go.

Bishop has all the oily charm of a quack abortion peddler, with his perverse implication that Ripley can exchange a malignant embryonic life-form for a benign one if she'll only cooperate. Unconvinced, Ripley wisely balances these concerns against the fate of humanity by thinking according to the infection model: "If it gets off this planet, it'll kill everything." Life may indeed require disease and death for Hegel and Schelling, but Ripley has decided that contagion will not win today or in this way, as we'll see in the final section.

Madness

Of course, Fury 161 is not just a prison but a life sentence for double-Y chromosome criminals.[12] Yet even if the YY condition is understood as a genetic deformity giving individuals a predisposition for violent crimes, both psychology and criminal justice tell us that these "maximum-risk" prisoners may not have been consciously responsible for the criminal acts they committed, and therefore deserve treatment and rehabilitation over punishment and exile. Nonetheless, "what's out of sight is out of mind." A deliberate judgment has been made that, in restricting the (impaired) autonomy of the YY's, others will find themselves more free in not having to worry about such "deviants." Perceived mental illness becomes social infection, and the social infection is quarantined.

Eugen Fischer claims that "mental 'illness' is constituted by a certain lack of autonomy," and that Plato's *Republic* first offered a view of mental health that still shapes our views of mental illness today: "the ideal of a balanced, rational agent who can master his feelings and impulses so as to be truly autonomous. We count as 'ill' when we fall significantly short of this ideal."[13] Because the goal of the *Republic* is ultimately moral in character, Plato compares virtue to "a sort of health, a fine and good state of the soul." Yet there is significant distance between Greek *mores* about mental health and our own, as revealed when Plato compares vice to "a shameful disease and weakness."[14]

As Foucault shows in *Madness and Civilization*, the ways in which western cultures treated the mad have varied widely. Prior to the origins of psychiatry in the late eighteenth century, he notes, madmen weren't treated as sick; rather, in the context of Christian beliefs, madness was seen as "the lower limit of human truth, a limit not accidental but essential."[15] By this, Foucault means that "the scandal of madness showed men how close to animality their Fall could bring them; and at the same time how far divine mercy could extend when it consented to save man."[16] According to this view, madness, not sanity, is treated as a better mirror of the "dizzying unreason of the world."[17]

The Christian religion provides a degree of order among the few remaining inmates of Fury 161, but not all the prisoners share its views of the essential separation of the sexes and its "happy ending" in the final resurrection. Similarly, the writers and production crew foreshadow the fact that this belief will not triumph in the end when Dillon's homily at the burning of the bodies of Hicks and Newt is juxtaposed with the birth of the "dragon" Xenomorph. "Within each seed there's the promise of a flower. And within each death, no matter how small, there's always a new life. A new beginning," he recites, unaware that in this case, new life is not always a good thing. Dillon, the self-appointed preacher, proves to be a more effective leader than superintendent Andrews when it comes to rallying the prisoners against the Xenomorph, yet at the same time, Dillon views Ripley's sex as both "intolerable" and a "temptation" despite his strength of will:

DILLON: You don't wanna know me. I am a murderer and a rapist. Of women.
RIPLEY: Really. I guess I must make you nervous.
DILLON: Do you have any faith, sister?
RIPLEY: Not a lot.
DILLON: We got lots of faith here. Enough even for you.
RIPLEY: I thought women weren't allowed.
DILLON: We never had any before. But we tolerate anybody. Even the intolerable.
RIPLEY: Thanks.
DILLON: That's just a statement of principle. Nothing personal. We got a good place here to wait. Up to now, no temptation.

Ripley is seen as a contagion that interrupts Dillon's patient waiting for the inevitability of salvation.

Before the nineteenth century in the west, madness was not seen as sickness of the body, true, but was conceived of instead as a *social* disease—something that could potentially be contagious if the mad, however benign, were not confined in places like London's Bethlem Royal Hospital (or "Bedlam") and Bicêtre Hospital in Paris. So psychiatrists in the time of philosophers like Hegel and Schelling, that is, the early nineteenth century, saw themselves as agents of "public hygiene."[18] They tried to link insanity to problems in living conditions of the time: "overpopulation, overcrowding, urban life, alcoholism, debauchery," while at the same time wondering about whether and how madness could be transmitted through newly understood mechanisms of heredity.[19]

These concerns over infectiousness pervade our picture of Xenomorphs in the *Alien* series. In fact, not only are the predation and procreation behaviors of the Xenomorphs (and our protagonists' reactions to them) clearly symbolic of disease and its related fears, but their habitats—or, if you prefer, hunting grounds—in the *Alien* films mirror the cramped, fetid everyday living conditions that early psychiatrists suspected spawned insanity. In this way, even if madness isn't seen as a disease, it can be linked to the same conditions that foster disease.

The society of the twenty-second century would seem to resemble the early nineteenth in writing off the mentally ill as suitable only for confinement. Clearly, the greatest madman of the lot on Fiorina 161 is Golic. His mind, never clear in the first place, seems to break after he witnesses two of the first prisoner deaths at the hands (claws, really) of the Xenomorph that had gestated in Murphy's dog Spike. In shock, he returns to the mess hall where he is discovered by the cook, drenched in blood and eating breakfast cereal. Golic is restrained for his own safety and sent to the infirmary, where Dillon and superintendent Andrews debate his case. For Andrews, Golic has clearly fallen below Foucault's "lower limit of truth":

ANDREWS: Keep him separated from the rest, I don't want him causing a panic. Clemens, sedate this poor idiot.

DILLON: Not until we know about the brothers... (*turns to Golic*) Now pull yourself together, man, talk to me. Where are the brothers?

GOLIC: I didn't do it!

ANDREWS: Hopeless. You're not to get a thing out of him...We'll have to send out a search team. I'm afraid we have to assume that there is a very good chance this simple bastard has murdered them.

DILLON: You don't know that. He's never lied to me. He's crazy. He's a fool. But he's not a liar.
(*Ripley walks up to the group from the shadows. All eyes turn to her.*)

RIPLEY: There's a good chance he's telling the truth. I need to talk to him about this dragon...

Unlucky Golic! The "dragon's" next victim is his medical caregiver and Ripley's only ally, Clemens. In this "bloody well" key scene in the infirmary, we learn that no one is safe, and at the same time we first begin to understand that the Xenomorphs can sense their own kind, even in embryo, as the "dragon" leaves both Ripley and Golic for later.

Golic is unusual among those on Fury 161 as he obsesses about the Xenomorph after it kills Raines and Boggs, even calling it "magnificent!" after it kills Clemens (this line and his full obsession appear only in the 2003 "Assembly Cut" of *Alien³*). In this regard, he is quintessentially "mad" in the sense explored by the idiosyncratic thinker Arthur Schopenhauer (1788–1860), a late contemporary of Hegel and Schelling. Schopenhauer thought that madness was a "violent 'casting out of one's mind' of something" that follows "a 'putting into the head of something else.'"[20] These ideas, crudely expressed as they are, were influential to early psychiatrists (or "alienists") in forming the more recognizable concepts of "dissociation" (Pierre Janet) and "repressed memories" (Freud). In his discussion of madness, Schopenhauer continues:

> The reverse process is rarer, namely that the "putting into the head" is the first thing, and the "casting out of the mind" the second. It takes place, however, in cases where a person keeps constantly present to his mind, and cannot get rid of, the cause of his insanity; thus, for example,...the case of madness that has resulted from horror at a sudden, frightful occurrence. Such patients cling convulsively, so to speak, to the conceived idea, so that no other, at any rate none that opposes it, can arise.[21]

The psychosis that made Golic a mass murderer before Fury 161 now makes him the obsessive protector of the Xenomorph. Yet another major divergence from the theatrical version in the "Assembly Cut" is that the attempt to trap the "dragon" in the nuclear waste dump succeeds; it is Golic who slits the throat of a prisoner standing guard and frees the Xenomorph, only to be slaughtered for his pains.

Death

At the end of *Alien³*, our heroine, Ripley, kills herself rather than allow her own Chestburster "contagion" to survive and—what may be worse—be captured by the Company. What's the significance of this tragic ending?

In examining the views of Hegel and Schelling on disease, we saw that although it seems paradoxical, contagion, decline, and death are all necessary for life. Madness, understood in parallel way (as a "disease of society"), was seen as equally necessary for a proper understanding of the human predicament and need for salvation in the history of Christianity, a view that changes around the time of Schopenhauer as madness is "medicalized." Foucault defines "medicalization" as the social changes leading "human existence, human behavior, and the human body" to be "brought into an increasingly dense and important network of [medical research, application, and treatment] that allowed fewer and fewer things to escape."[22] One interpretation of what this means would be to gesture to the same kinds of reasons that are today invoked in support of universal health care: more prevention, longer life spans, greater focus on individual wellness. These are new types of freedoms surrounding the healthy individual body and the increased abilities that accompany that health.

Another very different reason, as we have seen, is to promote the cause of public hygiene, with all this phrase implies about medical, legal, and political power being used to restructure living relations. These uses of power are perceived by some, particularly in the public debate about universal health care, as implying a *lessening* of freedom. Perhaps, as the German Idealists concluded with reference to contagion and Michel Foucault intimated about madness, we should not expect the one without the other, the good without the bad. Strangely, this suggests a kind of identity between what we consider to foster our freedom and what is inimical to it. Schelling called this hidden identity "indifference," and considered it the central focus of all philosophy.

Ripley's own personal solution to this dilemma—what to do about the contagion that becomes achingly clear over the course of *Aliens³*— also embraces this indifference, as a final quote from Schopenhauer makes clear:

> Suicide can also be regarded as an experiment, a question we put to nature and try to make her answer, namely, what change the existence and knowledge of man undergo through death. But it is an awkward experiment, for it abolishes the identity of the consciousness that would have to listen to the answer.[23]

Ripley's experiment ends as she falls into the molten lead, its results unclear except that "the experience and knowledge of man" may go on a little longer with two fewer Xenomorphs in the universe.

Unless there were to be some kind of...resurrection?

Notes

1. Arthur Schopenhauer, "On Suicide," in *The Essential Schopenhauer*, ed. Wolfgang Schirmacher (HarperPerennial, 2010), 183.

2. Mary Douglas, *Purity and Danger: An Analysis of Concepts of Pollution and Taboo* (Frederick A. Praeger, 1966), 35.

3. Michel Foucault, *History of Madness*, ed. Jean Khalfa, trans. Jonathan Murphy and Jean Khalfa (Routledge, 2006), 47.

4. Ibid., 78.

5. Susan Neiman, *Evil in Modern Thought: An Alternative History of Philosophy* (Princeton University Press, 2002), 238.

6. G.W.F. Hegel, *Philosophy of Nature: Part Two of the Encyclopedia of the Philosophical Sciences*, trans. A.V. Miller (2004), §338, 277.

7. Ibid., §357 *Zusatz*, 381.

8. Ibid., §371, 428.

9. David Farrell Krell, *Contagion: Sexuality, Disease, and Death in German Idealism and Romanticism* (Indiana University Press, 1998), 83–84.

10. Ibid., 92.

11. Among the Nuer people of south Sudan, for example, "A 'little incest' is something which could happen between the best families at any time," and is not to be condemned. Conversely, "they regard the effects of adultery to be dangerous to the injured husband; he is liable to contract pains in his back when he subsequently has intercourse with his wife." Douglas, *Purity and Danger*, 131.

12. And it's an odd sort of prison. It has no armed guards and just two authority figures—superintendent Andrews and his assistant, Francis "85" Andrews (the nickname is his IQ). Inmates seem to have free reign over the facility (indeed, the entire planet) and, given the difference in numbers between the convicts and their guardians, could've easily taken over the place. The planet thus bears a resemblance to the "ship of fools" mentioned by Plato in book VI of the *Republic*, ships that Michel Foucault claims really existed in the medieval centuries as cities sought to offload the mad to places where they could do no harm; see *Madness and Civilization* (Vintage Books, 1965), 7 ff.

13. Eugen Fischer, "Diseases of the Understanding and the Need for Philosophical Therapy," *Philosophical Investigations* 34.1 (January 2011): 44. See Plato, *Republic*, trans. C.D.C. Reeve (Hackett, 2004), 132–134 (443c–444e).

14. Plato, *Republic*, 134 (444c11–444e1).

15. Foucault, *Madness and Civilization*, 81.

16. Ibid.

17. Ibid., 13.

18. Foucault, "About the Concept of the 'Dangerous Individual' in Nineteenth-Century Legal Psychiatry," in *Essential Works of Foucault, 1954–1984*, vol. 3, ed. James D. Faubion (New Press, 2000), 184.

19. Ibid.
20. Schopenhauer, *The World as Will and Representation*, vol. 2, trans. E.F.J. Payne (Dover, 1966), 401.
21. Ibid.
22. Foucault, "The Birth of Social Medicine," in *Essential Works of Foucault, 1954–1984*, vol. 3, 135.
23. Schopenhauer, "On Suicide," 183.

Part V

SEX AND GENDER: "NONE OF THEM HAVE SEEN A WOMAN IN YEARS"

14
Ellen Ripley: The Rise of the Matriarch

Andrea Zanin

A mother's instinct to protect is an intuition that would have her dive in front of a bullet or offer a kidney without thought. Science knows it as "maternal aggression"—a motherly assault to protect offspring from harm. A mom knows it as the rising fury that threatens to rip the head off any human (or other) threatening the welfare of her child, and woe to any playground attendee who unbalances the status quo with ill-mannered running, wayward sand-throwing or impatient pushes when under the beady eye of all-seeing mom. Perhaps director Ridley Scott did not have this exact scenario in mind when he was figuring out how to scare the world into frenzied hysteria with the art of cinema and some fiendish extraterrestrials in a horror-sci-fi extravaganza of death and destruction. What he did do was set the world up for the evolution of Ellen Ripley into one bad-ass momma bear.

Motherhood is primal. The tiny seed that plants itself in a woman's body—feeding off her nutrients and life blood with parasitic fervor, tearing its way to freedom nine or so months later. Birth inflicts disfigurement on body and brain, fertilizing a new mother's mind with an insatiable need to protect the new life but also to be free from that life. In the films of the *Alien* franchise featuring Sigourney Weaver, Ripley's maternal instinct is an integral part of who she is as both survivor and protector—and as a destroyer, too.

Ripley's way of engaging with the world, her subjectivity (the consciousness, agency, personhood, reality, and truth of her existence) is informed by "the maternal," by "mothering." Philosophers know this as "maternal subjectivity," and focus on how conceptions of motherhood

Alien and Philosophy: I Infest, Therefore I Am, First Edition.
Edited by Jeffrey Ewing and Kevin S. Decker.

and self both reinforce and oppose one another. The contemporary philosopher Alison Stone argues that a traditional idea of subjectivity is at odds with motherhood because it implies subservience of the self to the needs of a child—a lack of autonomy, in other words. For mothers to preserve their sense of self, Stone argues, they need to break away from their children; they need to make themselves antithetical to the life they have brought forth. These ideas come across in the many versions of the role of "mother" that Ripley plays in the *Alien* films.

Über Mother

In *Alien*, Ripley's misplaced maternal instincts save her from the death-by-alien that is the fate of her crew mates as she hurries off in search of the ship's resident cat, Jones (better known as "Jonesy"). In *Aliens*, cat becomes daughter in the form of Rebecca "Newt" Jorden, whose family and colony have been wiped out by the film's nemesis. Ripley risks everything to protect her surrogate daughter, as any mother would. By identifying herself in terms of maternal categories, Ripley instills urgency to her survival in a situation that might otherwise have resulted in her demise. In subsequent films, Ripley's role as "mother" comes up again. In *Alien³*, she is host to a Xenomorph embryo that incites her suicide in an effort to destroy the creature that has laid claim to her body. *Alien: Resurrection* sees the debut of a hybrid human/Xenomorph, a by-product of corrupted cloning experiments conducted by scientists of the United Systems Military. The creature identifies Ripley as "mother," but she kills it anyway to save both the human race and herself. And she does it as a clone: Ripley-8, to be precise—a mother unto herself, produced from frozen samples of her blood recovered after her death and subsequently mixed with alien DNA to create a human weapon.

We also know that Ripley has, in the past, been mother to a child (a little girl) of her own, back on Earth, or so Ripley tells Newt in *Aliens*. Assuming Ripley's daughter was her natural daughter and not adopted, our heroine fits in with a central element in Stone's ideas on maternal subjectivity. This is the notion that becoming a mother and relating to one's child are bodily experiences. And yet, Stone also views mothering as a profoundly *relational* experience, which would explain Ripley's kinship with Jonesy, Newt, and even the human/Xenomorph thing that calls her mom. The maternal role that Ripley embraces on her apocalyptic *Alien* adventures incites a journey of self-actualization in which she embodies a new philosophical way to understand what makes the identity of a mother, as seen through the framework of Alison Stone's unique perspective on maternal subjectivity.

Of Cat and Girl

Stone argues that the kind of subjectivity someone has always reflects the body they have. This idea comes from the philosophers Friedrich Schelling (1775–1854) and Georg W.F. Hegel (1770–1831). Schelling said that although we, as human beings, are free and autonomous agents, we aren't separate from nature; we are a part of nature and emerge out of it. Hegel, who was a systematic thinker, theorized a comprehensive view of existence within which everything is understood in terms of its interconnections with everything else. Influenced by these philosophies, Stone's thoughts on maternal subjectivity resonate with the thought that as human beings, we can't escape the physicality of our existence and consequently thought and subjectivity emerge out of the body. This means that bearing a child, becoming a mother, relating to one's young, are all embodied experiences. This suggests a specifically maternal form of subjectivity—something unique to the act of carrying and birthing a child. And yet for Ripley, the maternal instincts evoked by Jonesy and Newt have no attachment to her corporeal person; these "children" did not gestate in her body. In fact, she barely knows them, *and one is a cat*. Still, she mothers them—saves and protects them.

When Ripley hears Jonesy's meow, she responds like a mother to a crying baby. She finds him and even though he almost swipes her face off, she doesn't give up! With Ripley's help, Jonesy escapes and the pair drift in space together for fifty-seven years before being discovered, an event that heralds the start of *Aliens*. In this film, Jonesy is replaced by Newt, who has lost her family and is left to fend for herself in the middle of a Xenomorph invasion. When the Marines find Newt hiding in a tunnel, the only survivor of what was a bustling colony, it's Ripley who calms the Mowgli out of Newt. Ripley cajoles information out of the girl and assumes a motherly role; she won't let Newt look at the disturbing visuals on the surveillance monitors and also tucks her in to sleep, saying, "I'm not gonna leave you, Newt. I mean that. It's a promise." When Newt is captured at the end of the film, Ripley goes back for her in spite of the odds, and so lives up to her promise. And by the end of the film Newt is calling Ripley "mommy" in response to the maternal care shown her.

If Ellen Ripley is anything to go by, maternal subjectivity is inspired by a feeling of kinship as much as by something physical. The question is, does one necessitate the other? Stone believes in the significance of the relational, intuitive understanding as much as the physical, and she would likely contend that the relational and the physical *are* interconnected—as Hegel and Schelling contend. Stone views maternal subjectivity as a matter of being in intimate, intense relations with a small, dependent being who expresses emotions in a very raw way—as Newt does to Ripley in *Aliens*. Stone might argue that Ripley's pre-*Alien* experience as mother has already shaped and defined her subjectivity into something maternal, and that it's only natural for her to exert that sense of herself when faced with the defenselessness of both cat and girl. Not that either Jonesy or Newt are entirely helpless—they both do pretty well fending for themselves, but it's Ripley who offers them life. And from this perspective, the role of mother, at the center of which is the ability to bring forth life, is one that embodies an almost god-like sense of empowerment. But it's not all peaches and cream—*nothing* is when there are acid-drooling Xenomorphs involved. Motherhood can be a decidedly bitter pill.

That Bitch!

As a macro-theme within the *Alien* franchise, motherhood is invoked right from the get-go. Ridley Scott's *Alien* begins with an image of near-naked bodies in capsules, awakening from sleep, slightly dazed, slightly confused—intimating birth, or rebirth. The crew of the *Nostromo*, a spacecraft traveling back to Earth, is awakened by MU/TH/UR 6000 or "Mother," a computer operating system that governs the ship while the crew is in stasis, after intercepting a transmission from an unknown origin. When Mother talks, everyone listens, as demonstrated when ship's captain Dallas abandons a perfectly pleasant meal with his compadres immediately after a bleeping summons from "mom." It's Mother that directs the *Nostromo* to the alien planet, Mother whose orders cannot be disobeyed. Mother has secrets, and answers, too. Mother is not what she seems. Suspecting something sinister, Ripley accesses Mother and discovers that android Ash has been ordered, on the sly, to return an alien to the Company, which considers the crew expendable. Ripley, furious at the deception, calls Mother a "bitch"—and rightly so. Mother hasn't been very motherly, has she, plotting against her children and leading them into an alien apocalypse? The ship, personified as a mother figure, stands in stark contrast to Ripley, who exudes real motherliness and primal affection for Jonesy. And so what the audience is left with in *Alien* is a rather confused notion of motherhood. By offering the typical characteristics of a good mother, evident in Ripley, but then imbuing them with a malevolent spirit, evident in Mother, the film unsettles the notion of motherhood and brings it to the fore as a thematic element continued throughout the Ripley films.

Drawing on the force and effect of the "bad mother" vibe in *Alien*, the word "bitch" is used again by Ripley in *Aliens*, when she commands the pulsating, slime-slobbering Queen Xenomorph to leave Newt alone: "Get away from her, you BITCH!" Before momma-alien makes a meal of the seven-year-old, Ripley, bedecked in the protective frame of an exosuit cargo-loader, expels said bitch through the ship airlock into outer space. It's an epic confrontation—mother against mother, Ripley protecting Newt and Queenie seeking vengeance for the million-strong mass of offspring that Ripley torched with a flamethrower not ten minutes prior. In this confrontational scene, the interplay is poignant because there seems to be a level of understanding between Ripley and momma-alien—both females are exercising their maternal aggression. Of course, the Queen's no match for Ripley, but the mother-to-mother interaction binds heroine and fiend, introducing a wrinkle into the mythology behind the concept of something being "alien." The wrinkle is represented by the affinity resonating between Ripley and the momma-alien. The easy distinction between "good" and "bad" mothers is sabotaged by a shared "motherly" rapport and, much like in *Alien*, the audience is confronted yet again with the notion of the "malevolent mother." It's an idea that not only resonates between Ripley and the Queen but also through H.R. Giger's design of the Xenomorph species. The Swiss surrealist said of his art, "I like to combine human beings, creatures and biomechanics. And I love to work with bones—they are elemental and function[al] and, after all, are part of human beings."[1] Giger's Alien has an amorphously human tone to it, which adds ambiguity to the familiar distinction of "man versus monster" that resonates throughout mythology.

Alien and *Aliens* depict motherhood as something two-sided and complex. A mother is something that protects but also destroys, something that's not always safe, alien, even. *But why?* Maternal subjectivity suggests the need for a complete break by new life from the maternal body, a violent separation between mother and child—also known as differentiation (or divergence)—which, according to traditional thought, needs to happen in order to enable an assertion of the child's subjectivity, autonomy, and freedom. This might explain the injurious aspects of mothering—a mother's inclination for the pernicious as much as the protective. In *Alien³*, Ripley, impregnated with alien spawn, ironically quips, "Now I get to be a mother again," and follows up with, "I don't have much time. I need you to kill me. I'm dead anyway. I can't survive it." She's talking both literally—a Chestburster will imminently rip itself from her body—and metaphorically, as describes a death of identity (the death of the self). It's a notion supported by the film's context. The isolation and desolation of the convict colony Fury 161 in which Ripley finds herself is an apt representation of what motherhood can be like—it invokes a desperate need for self-assertion, but there is also a sense of loneliness in this struggle, especially within a patriarchal society. Men don't give birth, so if Stone's emphasis on the physical aspect of the parent–child relationship is valid, women experience aspects of the relational nature of parenthood to which men aren't privy. In light of this point, it's interesting that Ripley lands up alone and "pregnant" on an island of men. The whole scenario plays havoc with her identity, her sense of self. In a face-to-face confrontation with the alien wreaking calamity in and on the colony, Ripley says, "You've been in my life so long; I can't remember anything else." The alien is a part of her; Ripley is alien—a foreigner unto herself—void of fathomable identity.

Rachel Cusk, a Canadian novelist, describes in her book *A Life's Work* the experience of becoming a mother and the chaotic disarrangement of her body:

> In the morning I would sit up in bed, the room listing drunkenly about me, and I would put a hand to my face, checking for some evidence of disfigurement: an eyebrow, perhaps, slipped down to my cheek, a deranged ear cluttering my forehead, a seam at the back of my skull gaping open.[2]

It's as if Cusk, like Ripley, woke up an alien in mind as much as in body. Ripley, rather than fighting the feeling of being alien on Fury 161, accepts it, at least initially. She changes to fit in, altering her clothes and hair—adopting the identity she needs to survive as a woman (carrying an alien baby) in a colony of sadistic, sex-deprived convicts. She soon realizes that "fitting in" will not save her. The truth is that nothing can save Ripley but violence—a savage separation. When she was impregnated with an alien embryo on board the *Sulaco*'s emergency escape pod, her autonomy, as well as her body, was irreparably violated. Death is the only solution: when the alien rips its way out of her, she'll die, so she may as well take the beast down before it does the same to her. The metaphor is poignant: an assertion of a mother killing her child to save herself (and the world—*there's that little thing, too*). Unable to find an assassin willing to do the job (in a colony full of violent offenders—oh the irony!), Ripley throws herself into a fiery furnace to destroy the horror (a queen, at that) that has invaded her body. She's a martyr for humanity, for herself—Christ-like in her cause; with arms stretched out on a virtual cross, she plummets to her death, taking her alien baby along with her. And it is only in death (death to motherhood and death to person) that Ripley achieves subjectivity, a fact poignant in its futility.

Stone argues that we need a new model of differentiation from the maternal body for both mother and child, one based on embodied, affective, and linguistic relationality, or connection, rather than on violence and a complete break from the maternal body. Stone makes a distinction between differentiation and separation: differentiation means both distancing and connection, while separation is based on break and discontinuity.

In her theory, Stone harks back to the approach of psychoanalysis, claiming that each experience of motherhood repeats the mother's own infantile past and her own traumatic separation from the maternal body. So really, moms aren't hating on their children in a desperate need to assert themselves, they're just reliving childhood. Stone refers to "maternal temporality," which involves this repetition, but with a difference—the maternal past in a new context provided by the new mother's relations to her child. This repetition, Stone argues, is a form of emotional, affective, bodily memory, which is different from conscious memory mediated through language and visual perception. It's instinctive, in other words—which explains Ripley's mothering of Jonesy and Newt, as well as her inclination toward death and destruction in *Alien*[3]. Ripley, to identify her strengths as both "self" and "mother," must connect with her "child" rather than disconnect from it. And because she has no biological child, she adopts a couple along the way: Jonesy, Newt, and, in *Alien: Resurrection*, an auton (Call) and an alien (sort of).

Resurrection

In *Alien: Resurrection*, Ripley is reclaimed through a purposeful symbiosis of mother and child; human and alien; self and "other." It's the ultimate example of connection: Ripley as clone, with alien blood— mother unto herself, forged from her own DNA, is a symbol of the rebirth of an idea and of Stone's take on maternal subjectivity. *Alien: Resurrection* begins with Ripley breaking out of a placenta-like sac. She is born into the world with the body of an adult but without some of the capabilities, and so she has to learn what she once knew. As part of her rehabilitation, Ripley is shown an image of a little girl, which evokes an emotive response, but, interestingly, Ripley is unsure why. The audience, privy to three previous films, understands that it's an image reminiscent of Ripley's own daughter as well as Newt. Ripley's maternal instinct responds to the picture. As Ripley-8, she doesn't understand what her response means because her memories are faulty, but the emotions are nonetheless there. She feels a connection.

Ripley's response can be explained with the help of Alison Stone, who cites the work of Helene Deutsch, a collaborator of Freud's who, according to many modern feminists, laid the foundations for subsequent feminist psychoanalytic work on mothering. Deutsch argues that a woman's desire to mother rests not primarily on her Oedipal wish for the penis (or the desire for sexual involvement with the opposite sex—or parent, if we want to get really Freudian) but on her wish to return, in fantasy, to the earliest conditions of her life. As a baby, Deutsch would say, Ripley loved herself and her own mother indistinguishably and then later loved her children as herself, first in pregnancy and then after giving birth. In a state of emotional fusion, the mother regresses, in fantasy, to her early loving identification with her own mother. Deutsch talks about a "quasi-infantile" state, in which mother Ripley feels that her own feelings and those of the child are indistinguishable. So when Ripley is shown that picture, there is a subconscious mental process that takes her back to the time when she gave birth and then further back to her own mother; and she identifies with both. Deutsch goes on to say that in order to function socially, a mother must snap out of the fantasy (the "quasi-infantile" state) by means of a nonviolent form of separation that is roughly equivalent to Stone's version of differentiation.

Ripley does indeed snap out of it: an alien threat will do that to a girl, even if the alien is your daughter. When Ripley blows the head off one of her pals, Call says, "I can't believe you did that. It's like killing your own kind," and Ripley quips, "It was in my way." The quasi-infantile fantasy does resurge, though: as the alien Queen (Ripley's child) prepares to give birth, Ripley perceives the creature's angst. The feelings of the being that inhabited her body are indistinguishable from her own, and as she mistakenly falls in amongst a hoard of pulsating Xenomorphs, drawn to their energy, it's as if she is home. The scene is weird—erotic and primal, and very uncomfortable from the audience's perspective, but it aptly encapsulates the sense of emotional fusion between a mother and a child—a "psychic umbilical cord," as Deutsch liked to call it. At the end of the film, the human/Xenomorph makes its way onto the ship (*of course it does!*) and Ripley nurtures it, allows it to embrace her, to "love" her, and she returns the sentiment. Yet in the very next breath, Ripley offers her child up to the forces of atmospheric pressure, which dismember, decapitate, and decompose that which looked upon Ripley as mother but a few seconds before. It's brutal. And Ripley cries. Her sense of loss is tangible. She feels compassion for the creature but she kills it anyway, saving Call (and the world—*again*).

Alien: Resurrection brings its audience back to the ambivalence and violence of motherhood, freeing two lives from each other by separation rather than differentiation. This seems to undermine what we took to be Stone's attempts to reimagine differentiation as a non-violent process. After all, birth itself is violent; even those with a happy-chappy childhood would have been wrenched from a mother's belly via scalpel or forceps. So, even under the eye of Stone's psycho-analytic gaze, the subconscious fantasy replaying history will always be aggressive in some manner or other. It seems inescapable, and yet Ripley survives *Alien: Resurrection* and remains the ever-present mother figure. In the film's final couple of scenes, Ripley and Call, her new ward, look toward the horizon, a symbol of hope, as the ship jets away from the enemy. We know, however, that the *Alien* franchise does not deal in happy endings, so at the very end, Ripley and Call look across the expanse of a broken Earth. Although this is the planet of her birth, Ripley calls herself a "stranger here."

I'm an Alien. And That's OK.

The notion of being alien to one's self is a theme that resonates through all the Ripley films. The theory of maternal subjectivity says that the sense of unfamiliarity pervading a mother's sense of self stems not only from change, but from loss. And what's more, this is a double loss: the loss of emotional intimacy with one's own mother and the loss of intimacy with a child. Loss is inherent in the very structure of the maternal experience. Psychiatrist and psychoanalytic theorist Daniel Stern articulates maternal loss succinctly when he says:

> There exists within most women an important identity as the daughter of her parents. Even if she is an autonomous, independent woman... this life-long identity as daughter occupies a kind of historical center of gravity. With the birth of her own daughter she must shift the center of gravity from being primarily the daughter-of-her-mother to being the mother-of-her-daughter. In one blow, part of [her] fixed representational world has shifted irreversibly...A world (even if part of it is illusion) is gone. And there is often a profound sense of loss that runs beneath the sense of worlds gained.[3]

Stone develops Stern's idea by saying that the mother doesn't altogether cease to be a daughter. In fact, in becoming a mother, she remains a daughter because she reenacts with her child her past relations with her mother. But the change of context over time means that the mother undergoes her own daughterhood again, in a new guise so she can never be the daughter that she used to be, which is (in effect) a loss of familiar self. Part of this loss is the fact that not only do mothers lose a sense of themselves as daughter, but each mother also loses her child in the child's process of becoming an independent, distinct adult— a loss referred to by Helene Deutsch as the "tragedy of motherhood."

In Ripley's case, a couple of her kids are born "different"—they're different before they even make it into the world by virtue of being another species entirely. This means that Ripley is dealing with loss before her child is even born—harking back to *Alien³*, when Ripley, after finding out about the alien inside of her, expresses her desire to die almost immediately. And yet in spite of the fact that Ripley enacts separation, she covets the differentiation that Stone believes possible. *Alien: Resurrection* is the closest Ripley gets to realizing Stone's maternal subjectivity. For one, she's alive at the end of the film; she's also come to terms with her new identity—as Ripley-8 and part-alien. There's no need to kill herself in order to manifest subjectivity, as was the metaphoric implication in *Alien³*. That which is alien, or motherhood, the thing that threatens Ripley's subjectivity, is also an undeniable part of who she is. American writer Harlan Ellison said of H.R. Giger, "This man knows what we fear. And he shows it to us again and again."[4] In so doing, we're confronted with an essential truth: motherhood, "the maternal," cannot be quashed, no matter how alien.

Notes

1. H.R. Giger, quoted in Justin Scuiletti, "Surrealist, Sculptor and 'Alien' Designer H.R. Giger Dies at 74," *PBS Newshour*, http://www.pbs.org/newshour/rundown/surrealist-sculptor-alien-designer-h-r-giger-dies-78 (accessed June 10, 2016).
2. Quoted in Alison Stone, *Feminism, Psychoanalysis and Maternal Subjectivity* (Routledge, 2012), 2.
3. Stern, quoted in ibid., 151.
4. Harlan Ellison, Introduction to H.R. Giger, *Biomechanics*, http://www.hrgiger.com/alien4a.htm (accessed June 10, 2016).

15

Is Ellen Ripley a Feminist?

Alexander Christian

Ellen Ripley stands out from the ordinary, stereotypical women in horror and science fiction movies up until the release of *Alien* in 1979. Novelist and film critic John Scalzi rightly describes her as "pushy, aggressive, rude, injured, suffering from post-traumatic syndrome, not wearing makeup, tired, smart, maternal, angry, empathetic, and determined to save others, even at great cost to herself."[1] This realistic depiction of a human being trying to survive under gruesome circumstances differs dramatically from other female characters in popular science fiction, who depend on strong, independent, and notably male characters. Think, for example, of Lt. Uhura in *Star Trek*, who seems to be on telephone duty during her entire service on the *Enterprise*. Although a bridge officer, she's depicted as little more than a space secretary whose job it is to answer urgent phone calls from Starfleet Headquarters in service to Kirk, an inveterate womanizer. Things hadn't changed much in science fiction a decade later when *Alien* was released. So, against this background, Ripley stands out as a feminist archetype.[2]

In fact, it isn't hard to interpret Ripley's fight against the Xenomorphs as a metaphor for the feminist struggle against sexual violence directed at women, or to see her actions as violent opposition to those who would deny her sexual self-determination. Beyond that, Ripley shows a great deal of care for humans (like the orphan Newt, on LV-426) as well as nonhumans (like Jonesy the cat) in need of protection. Confronting military personnel and stooges of the Weyland-Yutani Corporation, Ripley pleads for those who are particularly vulnerable

Alien and Philosophy: I Infest, Therefore I Am, First Edition.
Edited by Jeffrey Ewing and Kevin S. Decker.
© 2017 John Wiley & Sons Ltd. Published 2017 by John Wiley & Sons Ltd.

to decisions driven by militaristic or economic interests. Ripley's ethical code appears compatible with the view of morality found in works by feminist philosophers like Virginia Held, Nel Noddings, and Joan Tronto. But, as we'll see, Ripley's ethical code can't be treated as straightforwardly feminist ethics of care.[3]

"Have you ever been mistaken for a man?"

Feminism in philosophy is the lasting effect of a larger political, social, and cultural movement. As a political movement, feminism aims to establish a just society with equal rights for women.[4] Today, traditional ways of doing philosophy also include a feminist perspective—for example, analytical feminism, continental feminism, and psychoanalytic feminism.[5] These all criticize the unequal rights and opportunities for women that have resulted from gender stereotypes institutionalized in societies all over the world. Their second unifying feature is a research program that pays special attention to gender issues, like female-associated character traits in moral decision-making and the elimination of gender-based biases in science.

In ethics, feminism is primarily represented by care-focused and status-oriented approaches. Proponents of care-focused approaches observe that women have a special way of moral reasoning, whereas status-oriented thinkers seek to overcome gender-based inequalities and unjust social relationships through criticizing status differences between men and women, like stereotypes and differences in pay for the same work. Two brief examples from *Aliens* illustrate the difference between these approaches. A care-focused feminist would be interested in why Ripley cares for the orphan Newt and might suggest that Ripley's diligent devotion is a result of her maternal instincts, which lead her to consider the orphan's needs alongside her own wishes. Rescuing Newt, when this involves great risks for both their lives, could be seen as a paradigmatic example of how women often take care of those in need.

A status-oriented feminist, on the other hand, might have more to say about a character like Pvt. Jenette Vasquez, a smartgun operator on board the USS *Sulaco*. A member of the United States Colonial Marines, Vasquez has to cope with gender stereotypes. Rising to the challenge, Vasquez is one of the toughest and most professional soldiers in the battlefield. In addition, she seems more than capable in handling suggestive comments about her gender identity. After hypersleep, Vasquez and Pvt. Mark Drake, with whom she is chummy, warm up with some strength exercises. Pvt. William Hudson comments on her muscular figure, "Hey Vasquez, have you ever been mistaken for a man?" She responds, "No, have you?" A status-oriented feminist would interpret this exchange as evidence of a society in which women have to over-compensate for stereotypes and adopt physiological as well as psychological characteristics culturally identified as masculine in order to get the acknowledgment and respect of male soldiers.

Now, let's consider whether Ripley exercises a feminist ethics of care.[6] According to Rosemarie Tong and Nancy Williams, perspectives on feminist care ethics share the idea that traditional ethics exhibits an androcentric bias.[7] Further, "proponents of feminist care ethics, including Carol Gilligan and Nel Noddings, stress that traditional moral theories, principles, practices, and policies are deficient to the degree they lack, ignore, trivialize, or demean values and virtues culturally associated with women."[8]

Carol Gilligan, one of the founders of this movement, developed her ethical standpoint in critical response to Lawrence Kohlberg, whose account of moral development states that people go through six stages of moral development, the highest stage being a "post-conventional" moral perspective.[9] By this he means that a fully developed moral agent is free and self-governing, and applies universal ethical principles in her moral reasoning. Before reaching this stage, children think about morality on a pre-conventional level. Here, moral decision-making emerges from egoistic feelings of obedience and the avoidance of punishment. At the conventional level, adolescents seek conformity and interpersonal accord with peers, and soon after their moral decision-making relies on authorities and social order. Finally, on a post-conventional level, adults engage in reasoning according to the moral importance of contracts; some might ultimately apply universal ethical principles to justify their actions.[10] The later stages, according to Kohlberg, are typically not reached by most people, and Kohlberg later found that some people even regress to earlier stages.

But Carol Gilligan says that this account of moral development is biased towards a male perspective and favors character traits culturally associated with maleness, like rationality and rule following. In her pioneering contribution to feminist ethics, *In a Different Voice*, she criticizes Kohlberg for failing to equally represent female ways of dealing with moral dilemmas. Gilligan's claim is that women often approach moral problems with an emphasis on close relationships and responsibilities towards the particularly vulnerable. In contrast, men tend to aim at settling conflicts between rights holders, and they apply abstract moral principles—like the Kantian categorical imperative. This is an important difference: whereas men tend to embrace the idea of impartiality in their search for just moral solutions, women seem to stress the distinctive features of different moral problems.

This contrast can be illustrated by the moment when Ripley has to decide whether she should open the hatch for Kane, who is infested by an alien parasite. Opening the hatch would involve risk for the crew, because nobody knows whether the alien organism is dangerous or not. But leaving the hatch closed would mean certain death for Kane, a fellow crew member. According to Gilligan, a typical male point of view would be to solve the dilemma with rights and regulations: are there quarantine rules? Do the requirements of these rules override duties of assistance owed to Kane? The female voice would instead call for emphasizing the relationships and informal responsibilities of the crew members. Though male and female moral agents *might* reach the same conclusion, the way they get there makes the difference. In a professional context, universal regulations might be necessary in order to command a spaceship. But for a feminist care ethicist, morally right decisions sometimes need to be understood as resulting from emotional responses to individuals we're close to.

"Yes, I read you. The answer is negative"

Ripley's defining moment comes when Kane has discovered large eggs containing alien life-forms in the wreckage of a spacecraft on LV-426. One of those creatures attacks Kane, burns its way through his helmet with highly corrosive acid, and attaches itself to his face. He is rushed back to the *Nostromo* by Dallas and Lambert, who ask Ripley for entry through the ship's hatch:

DALLAS: We're clean, let us in.
RIPLEY: What happened to Kane?
DALLAS: Something attached itself to him. We have to get him to the infirmary right away.
RIPLEY: What kind of thing? I need a clear definition.
DALLAS: An organism, open the hatch!
RIPLEY: Wait a minute. If we let it in, the ship could be infected. You know the quarantine procedures: 24 hours for decontamination.
DALLAS: He could die in 24 hours. Open the hatch!
RIPLEY: Listen to me—we break quarantine we could all die.

LAMBERT: (*panicking*) Stop talking—open the god damn hatch! We have to get him inside.

RIPLEY: (*silent for a moment*) No. I can't do that. And if you were in my position, you'd do the same.

DALLAS: Ripley listen, this is an order: Open the hatch right now! Do you hear me?

RIPLEY: Yes.

DALLAS: Ripley, this is an order! Do you hear me?

RIPLEY: Yes, I read you. The answer is negative.
         (*Ash opens the hatch from inside*)

ASH: Inner hatch open.

The situation seems like a perfect moral dilemma: Ripley has to decide between two mutually exclusive actions, having obligations to do both of them. The crew has a duty to assist Kane, but they also must obey the quarantine rules, in effect to protect them and their mission.

Ripley sees a way to resolve the dilemma at hand. She refers to rules, regulations, and hierarchies of command. She references the reasoning behind quarantine regulations and appeals to these reasons in discussions with Science Officer Ash and Captain Dallas. On two occasions later in the film, this reliance on rules and codes is again addressed. First, she confronts Ash, who is examining the Facehugger, about his unauthorized decision to open the hatch and let Kane inside, thus endangering the whole crew:

ASH: Well it's an interesting combination of elements, making him [the Facehugger] a tough little son of a bitch.

RIPLEY: And you let him in.

ASH: I was obeying a direct order, don't you remember?

RIPLEY: Ash, when Dallas and Kane are off the ship, I am senior officer.

ASH: I must have forgotten.

RIPLEY: You also forgot the science division's basic quarantine law.

ASH: No, that I did not forget.

RIPLEY: Ah, I see, you just broke it.

ASH: But what would you have done with Kane, hmm? You know his only chance of survival was to get him in here.

RIPLEY: Unfortunately by breaking quarantine you risked everybody's life.

ASH: Maybe I should have left him outside. Maybe I have jeopardized the rest of us, but this was a risk I was willing to take.

RIPLEY: It's a pretty big risk, for a science officer. It's…not exactly out of the manual. Is it?

ASH: I do take my responsibilities as seriously as you. You do your job and let me do mine, yes?

Later, in a conversation with Captain Dallas, she takes a similar stance:

RIPLEY: Will you listen to me? Just tell me how you can leave that kind of decision to [Ash]?

DALLAS: Look, I just run the ship. Anything that has to do with the science division, Ash has the final word.

RIPLEY: How does that happen?

DALLAS: It happens, my dear, because the company wants it to happen.

RIPLEY: Since when is that standard procedure?

DALLAS: Standard procedure is to do what the hell they tell you to do.

In these conversations Ripley doesn't provide us with any evidence for care-based moral reasoning. Instead, she exemplifies a type of moral deliberation that leaves no room for personal feelings towards her fellow crew member or care for the injured Kane. In Kohlberg's terms, she seems to occupy the post-conventional level of moral reasoning, insofar as she's able to give an argument in favor of the quarantine procedures as applying to everyone equally. From a feminist standpoint, we might expect her to mediate between the different rights holders and avoid direct and aggressive confrontations with superiors. With the feminist critique of traditional ethics in mind, we could even say that her approach involves atypical female moral reasoning, which lacks the emotional responsiveness presented by feminists as a characteristic feminine approach to moral decision-making.

"Don't you think you're safer here with us?"

In the last scene of *Alien*, Ripley's strong identification with her professional role shows itself again when she makes a final entry in the *Nostromo*'s log. Before entering hypersleep, hoping for rescue while drifting in space, she dictates:

RIPLEY: Final report of the commercial starship *Nostromo*. Third officer reporting. The other members of the crew, Kane, Lambert, Parker, Red, Ash, and Captain Dallas, are dead. Cargo and ship destroyed. I should reach the frontier in about six weeks. With a little luck the network will pick me up. This is Ripley, last survivor of the *Nostromo*, signing off.

Notably, she has no words for her daughter Amanda or her husband. When Ripley is found after drifting in space for fifty-seven years, the narrative disposition in *Aliens* is radically different from Ripley's story in *Alien*. During her sleep, she's lost her daughter Amanda and the official investigation initiated by Weyland-Yutani resulted in the loss of her license as a flight officer. This process also leaves her with a deep mistrust towards the integrity of her former employer. This *Schicksalsschlag*, or "stroke of fate," with Ripley losing her private as well as professional identity while she sleeps, suggests that her traumatic experiences might have had an effect on her moral reasoning. There's evidence for this when Ripley's maternal feelings develop for an orphan found in the devastated colony on LV-426.

Deeply traumatized and haunted by nightmares, Ripley agrees to go along with a team of soldiers to investigate the loss of communication with the colony on LV-426. Although highly skeptical towards the intentions of Carter Burke, a representative of Weyland-Yutani, she accepts Burke's offer to become a flight officer and serve as a consultant on the mission. Arriving at LV-426, they find that almost all the colonists have fallen prey to a Xenomorph infestation. Only Rebecca Jorden, "Newt," survived the incident. After Ripley lures Newt from her hiding place in a ventilation shaft, the Marines try to interrogate the frightened girl:

GORMAN: What's her name again?
DIETRICH: Rebecca.
GORMAN: Now think, Rebecca, concentrate! Just start at the beginning, where are your parents? Now look, Rebecca, you have to try and help...
RIPLEY: Gorman, give it a rest, would you?
GORMAN: Total brain lock.
DIETRICH: Physically she's ok. Borderline malnutrition, but I don't think there's any permanent damage.
GORMAN: Come on, we're wasting our time.

Ripley, though, is able to establish an emotional connection to Newt. She uses quite a different voice than the one we heard in conversations with Dallas and Ash:

RIPLEY: Try this... (*Ripley carefully hands over a cup to Rebecca*) ...it's a little hot chocolate.
            (*Rebecca drinks, staring emotionless*)
RIPLEY: There you go. Oh, that good, huh?
            (*Ripley cleans Rebecca's lips with a napkin*)
RIPLEY: Oh, oh, I made a clean spot here. Now I've done it, I guess I have to do the whole thing.
            (*Ripley cleans Rebecca's whole face*)

RIPLEY: Hard to believe there is a little girl under all this—a pretty one too. You don't talk much, do you? [...]

RIPLEY: I don't know how you managed to stay alive. But you are one brave kid, Rebecca.

REBECCA: (*very quietly*) ...Newt.

RIPLEY: What did you say?

REBECCA: Newt, my name is Newt. Nobody calls me Rebecca. Except my brother.

RIPLEY: Newt. I like that. I'm Ripley. It's nice to meet you....And who is this?

(*Ripley grabs the girl's stuffed puppy*)

REBECCA: Casey.

RIPLEY: Hello Casey. What about your brother? What's his name?

REBECCA: Timmy.

RIPLEY: Is Timmy around here too? Maybe hiding like you were? Any sisters?

(*Rebecca slowly shakes her head*)

RIPLEY: Mom and dad?

(*Rebecca slowly nods*)

RIPLEY: Newt, look at me. Where are they?

REBECCA: They are dead, alright? Can I go now?

RIPLEY: I'm sorry, Newt. Don't you think you're safer here with us?

(*Rebecca slowly shakes her head*)

RIPLEY: These people are here to protect you. They're soldiers.

REBECCA: It won't make any difference.

From the perspective of feminist care ethics, Ripley's way of handling the situation can be seen as an example of women's disposition to care for those in need and to use inclusive and empathic language, while men like Gorman appeal to obligations and verbalize them harshly ("Now think, Rebecca, concentrate! Just start at the beginning, where are your parents? Now look, Rebecca, you have to try and help..."). Ripley's changed voice works when the male way of reasoning and speaking fails to address the traumatized child's need.

One might object that Ripley's care for Newt should not be interpreted in feminist terms, since there's no real moral dilemma here. But such a concern can be met by looking at Ripley's later efforts to escape with Newt from the colony. Before leaving Hadley's Hope, Newt was taken by a Xenomorph to the hive and Ripley—without a moment of hesitation—rescued her. Here we can find a genuine moral dilemma: if Ripley rescues Newt, then she endangers her own life and possibly the lives of others, and if she leaves Newt in the hive, then the orphan's death is only a matter of time. Ripley's decision might be influenced by her emotional bond with Newt—her motherly feelings for the girl—and a refusal to lose another child, but this does not diminish the momentousness of her moral decision, nor does it count against a feminist interpretation of her decisions. Rather, it speaks in favor of the idea that Ripley's moral calculus in this context exhibits features of feminist care ethics.

"A lot of innocent people will die..."

So far we've considered the idea that Ripley's behavior could be understood in terms of a feminist ethics of care, but how crucial is the example of her interaction with Newt for understanding Ripley's way of moral thinking? Is her selfless behavior on LV-426 evidence enough to classify her moral calculus as through and through feminist?

After the escape from LV-426, the USS *Sulaco* ejects the cryo tubes of the four survivors (Ripley, Newt, Corporal Hicks, and Bishop) because of an electrical defect. The escape pod crashes near the penal colony Fiorina ("Fury") 161 with Ripley as the sole survivor. The inmates of Fury 161 are murderers and rapists—so, not exactly a holiday resort! With Newt drowned in her cryo tube and Hicks impaled by a fragment of the escape pod, Ripley yet again suffers the loss of everyone close to her. Even worse, she discovers that she's not only impregnated with a Xenomorph embryo that sooner or later will burst through her chest, but another Xenomorph also starts to decimate the prison's population.

Against all odds and with many casualties among the inmates, the prisoners and Ripley manage to capture the alien and later discover that Weyland-Yutani wants to take the specimen into possession. In a short conversation with Dillon, the religious leader of the inmates, Ripley explains her reasons for killing the alien before the arrival of a Weyland-Yutani taskforce:

DILLON: So you're telling me they're coming to take this thing with them?
RIPLEY: Yeah, they're gonna try. They don't want to kill it. We got to figure out a way to do it before they come here.
DILLON: Why do we have to kill it? You just said the company is coming for it.
RIPLEY: That's right. They want to take it back. Some kind of work with it.
DILLON: What's wrong with this?
RIPLEY: They can't control it. They don't understand; it'll kill them all.

DILLON: Well that's it. What's wrong with that?
RIPLEY: Well nothing's wrong with that, except a lot of innocent people
         will die....I thought you were a religious man.
DILLON: You don't understand, do you? That world out there doesn't exist
         for us anymore. We got our own little world out here. It ain't
         much, but it's ours.
RIPLEY: So, fuck everybody else?
DILLON: No, fuck them.

Here, Ripley does not appeal to professional standards, as in the conversations with Dallas and Ash, nor does she appeal to moral reasoning based on a close and empathic relationship to an individual, like Newt. Instead, she refers to the welfare of an abstract class of rights holders—innocent people like the Hadley's Hope colonists—who might suffer from bioweapons research conducted by Weyland-Yutani (or, more likely, suffer at the hands of the wily Xenomorph specimen when it escapes). Ripley again operates on a post-conventional level of morality, considering her social responsibilities. The prospect of an industrial–military complex with control over a Xeno specimen is reason enough for her to even commit suicide by leaping into a furnace filled with molten lead. These decisions reveal that although Ripley is capable of recognizing the interests of those who are particularly vulnerable and in close social proximity, she's equally dispositioned to extend her moral calculus, in order to take into account the needs of a larger and anonymous group of individuals.

A Professional, a Mother, and Someone Who Cares

Our initial question was whether Ripley's moral thinking can be called feminist. Only on one occasion does Ripley use moral reasoning that could be interpreted in terms of a feminist ethics of care, namely, when she emotionally bonds with Newt in Hadley's Hope and flees with her from LV-426. The feminist interpretation makes sense there, because this takes place against a background familiar from feminist criticisms of male-oriented societies, in which women are forced to accept responsibility for those who are particularly vulnerable. Also, Ripley's way of relating to Newt exemplifies caring behavioral dispositions, which feminists associate with the female moral reasoning.

Nonetheless, there is not quite enough to substantiate the claim that Ripley's ethics are properly understood in care feminist terms. In many other situations, Ripley invokes impartiality, professional standards, and general social responsibilities in her moral reasoning. Even after losing her professional status, her ethical decision-making does not, for the most part, depend upon care feminist values or a supposedly feminine attention to empathic communication, nor is it oriented toward gender issues in general.

From the feminist viewpoint, Ripley appears to be an atypical woman who only occasionally refers to care-based reasoning; she otherwise applies a moral calculus that aligns with a high level of reflection and abstraction on Kohlberg's scale. Maybe this is why Ripley is appealing to the viewer: she is at the same time a professional, a mother, and someone who cares.

Notes

1. "Ellen Ripley Is Clearly the Best Female Character in Scifi Film, and That's a Problem," http://www.amc.com/talk/2011/09/ellen-ripley-is (accessed January 2, 2017).
2. I would like to thank Frauke Albersmeier, Kevin Decker, Jeffrey Ewing, and Bill Irwin for their kind comments, corrections, and suggestions for stylistic improvements.
3. By focusing on the cinematic presentation of Ellen Ripley by Sigourney Weaver and ignoring novelizations by Alan Dean Foster (*Alien*, *Aliens*, and *Alien³*) and Ann C. Crispin (*Alien: Resurrection*), one leaves aside an auctorial perspective on the story, told by an omniscient narrator which provides no insight into Ripley's moral reasoning. Furthermore, I will stick to the classical universe depicted in the movies, since the various spin-off comics, novels, and video games don't share a common timeline and artistic vision. I will also exclude *Alien: Resurrection*, since the main character in this movie, the clone Ripley-8, doesn't possess the psychological or physiological features essential to Ripley's credibility in the first three parts of the series.
4. Chris Beasley, *What is Feminism?* (Sage, 1999), 3–11.
5. Nancy Tuana, "Approaches to Feminism," in *The Stanford Encyclopedia of Philosophy* (Spring 2011 Edition), ed. Edward N Zalta, http://plato.stanford.edu/archives/spr2011/entries/feminism-approaches/.
6. We'll leave behind status-oriented feminist criticisms for lack of space.
7. Rosemarie Tong and Nancy Williams, "Feminist Ethics," in *The Stanford Encyclopedia of Philosophy* (Fall 2014 Edition), ed. Edward N Zalta, http://plato.stanford.edu/archives/fall2014/entries/feminism-ethics/.

8. Ibid.

9. Lawrence Kohlberg, *From Is to Ought: How to Commit the Naturalistic Fallacy and Get Away with It in the Study of Moral Development* (Academic Press, 1971).

10. Lawrence Kohlberg and Thomas Lickona, "Moral Stages and Moralization: The Cognitive-Developmental Approach," in *Moral Development and Behavior: Theory, Research and Social Issues* (Holt, Rinehart and Winston, 1976).

16
Alien Violation: Male Bodily Integrity in an Equal Opportunity Rape Culture

Tim Jones

There are lots of reasons to feel scared when we watch the *Alien* films. There's the fear of isolation in a tight, claustrophobic environment, with no hope of making a break for safety because all that's outside is deep, inhospitable space. There's the fear of knowing that when the creatures attack from the shadows, they won't be bargained or reasoned with, since there's nothing they want that they can't just rip from us, and even if there were, there'd be little hope for us to communicate. And there's the even simpler and starker fear of death—of annihilation of mind and body.

No wonder these films get us peeking out from behind a cushion or reaching to turn the light switch back to "on." But we haven't even mentioned the worst fear of all, the fear that leaves us the most deeply unsettled. This is the fear of physical violation.

The *Alien* films are steeped in the horror of sexual violence and the effects that it can have on survivors. Sure, they rarely address the subject head-on, beyond the odd line from Dillon in *Alien³* and the prisoners' attempted rape of Ripley in the same film. But if we look at what the alien Facehuggers do to their victims, there are clear allusions to rape throughout the entire franchise. Just think of the nonconsensual nature of the physical contact Xenomorphs make with their victims. While this is obviously a component of most violence, once the Facehuggers are attached, they forcibly insert a tube-like proboscis down the throat and implant their seed into the unwilling human's body. Sometime later, the human is forced to hatch the Facehugger's offspring.

Alien and Philosophy: I Infest, Therefore I Am, First Edition.
Edited by Jeffrey Ewing and Kevin S. Decker.

With just a little imagination, we can see the parallels between these fictional violent acts and rape—particularly the most common form of rape, which remains the forcible penetration of a woman by a man, using his penis, and which usually results in his ejaculation into the woman. Men can rape men too, just as women can rape people of both sexes, but (as we will see) none of these other possibilities is statistically anything like as common as male-on-female rape.

No wonder the female half of the audience feels genuinely unsettled by what the *Alien* films depict; it's a little too like an ever-present threat in the real world. But what about the other half? The films place *male* viewers into a position they're not usually forced to confront in their own lives, during which they can only wonder what it would be like to have to worry about sexual violence just as much as women. After all, the Xenomorphs and the Facehuggers don't seem particularly picky about which sex they violate.

Bodies That Matter

Much of our identity hinges on our relationship with our bodies. We display our personality by adorning bodies with clothing, jewelry, or makeup; like Fifield in *Prometheus*, some of us cover our bodies with intricate tattoos. We train our bodies and build them up in various ways so that they become physically suited for the tasks we need to accomplish. They shift with our moods: if we're feeling happy and relaxed, we can look and feel healthier, and if we're feeling down, our bodies feel inert and sluggish. There's a lot more to us than just our bodies, sure, but there's an inextricable link between them and the very core of who we are. Bodies are far more than just mechanical automatons of muscle and bone like the powered exoskeletons the Marines drive in *Aliens*.

Carolyn M. Shafer and Marilyn Frye's "Rape and Respect" stresses the body's importance through the concept of the "domain," which describes the total sum of objects and properties that a person can rightfully consider to reside under his or her control.[1] A person's body lies at the very center of this "domain," and so an attack on the body is an attack on the victim's personhood. This is one reason why the physical violation of rape is often judged to be the most devastating crime of all.

In the *Alien* films, human bodies are reduced to being mere incubators for alien life. People who have been raped often talk about having their bodies taken away from them—about having them fall under the control of the rapist, to be used by him for his ends and his pleasures, rather than the survivor's own. They speak of having their agency over a crucial part of their identity removed, so that it becomes a mere object or tool for someone else's degraded fantasy. Shafer and Frye argue that rape casts its object as a being who exists as an appendage of someone else's "domain," rather than a subject with a "domain" of his or her own. Ann J. Cahill explains this powerfully, too, when she describes rape as a "total denial of the victim's agency, will and personhood."[2] And your body is something you're necessarily stuck with for your life, so it's not like a survivor can ever really escape the place where their very self was attacked in this way. A main goal of counseling for rape survivors today is helping them "reclaim" ownership of their bodies from the attacker. They're coached on how to take back the right to feel that their body is their own and that they deserve to take all the pride and the pleasure from it that they did before.

The *Alien* films are powerful in the unique way they convey the threat of the loss of bodily agency to *men*. It's important that I stress that women comprise the majority of rape survivors. The statistics from the Rape, Abuse and Incest National Network show that 1 in 6 American women have been subjected to a completed or attempted rape, as compared with the much smaller figure of 1 in 33 American men. We should acknowledge that rape is more likely to be underreported for male survivors than for females (for reasons I'll get onto in a moment), but the gulf between sexes is still likely to be pretty large, even taking this into account. By exploring how these films are intimating hypothetical acts of sexual violence towards men, I don't want to suggest that this is as common a threat outside the films for men as it is for women, or that we should focus on male survivors to the exclusion of the more numerous female ones.

Still, there's something darkly distinctive about the imaginative experience the *Alien* films deliver for a male audience. Some people still find it hard to imagine that rape can happen to men at all, and it is certainly very little talked about or represented in fiction or the media. Simultaneously, this is yet another problematic manifestation of the same patriarchal model that casts men as powerful and women as passive, men as strong and women as weak. In patriarchal culture, the idea is that a female rape survivor is more closely playing the role that patriarchy has cast women into than a male survivor would be. Men are supposed to be dominant and in control, so the very idea of a man being victimized in this most dehumanizing of ways is harder to face. A "real" man (patriarchal culture tells us) would be able to fight back and stop it from happening. The argument goes, whatever you may make of it, that a man could potentially be emotionally injured even more by rape than a woman, since for a man to be rendered the powerless object of another person's physical urges is even more of a patriarchal taboo. From this perspective, however hard it is for women to talk about rape, patriarchy makes it harder still for men (which isn't to say that it's easy for either).

Ultimately, there is a combination of factors that make rape a much less common subject for men to discuss and think about. Firstly, it happens less. Secondly, it's significantly less talked about by the men it does affect, resulting from its status as an even greater taboo for a man to bring up. So it doesn't happen as much, and when it does, it is more likely to be kept invisible: the first of these factors is an advantage of male privilege, while the second is the result of patriarchy actually serving to hurt men as well as women, even if not as greatly or as frequently.

This is the key difference between the world of the *Alien* franchise and the world outside it. Bodily violation is just as common and just as visible in these films for men as it is for women, so male audience members suddenly have a window into an unfamiliar world of sexual violence that the patriarchy today does its very best to keep hidden from them.

Rape Culture

We need to look more closely at what it's like for women in both the real world and the world of the *Alien* films. Some feminists argue that sexual violence against women is such a huge problem that we live in a "rape culture." This label, coined by American second-wave feminists in the 1970s, describes a society that in many ways, both large and small, both visible and invisible, continually normalizes (and even advocates) sexual violence against women, while simultaneously reducing the responsibility of the perpetrators for their own actions.

Rape culture can be seen in frequent comments that women who wear particular clothing are "asking for it," alongside a media that's more likely to comment on a woman's physical appearance than her mental skills or qualifications. It's reinforced through the interrogation of rape survivors about why they chose a particular route home, to hang out with strangers, or to "drink too much"; and it's strengthened through all of the prominent advice about preventing rape, casting it as the responsibility of female victims to act in ways less likely to encourage it, rather than as the responsibility of male perpetrators not to rape. It's perhaps no wonder, then, that women comprise the majority of survivors, when these cultural trends appear to depict sexual violence as almost inevitably their lot in life. Society likes to make a big *fuss* about rape being the worst crime of all, while actually encouraging it much more than it tries to stop it. These cultural signals all explain why radical feminist Andrea Dworkin is able to argue in *Our Blood: Prophecies and Discourses on Sexual Politics* that "rape is not committed by psychopaths or deviants from our social norms—rape is committed by *exemplars* of our social norms…Rape is no excess, no aberration, no accident, no mistake—it embodies sexuality as our culture defines it."[3] Rape culture leads to sexual violence against women being so normalized that a regular guy can do it without even realizing that his actions are wrong, merely by treating the opposite sex exactly how society tells him he should.

You'd like to think that things would've improved by the early twenty-second century, but the *Alien* films suggest that a rape culture is still just as entrenched then as now. This is especially true of *Aliens* and *Alien*[3]; not that surprising, considering the glut of alpha-male space Marines in the former and violent offenders in the latter. Listen to the Marines' banter on the shuttle en route to the colony on LV-426, when they joke about rescuing colonists' daughters "from their virginity." It's as if they're saying these women have no other way of showing their gratitude than by giving men their bodies, which they are obligated to do regardless of whether or not they actually want to. "Isn't this just harmless joking around between a bunch of guys about to risk their lives in battle?" you might ask. But a lack of intention to actually follow through on such remarks wouldn't stop it from fueling rape culture—such jokes normalize and even valorize it. For example, even if it's a joke, it still keeps the idea that women are only valued for their bodies in currency, and—a point it's important to keep in mind whenever anyone says that any racist, sexist, or homophobic remark is just harmless fooling around—can the Marine who says it's a joke really be entirely sure that everyone around him *recognizes* it as such? If one of his fellow Marines *were* actually looking forward to ravishing the local population, he'd just take the joke as further support that harming women in this way is a completely valid and normal activity. You can joke about a woman's outfit meaning that she's "up for it" and genuinely intend her no harm whatsoever, but the people around you might not *know* it's just a joke and so this might turn into a cause of harm to women in spite of your benign intention.

Many more examples might seem like innocent background noise but actually further normalize women as subjects of sexual violence. Rape culture can be promoted even by seemingly tiny remarks, like Dr. Elizabeth Shaw in *Prometheus* being greeted with "Hey baby!" as soon as she wakes from stasis—a seemingly innocuous couple of words that further push a woman into a subservient victim role by infantilizing her and diminishing her considerable mental achievements (female academics are already fed up with this in 2017, let alone it should continue until 2093!).

Look at Ripley being told not to "parade around" in front of the prisoners on Fiorina 161. If anything happens to her, the implication is, it'd be her responsibility for having encouraged the urge to assault her, rather than the fault of the male prisoners for having failed to keep this urge in check (as if adult males have no more control over their actions than a Xenomorph running purely on instinct!). And in *Alien: Resurrection*, Johner's first reaction to seeing Ripley playing basketball is to joke about how he knows "some other indoor sports" he'd like to try out with her. To see how this becomes part of a wider cultural trend, rather than just an isolated incident of one horrible man making a crude remark, note that the other members of the *Betty* crew don't do much to point out to Johner why it's inappropriate to admire a woman playing sports for how much the sight makes him want to fuck her, rather than for her actual prowess on the court. His belief that a female athlete is there for his sexual pleasure isn't called out or challenged, and is therefore normalized by default.

It would be pretty understandable if Ripley were as scared of the guys in these films as of the aliens. Perhaps the reason that she isn't is that by the time a woman living in a rape culture has reached her early thirties, the phenomenon has gotten so depressingly mundane that she doesn't see the point of calling it out anymore. Or worse still, it's become so normalized that even she doesn't see how wrong it is.

Equal Opportunity Offenders

So how do these points about Ripley living in a rape culture lead to my suggestion that the film uses sexual violence towards *men* in a way that can give its male audience a uniquely unsettling experience? While Ripley isn't any different from women in our own society in encountering rape culture, often on a daily basis, one huge aspect of male privilege is that men simply aren't subjected to this sort of thing.

Men are raped, but men are not continually encouraged to second-guess their actions, every day, through the background of sexual violence being normalized as both their destiny and their responsibility. Men don't live with the same background noise as most (some would say *all*) women.

While the men in these films direct their ugly comments towards female characters like Ripley or the hypothetical colonists' daughters, the aliens themselves are far less discerning. They're equally happy to violate the bodily integrity of either gender. So the men in these films, on the *Nostromo*, on LV-426, on Fiorina 161, on the USM *Auriga*, get to share an experience akin to what women do in a patriarchal society. They face the threat of knowing that indiscriminate Facehuggers are out there, sizing them up as natural objects of violation, and they have to check every single move they make in order to protect themselves from this ever-present danger. In the world of the *Alien* films, it's not just women who endure the fear and anxiety that come from living in a rape-culture-like environment. The privilege that protects men from experiencing this culture is taken away.

But the films' removal of this one manifestation of male privilege goes much further than this. It is probably insensitive to argue whether rape may or may not be worse for one sex or the other. Yet we can definitely say that there's one potentially devastating effect of rape that cisgender male survivors will never have to face, since they're protected by their very biology: pregnancy.

Women who've been raped have to live with the possibility that the rapist's child will grow inside their body over the next nine months. If they keep it, that child will be an ever-present reminder of what happened for the rest of their lives. This is an especially real threat for women in countries that don't provide any legal access to abortion. And let's not forget that even in the twenty-first century, pregnancy can be fatal. While this is true even in the developed world, some countries outside it have a maternal mortality rate as high as 1 in 7. Even if we look at pregnancy in the context of consensual sex, pregnancy and childbirth are still consequences that many women face entirely alone. The Marines don't seem at all bothered by the possibility of the female colonists on LV-426 getting pregnant after giving their rescuers their amorous "reward," forced or not—because if they did, it'd be the women living with the potentially life-long consequences, while the Marines would just fly off to their next mission.

However horrible the possibility would still be, if the Marines went after men instead, this is one consequence that male colonists would undeniably not have to face. And yet this *isn't* true of the male characters who're violated by the Facehuggers. The very first human victim we see in the films, Kane, is a man whose body is violently penetrated by a Facehugger, forced to carry its offspring inside him, and then killed by the birthing process. The male Engineer at the end of *Prometheus* meets the same brutal fate after being impregnated by Shaw's squid-like offspring. And in the director's cut of *Alien*, Ripley, in her escape from the *Nostromo*, meets the cocooned Dallas; he knows he's been impregnated and what's about to happen to him, and begs Ripley to end his life. So as well as placing male viewers in an environment in which physical violation is just as much an ever-present threat for men as rape culture is for women, the *Alien* franchise also removes the privilege of being protected from the specific consequence of pregnancy.

If men who feel particularly unsettled by these films think about why exactly this might be, and if they work with the results of their thinking, there could be beneficial effects for society. Dealing with this filmic discomfort could reduce the taboo faced by male rape survivors that makes acknowledging and processing their experiences so difficult. And identifying with the horror of the situation might encourage men to look at how they can contribute towards a society that's a less scary place for women.

Notes

1. Carolyn M. Shafer and Marilyn Frye, "Rape and Respect," in *Feminism and Philosophy*, eds. Mary Vetterling-Braggin, Frederick Elliston, and Jane English (Rowman and Littlefield, 1977).
2. Ann J. Cahill, *Rethinking Rape* (Cornell University Press, 2001), 132.
3. Andrea Dworkin, *Our Blood: Prophecies and Discourses on Sexual Politics* (Perigee Books, 1976), 45–46.

Part VI

CONTINENTAL PHILOSOPHY: "I'M THE MONSTER'S MOTHER"

17

The Alien as Übermensch: Overcoming Morality in Order to Become the Perfect Killer

Robert M. Mentyka

During the android Ash's confession in *Alien*, we learn a lot about the creature that has been stalking the crew of the *Nostromo*. Rather than give the human survivors some hope about their chances of overcoming the Xenomorph, Ash waxes poetic about the alien's nature, describing it as the "perfect organism." He goes on to explain that, "Its structural perfection is matched only by its hostility," and that it is "a survivor…unclouded by conscience, remorse, or delusions of morality." The scene helps the movie establish the utterly inhuman character of its predatory antagonist, driving home the fact that this is not a being that can be reasoned, pleaded, or bargained with.

To the moviegoing public, such a wholly amoral life may well seem completely alien to human existence. Within the study of philosophy, however, this notion has been explored extensively, perhaps most notoriously in the writings of the German philosopher Friedrich Nietzsche (1844–1900). Widely known for inflammatory quotes such as "God is dead," Nietzsche fancied himself a kind of prophet of immorality, blowing a clarion call to the men and women of his era to abandon the restrictions of Judeo-Christian ethics and embrace the "fullness" of living that lay beyond its limits.

One of Nietzsche's most enduring ideas is the concept of the *Übermensch*, commonly translated as "superman" or "overman," which he held out as a sort of rationalist alternative to the Abrahamic notion of the Messiah.[1] Much has been written on this controversial

Alien and Philosophy: I Infest, Therefore I Am, First Edition.
Edited by Jeffrey Ewing and Kevin S. Decker.
© 2017 John Wiley & Sons Ltd. Published 2017 by John Wiley & Sons Ltd.

aspect of Nietzsche's philosophy, but a striking amount of the literature about it also seems strangely applicable to the Xenomorph stars of the *Alien* franchise.

The nature of the Xenomorph illustrates some of the core principles of Nietzschean philosophy. This chapter will focus on the idea of the Übermensch and how the aliens from this beloved franchise so perfectly realize, in fiction, the kind of existence Nietzsche hoped to make a reality. While this can be most clearly seen in their lack of human ethics, the Xenomorphs' ability to appropriate traits from their infested hosts also connects with Nietzschean thought, which bears an emphasis on the transitory nature of personal being.

For analysis, we'll draw on not just the four films of the *Alien* quadrilogy, but also the franchise's expanded universe of comics, novels, video games, and other product tie-ins. More recent additions to the franchise, such as the *Aliens vs. Predator* movies or *Prometheus*, may be alluded to, but we'll refrain from using them as a primary source of information as their connections to the original films remain nebulous.

"You still don't understand what you're dealing with, do you?"

When the crew of the doomed ship *Nostromo* encounters the first Xenomorph in *Alien*, they are completely dumbfounded as to what exactly they are dealing with. Emerging from an egg as a spider-like Facehugger with acid blood, then bursting forth from the crewman Kane only to morph into an imposing biomechanical terror, the Xenomorph is an ever-changing variable, adapting to everything used to stop it. This sense of mystery regarding both the creature's form and abilities grounds much of the original film's horror, as neither the crew nor the audience are ever quite prepared for what's waiting for them in the darkness.

Nietzsche's readers were left with a similar sense of confusion when he first introduced the "overman" in the opening pages of his influential work *Thus Spoke Zarathustra*. Published relatively late in his career, the book was written in a way that, to many, seemed thoroughly unphilosophical.[2] Unlike the dry, academic tracts commonly associated with philosophers, Nietzsche's *Zarathustra* was presented as a sort of mythical allegory, a pagan bible to teach the new truths he was trying to convey. In many ways, his writing mirrors the fanatical, over-the-top theatrics of Dr. Jonathan Gediman in *Alien: Resurrection*.

In order to introduce his cinematic terror in *Alien*, director Ridley Scott had to transport viewers to a harsh, distant world where strange vessels house even stranger mysteries. Nietzsche, on the other hand, sought in his writings to bring new ideas to us by having his fictional prophet, Zarathustra, leave the shelter of his hermitage to preach to the people. He begins, "*I teach you the overman*. Man is something that shall be overcome. What have you done to overcome him?"[3] Much like the android Ash, Nietzsche's Zarathustra has been given the task of introducing a whole new form of life to humanity, and he will not fail at that directive.

In the *Alien* franchise, one of the driving plot points is the desire by the Weyland-Yutani Corporation to acquire a specimen of the Xenomorphs for their research and development team. This is, of course, opposed by the protagonists of each film led by Ripley, who understands that letting just one of these aliens reach Earth could well mean the end of the entire human race. When the Xenomorphs do finally reach Earth in the expanded universe, they quickly multiply and infest the entire planet within two years' time.[4]

Nietzsche's new form of life, the overman, is not a new physical species or the next step in humanity's biological evolution, but rather a new approach to living and ethical decision-making. The overman is an ideal whose character we are drawn to emulate. Zarathustra famously states that, "Man is a rope, tied between beast and overman—a rope over an abyss."[5] Human nature is not static being, but dynamic becoming, as our choices continually mold and shape us either towards or away from such heroic ideals.

This metamorphosis, however, is not one that can be passively avoided. Any time a human character comes in contact with the Xenomorph species, they are soon drawn into a desperate, life-or-death struggle. There's no middle ground in dealing with the aliens, as their complete annihilation is "the only way to be sure" of defeating them. So too, according to Nietzsche, every person must make a choice between who they are and who they could be. Humanity has risen above the nature of brute animals, but unless men and women choose to become authentic overmen, they are doomed to regress into a state of moral and cultural stagnation and decline. It is for this reason that Nietzsche considers the gestation of such overmen the most important mission of philosophy and the defining goal of his entire career as a writer.

Nietzsche sees ordinary men and women hovering on the brink of despair. His infamous quote, "God is dead," is intimately connected to this viewpoint, as he surveyed society near the end of the nineteenth century and saw that people no longer believed in the core ideas that used to shape their lives.[6] People were losing faith in religion, government, and even the progress of science, but they had yet to fill this void in their lives with an unshakeable faith in themselves. This was the reason why Nietzsche's Übermensch was so vital to humanity, as both the new goal to be sought by human existence and the very means by which it might be obtained.

"You know, Burke, I don't know which species is worse"

One of the most enduring themes of the *Aliens* franchise focuses on the contrast between humanity and the Xenomorph menace. Outwardly, the Xenomorphs appear to be nothing more than monsters, perversions of being bent only on procreating and spreading their horror across the stars. Even in the expanded universe, we see very little of anything they contribute to the world around them. They showcase no great achievements in science, no cultural developments of society, nor any great contributions to art to offset the mind-numbing terror they inspire.

For all their outward monstrosity, however, the Xenomorphs are consistently shown to be less inhumane than many of the human villains of the *Alien* franchise. We see this inhumanity clearly in the orders given to Mother in the first *Alien* film, as well as in Carter Burke's scheming in *Aliens*. In both cases, greed and ambition cause humans, either as individuals like Burke or through massive corporations such as Weyland-Yutani, to consciously betray their fellow men and women in the most heinous ways possible. By contrast, as Ripley herself pointedly sums up about the Xenomorphs in *Aliens*, "You don't see them fucking each other over for a goddamn percentage."

For his part, Nietzsche also frequently relies on comparisons in describing the overman. One of the best ways to describe the overman is by contrasting him with his most direct adversary, whom Nietzsche called the "last man."[7] Again reflecting the comparison between humanity and the Xenomorphs, the differences between Nietzsche's overman and the "last man" are marked by the fact that most readers would expect the latter of these two to be the more desirable type of human character.

Nietzsche's last men are akin to the vast majority of people populating the crews of starships like the *Nostromo* or *Sulaco*. They are mean, petty types so focused on survival that they have forgotten just what it means to truly live. Like the technicians Brett and Parker in the first *Alien* film, they remain nonplussed by the prospect of contact with an alien species, but are singularly focused on the paycheck they will receive for retrieving a specimen. It's not that these last men harbor particularly detestable vices or live especially villainous lives; rather, it is their very mediocrity that Nietzsche condemns.

The overman, on the other hand, is the height and glory of the character he has chosen to fulfill. He will certainly have flaws and vices, but even these are possessed by him in their fullness. For instance, an overman would not struggle with a tendency for gambling, but could be a card shark of the most notorious and successful ilk, well known in all the major casinos across the land. This is similar to the Xenomorph's role as hunter. Every part of its body, even the acidic blood it utilizes for defense, is oriented towards its aggressive, predatory function. Just as the Xenomorph is not merely a killer, but the ideal killing machine, so too is the overman the perfection of the characteristics inherent to him.

Nietzsche wholeheartedly believed in extremes, but he also realized this kind of thinking was not particularly popular. After the vision of ideal humanity is introduced in *Thus Spoke Zarathustra*, the townspeople of that fictional world reject the idea, clamoring instead, "Give us this last man, O Zarathustra...Turn us into these last men!"[8] They would rather stay safe in mediocrity than risk the upheavals that authentic virtues and vices would bring to their world. Like the colonists and ship crews of the *Aliens* movies, who steer a wide berth around the Xenomorph menace, ordinary people prefer to remain who and what they are instead of being challenged to become something greater.

At this point, it seems that Nietzsche would fit in quite nicely among the upper levels of Weyland-Yutani management. His argument bears a lot of parallels with the justifications given by Ash and Burke for their actions. Sure, some expendable crew members might die in the process, but this sacrifice is acceptable given the wealth of scientific discoveries and monetary profits that would be made possible by research on the Xenomorphs. Indeed, this is one of the major reasons Nietzsche has such a notorious reputation among philosophers. In his passion for creating ideal men and women, his callous disregard for established beliefs and ideas paints him as quite the rebel even today, more than one hundred years after his death.

Remember, however, that the real villains of the *Aliens* franchise are human beings, not the terrifying Xenomorphs. H.R. Giger's biomechanical beasts are indeed nightmare-inducing, but they also possess a type of nobility that leads us to respect them as much as we fear them. Much like Ash, audiences find themselves intrigued by the Xenomorphs, fascinated by the specter of so ruthless and perfect a killing machine. We too "admire its purity," as a memorable threat for heroes like Hicks, Newt, and Ripley.

Nietzsche's overman is a similarly radical departure from the ordinary lives that most of us live. While many individuals long for stability and a sense of normality, the overman sticks out as exceptional and extravagant. He draws attention to characteristics that are often downplayed in "proper" society, and he lives a life completely unchained from other people's opinions of him. The sheer excessiveness of Nietzsche's overman may shock and offend us, but the underlying idea is something we can respect much like we appreciate a Xenomorph. Whatever we may think of Nietzsche himself or his philosophy, his thoughts about the overman could well prove fruitful and fulfilling in our own attempts to become the kind of men and women we long to be.

"For within each seed, there is a promise of a flower, and within each death...there's always new life"

The most memorable characteristic of the Xenomorphs is their grotesque, invasive process of metamorphosis. More so than anything else, the Xenomorph's mutable physical form has cemented it as one of the most nightmarish monsters in all of cinema. This mutation goes deeper than the growth of the organism from immaturity into adulthood, as the Xenomorph's appearance and functions are altered based on the biological hosts they spring from. These aliens are so terrifying precisely because they can take the greatest strengths from any of their enemies and quickly assimilate these traits as their own.

Far from being the endpoint of humanity, the overman himself is a source of constant creative development. Nietzsche's thoughts here are bound up with transition and change, as this is one of the prime reasons why so much of his writing on the subject reads as allegory and myth. While he can paint, using broad strokes, a rough picture of the kind of figure an overman would be, the actual historical realization of Nietzsche's ideas might well appear unrecognizable to the philosopher who preached the overman in the first place.

During the course of its lifetime, every Xenomorph goes through several radically different stages. It begins life as an egg, or "Ovomorph," anchored to a particular surface to await the arrival of suitable biological material. Once such matter has come close enough, the Ovomorph opens to reveal a spider-like "Facehugger" that latches onto its victim and impregnates it with the infant Xenomorph commonly called a "Chestburster." Once this stage of the Xenomorph has lived up to its name, escaping from its host by literally eating its way out, the Chestburster matures into a full-grown Xenomorph.[9]

At this point in its life cycle, the creature's form is further shaped by its role within the hive, adopting differing characteristics based on whether it serves as a drone, warrior, or the heart of the hive, the queen. According to the expanded universe, this categorization is not permanent, as each Xenomorph can change its class based on the hive's needs. This is why the presence of even a single Xenomorph is enough to doom the Earth, as that individual alien drone could quickly morph into a queen capable of producing hundreds of eggs, thus beginning the cycle anew.

In *Thus Spoke Zarathustra*, Nietzsche outlines his own threefold metamorphosis. "Of three metamorphoses of the spirit I tell you," Nietzsche speaks through the mouth of Zarathustra, "How the spirit becomes a camel; and the camel, a lion; and the lion, finally, a child."[10] One interpretation of the three figures is that they are meant to represent the differing types of morality Nietzsche saw at work in the moral life. These can be broadly categorized as the repressive, the destructive, and the creative, but these descriptions, and the metaphors used to introduce them, can perhaps better be explained by referring back to the Xenomorph life cycle laid out above.

The repressive moral system, originally equated with the camel by Nietzsche, can be matched with the Ovomorph in that both are largely passive elements in the moral life. They have no say in the systems of value that govern their lives, instead waiting for others to offer beliefs and ethical laws that they must follow. Nietzsche locates most of humankind in this stage, teetering on the verge of complacency that leads to the last man described in the previous section.

The destructive morality, symbolized by Nietzsche as the lion, matches up with the intermediary stages of the Xenomorph: the Facehugger and the Chestburster. Faced with the dictates of a foreign ethics, the destructive morality answers with a definitive "No" and proceeds to destroy what once oppressed it.[11] Caring little for consequences, it seeks only to rip apart that which is its enemy, much as the

Facehugger and Chestburster have no qualms about the destruction they bring to any victim unfortunate enough to have been impregnated for the hive.

Just as the Chestburster kills its host in order to bring forth the new life of the mature Xenomorph, the destructive morality does not merely end in violence alone, but rather uses it to clear a path for the creative morality. Described by Nietzsche using the image of a child, this creative ethics sets up a new system of morality based on its own will. It chooses what is right and wrong based on what is fulfilling for its own life, rather than on what others claim to be helpful or hurtful for it. It has become the active principle in its moral life, much as the adult Xenomorph has left behind its passive existence as an egg to become the hunter of those who once hunted it.

If Nietzsche connects the first of these stages with ordinary human life, then it makes sense for the overman to be tied to the later stages. Most scholars equate the overman with the third level of morality, the creative, but many of Nietzsche's writings on the subject, as well as the popular view of his thoughts, tie it more closely to the violent level of the lion.[12] Ultimately, both aspects are important to the concept of the overman as a complete person who has the power to both tear down oppressive moralities and replace them with his own system of life-affirming value. Once again, the Xenomorph presents a strikingly on-point image: much as the lowly Xenomorph warrior can evolve into a queen in order to serve his hive, the overman can shift seamlessly from acts of creation to movements of destruction in order to serve both humanity and his own vital flourishing.

"You are...a beautiful, beautiful, butterfly"

Now, like any proper horror film, we must reveal our subject in full, just in time for the harrowing climax of our narrative. Nietzsche's Übermensch is both a goal to inspire and guide us and a description of the kind of human beings Nietzsche thought would rise up in light of the moral disillusionment of so many thinkers at the end of the nineteenth century. As such, the overman exists as both an important historical concept influential to philosophers and many other important figures over the past hundred years and the core of a philosophical viewpoint that continues to shape our ethical considerations today.

Though it's not certain whether Nietzsche's teachings were influential in designing the Xenomorphs, the fact remains that these horror icons expertly showcase features central to Nietzsche's thought. Their utter disregard for human "conscience, remorse, or delusions of morality" as well as their unconquerable will to survive bring Nietzsche's overman to life in a way that makes his own attempts seem pale by comparison. Perhaps fittingly, the very monstrosity of these "ideal" beings could well make Nietzsche himself think twice about the kind of vital perfection he tried to bring into the world. A self-appointed prophet of the extreme, Nietzsche could not fully anticipate the excesses that his teachings would inspire and the immoral decisions that his works would be used to condone.

Notes

1. For this chapter, I'll avoid translating *Übermensch* as "superman" so as not to confuse the idea with DC Comics' widely known superhero. Instead, I will rely on both the original German word and the translation "overman" that captures much of the same spirit without the connotation of flying men in tights.
2. Robert Wicks, "Friedrich Nietzsche," in *The Stanford Encyclopedia of Philosophy* (Winter 2014 Edition), ed. Edward N. Zalta, http://plato.stanford.edu/archives/win2014/nietzsche.
3. Friedrich Nietzsche, *Thus Spoke Zarathustra*, in *The Portable Nietzsche*, ed. and trans. Walter Kaufmann (Penguin, 1982), 112–439; 124.
4. Steve Perry, *Aliens Book 1: Earth Hive* (Bantam Spectra, 1992), 259.
5. Nietzsche, *Thus Spoke Zarathustra*, 126.
6. See ibid., 124, for the most famous statement of this infamous phrase.
7. Ibid., 129–131.
8. Ibid., 130.
9. A fairly concise summary of this process is contained in Perry, *Earth Hive*, 40–48. Numerous unofficial fan websites are similarly dedicated to exploring this cycle.
10. Nietzsche, *Thus Spoke Zarathustra*, 137–140.
11. Friedrich Nietzsche, "Ecce Homo," in *Basic Writings of Nietzsche*, ed. and trans. Walter Kaufmann (Modern Library, 2000), 655–800; 761–762, 765.
12. Numerous writers have investigated this topic, but a more synthetic view like the one adopted in this chapter can be found in Michael A. Gillespie, "Slouching Toward Bethlehem to Be Born: On the Nature and Meaning of Nietzsche's Superman," *Journal of Nietzsche Studies* 30 (2005): 49–69.

18

"Why Do You Go On Living?": Ripley-8 and the Absurd

Seth M. Walker

The ship is overrun with terrifying extraterrestrial killers, slowly picking off the remaining crew and passengers one at a time. Your group is heading to a docked craft, trying to stay ahead of the horde so you can escape, and something catches your eye. A door. Discreet and not particularly inviting. But, there's something curious about it—or at least what it has on the other side. Your companions urge you to leave it alone and keep going, but you just *can't*. The door opens. You slowly survey the room, taking in container after container of grotesque and deformed human–Xenomorph hybrids, horrifyingly preserved and left on display. These are the *mess-ups*, you quickly realize. Strolling through the crowded vessels of carnivalesque freaks, you make your way to a table in the back of the room. Sprawled out, mutated, and noticeably in great pain, an all-too-familiar face pleads for you to end her suffering: "Kill me." You've known for most of your short, accelerated life that you started out in this room, too. But it didn't quite sink in until now—now that you've come face to face with the previous, failed attempts. You respond with a wash from a flamethrower, granting her wish, and destroy the remaining, disgusting trophies, enveloping the room in explosive flames. These…things. These creations. You're one of them. But, standing before the torturous ruin, you realize what makes you different: you're going *to live*.

Alien and Philosophy: I Infest, Therefore I Am, First Edition.
Edited by Jeffrey Ewing and Kevin S. Decker.
© 2017 John Wiley & Sons Ltd. Published 2017 by John Wiley & Sons Ltd.

Number 8

Lieutenant Ellen Ripley just can't seem to rest in peace in the *Alien* saga—even after she actually *dies* at the end of *Alien³*. Fast-forward two hundred years to the opening sequence of *Alien: Resurrection* where United Systems Military (USM) science officers aboard the *Auriga* are toying with her DNA—salvaged from frozen blood samples on Fiorina 161—to try to create a cloned version of the alien queen that was growing inside her at the time of her death. The only problem: they need to successfully clone Ripley in order to get at a cloned Xenomorph embryo. Shortly after the film begins, when we witness a supposed clone-job and alien-extraction gone right, we notice it took the USM eight attempts to succeed. This cloned version of Ripley survived the disturbing caesarean section-like procedure and has been kept alive by the science officers as an "unexpected benefit." A number "8" is tattooed on Ripley's forearm, hence her official title in the film: Number 8, or, eventually, Ripley-8. And it doesn't take her long to start developing at an extremely fast rate and realize what she *is* and what *they* have done.

Part of this advanced level of learning and comprehension is a result of Ripley's DNA hybridizing with the Xenomorph during the cloning, the effect of which we see more clearly in those failed attempts she discovers on display in the laboratory. Ripley-8 is much *cooler* than that Ellen Ripley from two centuries ago everyone keeps talking about: she's part alien. She's got heightened levels of sense perception and memory recovery, exaggerated levels of strength and precision (remember that next time you try to shoot some hoops with her, Johner!), an incredible tolerance for pain, and that infamous acidic blood we've all grown to both fear and find totally awesome. It's pretty clear why the science officers wanted to keep her around to study and observe. But, when she does make that alarming discovery about who—or, what—she is, she's confronted with a crisis of identity and meaning that continues throughout the remainder of the film: not only has she genetically merged with a species she's been fighting for almost three hundred years, but she's also not *really* Ellen Ripley. So, let's take a closer look at this crisis and her place in the world around her—a crisis that I think we can rightfully say seems pretty *absurd*.

A Serious Philosophical Problem

The French essayist, journalist, playwright, and novelist (yeah, busy guy!) Albert Camus (1913–1960) made a name for himself in French intellectual circles as the fellow who thought life was characterized by "absurdity," and it's easy to see some parallels between his views and the situation of Ripley-8 throughout *Alien: Resurrection*. According to Camus, "the absurd" arises from the desire for meaning and intelligibility in an unintelligible world—or, in other words, "the confrontation between the human need and the unreasonable silence of the world."[1] It's not that the *world* is absurd. The absurd is what links the two—Ripley's desire to make some sense out of her troubling existence and the fact that the world is unable to offer her any such sense. Camus repeatedly stresses this point in different, sometimes rather poetic, ways throughout his classic essay, "The Myth of Sisyphus." But the point is always the same: we yearn for the world to make sense to us, and its response is that it couldn't care less about what we do or how we feel.

Let's face it, Ripley-8 has one messed-up and confusing life. How could she not feel like a lab-created freak who only exists because of some unforeseen outcome of the latest, most successful cloning attempt? Sometimes, she's rather clear about this feeling, too—like when she confesses to the synthetic, Annalee Call, that her alien-filled nightmarish dreams are more of a comfort now than anything else:

RIPLEY: When I sleep, I dream about them. It. Every night. All around me. In me. I used to be afraid to dream, but I'm not anymore.
CALL: Why?
RIPLEY: Because no matter how bad the dreams get, when I wake up, it's always worse.

That's how depressing her life is. It's hard not to feel bad for Ripley: she's not only struggling with the fact that she was created in a lab as part of some sort of twisted science experiment, she's also dealing with an internal biological battle of human versus alien. Not only that: since she has been fighting this alien race for most of her life, how could she *not* completely and utterly despise what *she* is now? This is where Camus comes in: maybe she should just kill herself.

Camus begins "The Myth of Sisyphus" with one of the most startling opening lines ever written and one of the most important and pressing questions you'll likely ever ask yourself: "There is but one truly serious philosophical problem, and that is suicide. Judging whether life is or is not worth living amounts to answering the fundamental question of philosophy. All the rest…comes afterwards."[2] And that's it. Close your copy of Camus, grab a beer, and give that question some thought before you even decide whether or not to bother reading the rest of his essay: is life worth living, especially after recognizing its absurdity?

Now, before you start to think, "well, yeah, of course it's worth living—I have a great job, wonderful friends and family, and even on the worst days, I still find joy in the beauty of the natural world," keep in mind that those *valuable* aspects of life aren't exactly what Camus was talking about. We can have joyful experiences and delight in our activities—and for Camus, that's really the only point of our existence. Remember, he perceived the world as completely unintelligible—*not* as devoid of happiness and pleasure—and our effort to make some over-arching, intelligent sense out of it all is what causes our pain and turmoil. Ripley-8 seems to grasp this, too. Call asks Ripley at one point if she understands her desire to save everyone on the *Auriga*: "I did once. I tried to save…people. It didn't work out." Reflecting back on her previous—and all-human—life, Ripley has finally realized that the world (and universe!) is a mess, so why bother trying to make sense of it all?

I Can Make it All Stop

This brings us to some of the options Camus offers for responding to the absurd: Go ahead and kill yourself, Ripley. Just end it—hopefully, this time, for good. Label this option "physical suicide." Or maybe: This universe may seem like it doesn't make any sense, Ripley, but you must have faith that it does, even if you can't figure it out. Camus calls this one "philosophical suicide." A third option: Life is absurd? Okay. Now we know what we're up against, Ripley. Let's get off this ship before it blows. This one is Camus's favorite, and, for him, is really the only sound option out of the three: "revolt" against the absurd.

But, let's back up a little bit here. What's so wrong with the first two? If the meaning of life is the most urgent question to be asked, and if it's necessarily characterized by a *lack* of meaning, why *shouldn't* Ripley-8 just kill herself? Well, for starters, physical suicide amounts to a submission—a submission and a confession that life is just too much to handle. And it really dodges the problem we're dealing with here: there's no meaning in death either, so why give in and preclude any further responses to absurdity? A strong human(ish) woman like Ripley-8 is certainly unlikely to go for this as well, even in such crummy circumstances. The first time she meets Call, Call sneaks up on her with a knife:

CALL: I can make it all stop. The pain. This nightmare. That's all I can offer.
RIPLEY: What makes you think I would let you do that?

There's a confusion of meaning involved here, which is probably making you scratch your head at this point: life not having any meaning does not exactly translate to a life not worth living. We can be happy and have valuable experiences, and, as we'll see, that might just be enough—or at least all we can ask for.

You're Programmed to Do That?

When Camus talks about philosophical suicide, he's really talking about an irrational "leap of faith." Typically, this involves belief in a deity or some other source of supernatural power, the existence of which solves the problem of unintelligibility—either in this life or in another after death. Camus refers to this option as a negation of human reason, and, just like physical suicide, it too evades our rather serious problem. What he means is that humans have limitations on their knowledge: Ripley can't possibly know everything about the universe, where "she" *was* for two hundred years before resurfacing in her new, Xeno/Ripley state, or the origins of both the human and Xenomorph species, among so much else. Instead of rationally recognizing this limitation on reason, people commit philosophical suicide by sacrificing it for an irrational explanation: "when, starting from a philosophy of the world's lack of meaning, it [the mind] ends up by finding a meaning and depth in it."[3] It's tempting to give in to this sort of thing: "History is not lacking in either religions or prophets, even without gods," Camus assures us.[4] Our goal, he instead advises, is to stay strong and only accept what little we can observe and truly understand.

We don't really see this taking place in *Alien: Resurrection*. And, actually, the only time "religion" comes up is when Ripley and Call enter the *Auriga*'s chapel and Call crosses herself: "You're programmed to do that?" Ripley judgingly asks (we can hear the chuckle just waiting to burst out of her chest, too…pun intended). But, the fact that Call *was* programmed to react that way in a chapel does imply that the universe hasn't exactly been purged of what Camus would call irrational ideologies. This scene illustrates a tendency Camus recognized throughout history that humans might continue to have a hard time avoiding when confronted with the nature of their existence—even in the face of advanced technological development and futuristic space travel and colonization.

I Rebel—Therefore We Exist

This brings us to the third option: permanent revolution—an acceptance of one's fate, and a revolt against absurdity. This option is equally a rejection of physical resignation and of any possible explanation beyond the observable facts of life. And we see this taking place with Ripley-8: she's not interested in ending her own life, no matter how crummy it may be, and she's not interested in *allowing* Call to do it for her—and she's certainly not "finding God" behind the door of the laboratory. One must *live*, Camus claimed, in order to reject "the most obvious absurdity": death.[5]

For Camus, this revolt doesn't just remain a solitary experience either, which is a theme he takes up in *The Rebel*. What we can't forget is that Ripley-8 isn't alone in this absurd scenario. Everyone else aboard the *Auriga* is faced with a similar, urgent question. Ripley's might be the most apparent, considering her unnatural and troubling creation, but she's *rebelling* just as much as everyone else. Camus tells us that "from the moment when a movement of rebellion begins, suffering is seen as a collective experience" and "the first progressive step for a mind overwhelmed by the strangeness of things is to realize that this feeling of strangeness is shared with all men...I rebel—therefore we exist."[6] But, one of these other passengers is actually rebelling under very similar circumstances: Annalee Call.

Little Hunk of Plastic

Ripley and Call are both artificial creations living a similar sort of existence. Ripley-8 *is not* Ellen Ripley: "You're a thing. A construct. They grew you in a fucking lab," Call tells her. But, Call isn't exactly the young woman she presents herself to be either. When she's shot in the chest by Doctor Mason Wren during the group's escape to the *Betty*, we were certainly surprised to see her come to their rescue shortly thereafter—with a gaping hole in her torso, oozing the white, gooey android "blood" we've seen in previous *Alien* films. "You're a robot?" Ripley rhetorically asks after seeing the "wound." "Son of a bitch!" Johner adds. "Our little Call is just full of surprises." But, she's not *just* a robot. She's apparently "second gen"—a robot designed by robots, or, an "auton," making her that much further removed from humanity and different from her companions. Just like we felt sorry for Ripley-8, it's hard to not feel something similar for Call when everyone starts to talk about her as if she's a lesser creature.

When Call and Ripley are sitting in the chapel after the gunshot incident, after Call has plugged into the *Auriga*'s computer to reroute the ship for its Xeno-destroying crash landing, she tells Ripley, "At least there's part of you that's human. I'm just...look at me. I'm disgusting." This brief exchange is actually pretty telling: it's clear that Call has been struggling with the same sort of issues Ripley has, but in a different way. Just as Ripley is disgusted with herself—for being genetically intermingled with her archenemy—Call is disgusted with an artificiality of a different kind. And both are equally rebelling against their absurd circumstances: during their first exchange, Ripley tells Call that she'll never get off the ship alive. "I don't care," Call replies. "Really?" Ripley counters. Grabbing Call by the throat, she whispers into her ear: "I can make it stop." But, we know it doesn't end for either of them in that scene. Both Ripley and Call, plagued by their equally absurd existences, could've ended each other's lives right there. But, instead, they both chose to rebel—both individually and collectively—forming a bond as *others* taking charge of their fates.

One Must Imagine Ripley Happy

At the end of the film, Ripley and Call are shown sitting in a deserted landscape, staring out towards what remains of a crumbling Paris, France—a scene Camus himself may have observed hundreds of years earlier under better circumstances, when it was still the dazzling City of Light. As they're contemplating their next move, Call turns to Ripley and asks, "What do you think? What should we do?" "I don't know," Ripley responds. "I'm a stranger here myself."

As we've pointed out above, they've already responded to the "now what?" suggested by the absurd: they're *living*, they're choosing to rebel against an apparent lack of meaning and intelligibility in the world. They might not know how things are going to turn out for them—it's not really clear how long androids *last* or if they naturally "die," and Ripley's life expectancy, with Xeno-spiked blood flowing through her veins, is equally unclear—but trying to answer these types of questions risks what Camus warns us against: there are limits to what we can know, and our revolt acknowledges this fact.

Camus ends his essay by showing us an image of the absurd hero *par excellence* from Greek mythology: Sisyphus. Sisyphus is punished by the gods for skipping out on a pleasant stay in the Underworld, and is tasked with rolling a large boulder up to the top of a mountain, only to watch it fall down. Then he's to roll it back up. Again. And again. For eternity. You're probably wondering, what's so heroic about that? Well, the thing to understand about Sisyphus, Camus tells us, is that he can't stand the gods (obviously!), and that he equally hates death and loves life. Sound familiar? Put another way, Sisyphus has no interest in either philosophical or physical suicide. But, his existence is rather meaningless: he's just repeatedly rolling a boulder up a mountain forever. And that's the "catch" Camus is getting at: "The absurd has meaning only in so far as it is not agreed to."[7] The only way we can have a meaningful existence in this world is by not caving in to its inherent meaninglessness (that's a head-spinner, I know). Even so, drawing some noticeable parallels between Sisyphus and Ripley might help us make some sense out of Camus.

When Call asks her, "Why do you go on living? How can you stand being what you are?," Ripley simply responds: "Not much choice." That's just who she *is*: someone living in the face of the absurd, understanding her limitations without sacrificing her reason to irrational appeals for meaning, looking death in the face and telling it to wait another three hundred years. Camus is most interested in that moment right before Sisyphus starts back down the mountain to retrieve the boulder and begin again: when he's fully aware of what he's doing as an endless and pointless task. But, we can imagine Sisyphus finds joy, Camus argues, in his choice to keep going—when *he* takes charge of his own fate. Just like Ripley.

We see that Ripley-8 is living in revolt of the circumstances of her life, but perhaps she didn't really grasp the similarly endless and pointless mission she's destined to have until the end of the fourth film. Maybe the "here" where she's a stranger isn't Earth per se, but the state of conscious awareness that she, like Sisyphus, is fated to repeat the same, meaningless task: exterminating the Xenomorph species to save humanity. Starting with rolling the boulder of self-destruction aboard the *Nostromo* in *Alien*, she's been returning to the bottom of the mountain in each addition to the saga ever since—from beating a Xeno queen in an exoskeleton-suit duel on the *Sulaco* in *Aliens*, to her self-sacrifice in *Alien³* to keep the Xenomorphs extinct once and for all. The cycle never ends, and each grand finale is made meaningless by the continuation of the narrative in the next film.

Until *Alien: Resurrection*, we could argue that Ripley wasn't conscious of her fate, nor was she even living in revolt—a fear of death is not the same as its rejection, and the hope for a better, Xeno-free existence was clearly a pipedream. When the queen is fully grown, we might argue that Ripley finally realizes the repetitive nature of her absurd story: "It's too late. You can't stop it. It's inevitable," she tells Call. But when Ripley decides she's going to live despite this endless toil, now manifest in the extreme—she's part alien now!—she's entered the "hour of consciousness" shared by Sisyphus on the top of his mountain.[8] But, again, we *can* find joy in this. Just as Camus tells us of Sisyphus, we must imagine Ripley happy as well.

Notes

1. Albert Camus, *The Myth of Sisyphus and Other Essays*, trans. Justin O'Brien (Vintage International, 1955), 28.
2. Ibid., 3.
3. Ibid., 42.
4. Ibid., 53.
5. Ibid., 59.
6. Albert Camus, *The Rebel: An Essay on Man in Revolt*, trans. Anthony Bower (Vintage International, 1956), 22.
7. Camus, *The Myth of Sisyphus*, 31.
8. Ibid., 121.

19

God Save the Xenomorph Queen: Defending Xenomorph Self-Defense

Jeffrey Ewing

It seems so clear that we're supposed to root *for* humanity and *against* each and every Xenomorph. But in *Doctor Who*, the Doctor muses, "There's a horror movie named *Alien*? That's really offensive. No wonder everybody keeps invading you." So, what if things aren't exactly as they seem? What grounds do we have to root for the humans at all? Perhaps our usual interpretation of the *Alien* films suffers from anthropocentrism—human-centeredness. After all, if we didn't automatically equate "human" with "good," and "Xenomorph" with "bad," wouldn't it be possible to see the scary, slimy aliens as merely defending themselves against the humans they perceive as constantly trying to kill them? Jean-Paul Sartre (1905–1980) might think so. If we take his famous defense of violence, and if we don't assume an anthropocentric view, we may actually have reasons to root *for* the Xenomorphs.

Existentialism is an Alienism

Jean-Paul Sartre was the most beloved French philosopher and perhaps the best known European public intellectual of the twentieth century. Sartre's works on existentialism and Marxism provide a number of insights on topics like secular morality, existence, resistance, and freedom, but Sartre may seem like a strange choice for defending Xenomorphs. This is because Sartre's philosophy often

Alien and Philosophy: I Infest, Therefore I Am, First Edition.
Edited by Jeffrey Ewing and Kevin S. Decker.

ignores the moral status of nonhuman species, and is often taken to be *anthropocentric*—the opposite of the argument we will be trying to make. This anthropocentric approach comes from Sartre's attempt to steep his philosophical projects in the view of "humanism," characterized by a firm separation of the human self and the natural world. For example, in his novel *Nausea*, Sartre offers an in-depth description of the alienation of humanity from the natural world through the novel's main character, Roquentin, who comments:

> I am afraid of cities. But you mustn't leave them. If you go too far you come up against the vegetation belt. Vegetation has crawled for miles towards the cities. It is waiting. Once the city is dead, the vegetation will cover it, will climb over the stones, grip them, search them, make them burst with its long black pincers; it will blind the holes and let its green paws hang over everything. You must stay in the cities as long as they are alive.[1]

The natural world is not a comfort—it is a destructive force which will outlive and erase human civilization.

It seems, at first glance, that Sartre would defend humanity against what is *alien*, relate to our fear and the fear of protagonists like Ripley and Newt, and justify the destruction of the Xenomorphs. How can Sartre possibly be used to defend them? Well, to begin with, Sartre makes an important presupposition about human beings—namely, that they are the only species that have conscious awareness of their own selves. Unlike other creatures, which are "passive, inert nature," we are capable of reflection on, and transformation of our own practices and ourselves in unique ways. Further, humans are *free* in their self-consciousness, and so not determined by external forces and limitations in the way non-human natural things are. But what if Xenomorphs are not passive, inert nature? If they show a similar capacity for self-conscious awareness, that is, if they can acknowledge Descartes's foundational discovery of "I think, therefore I am" (and everything that follows from this), then Sartre's views about the distinctiveness of humanity can also be applied to them. So a Sartrean defense of the Xenomorphs would have two steps: first, to examine why Sartre justifies revolutionary violence, and second, to show that Xenomorphs meet the criteria that Sartre uses to defend revolutionary violence.

Sartre's existentialist philosophy is grounded in the idea of freedom and the responsibility that results from it—in an early phrasing, "man makes himself."[2] While external forces may constrain us, we are always free to resist and try to change them. Similarly, a person's consciousness and essence are not pre-formed and constant. Rather, a person creates herself through her own activity and choices—in Sartre's formula, "existence precedes essence."[3] In short, for Sartre, our human capacities for knowing and understanding are the source for the potential of human freedom, and through that freedom we create the beings we are. While external powers and limits may constrain our free self-creation, we can resist rather than submit, fight rather than fall. It is this insight that connects Sartre's approach to the self to his defense of revolutionary violence.

After World War II, Sartre's philosophical interests turned towards the political with his *Critique of Dialectical Reason* (1958–1959), an existentialist defense of Marxism, and his preface to Frantz Fanon's *Wretched of the Earth* (1961). In the preface, Sartre both condemns European colonialism and defends the rightness of decolonization. First and foremost, Sartre identifies the core of the colonial project—the denial of the humanity of the colonized subject. Sartre argues:

> By rejecting metropolitan universalism, our soldiers overseas apply the *numerus clausus* to the human species: since none can rob, enslave, or kill his fellow man without committing a crime, they lay down the principle that the colonized subject is not a fellow man. Our military forces have received orders to change this abstract certainty into reality: orders are given to reduce the inhabitants of the occupied territory to the level of a superior ape in order to justify the colonist's treatment of them as beasts of burden. Colonial violence not only aims at keeping these enslaved men at a respectful distance, it also seeks to dehumanize them.[4]

While Xenomorphs are surely enough not biological *humans*, they may yet have the factors Sartre thinks characterize our "fellow man," or *people*—rationality, consciousness, even emotions—and so have the self-creating power we just discussed. If this is true, we may find that Xenomorph violence can be defended for the same reasons underlying Sartre's defense of the decolonization project. If these aliens are consciously self-aware, then perhaps the attempts of the human military to destroy them are indeed a type of colonial violence, attempting to dehumanize and destroy an intelligent species.

In this light, Xenomorph "attacks" could be interpreted as self-defense (rather than predatory violence), and attempts to resist human domination. Perhaps the human military can't see this, like the colonizer who "cannot recognize his own cruelty now turned against him

[…] he can't see his own savagery as a colonist in the savagery of these oppressed peasants who have absorbed it through every pore and for which they can find no cure."[5] In this light, the colonizer's brutality against the colonized is responsible for the latter's violent response to oppression—violence becomes necessary as a route or means to the preservation of personhood under repressive conditions. In this context, for the colonized:

> it is through this mad rage, this bile and venom, their constant desire to kill us, and the permanent contraction of powerful muscles, afraid to relax, that they become men….The false "natives," therefore, are still humans owing to the power and powerlessness of the oppressor that are transformed into the natives' stubborn rejection of their animal condition.[6]

Subjected to extreme human violence, Xenomorph attacks may look like animalistic malice, but as Sartre points out, "in a time of helplessness, murderous rampage is the collective unconscious of the colonized."[7]

A Funny Habit of Shedding His Animality

The intelligence of the Xenomorph species is an incredibly difficult thing to measure. A number of factors could hypothetically impact it, from age or the stage of a particular alien's development, to the base intelligence of the host species, to the distinct traits of the Xenomorph Queen. Xenomorphs are often treated like animals *despite* their intelligence. For example, in *Alien*, the crew of the *Nostromo* hypothesizes about potential Xenomorph weaknesses:

ASH: Yes, well, it's adapted remarkably well to our atmosphere considering its nutritional requirements. The only thing we don't know about is temperature.
RIPLEY: Ok, what about temperature? What happens if we change it?
ASH: Let's try it. I mean, most animals retreat from fire, yes?

Interpreting the Xenomorph straightforwardly as an animal makes sense—the crew had never before encountered one, and despite its relatively quick development, it was nonetheless born not too long prior. In *Aliens*, a conversation between Ripley and Pvt. Hudson further reveals the common tendency for humans to impose the label of "animal" on Xenomorphs *despite* their evident intelligence:

RIPLEY: They cut the power.
HUDSON: What do you mean, *they* cut the power? How could they cut the power, man? They're animals!

So, what evidence can help us identify the intelligence level of Xenomorphs?

Well, in *Alien*, the Xenomorph exhibits at least some degree of predator cunning—making use of hiding spaces and darkness on the ship to pick off the crew one by one, and finding its way to the *Narcissus* in advance of the *Nostromo*'s destruction. Even though the alien on the *Nostromo* isn't close to doing calculus or reading Sartre's massive book *Being and Nothingness* (as far as we can tell), this reflects more on the circumstances it was born into, rather than its characteristics. In the book *Alien Vault*, which chronicles the creation of the by-now classic first film, writer Dan O'Bannon clarifies that the Xenomorph aboard the *Nostromo* has "never been subject to its own culture," and has furthermore "never been subject to anything except a few hours in the hold of the ship. Quite literally, it doesn't have an education. The alien is not only savage, it is also ignorant."[8] Absent the tutelage of others of its species or the luxuries of time to develop, the Xenomorph in *Alien still* manages to outsmart most on board the ship, nearly escaping the film intact. Meanwhile, O'Bannon suggests that the Xenomorphs may be expected to have something akin to *culture*—a marker of intelligence, even personhood.

When the Xenomorphs cut the power their behavior suggests tactics and planning, alongside an understanding of the humans' dependence on electricity. Simultaneously, the aliens had built their lair beneath a reactor, a valuable form of protection from oppositional fire—it could be mere coincidence, or it could be the product of intentional defense.

In 1986's *Aliens* the species' potential really starts to shine with a number of other elements that complicate the picture further—considerations of Xenomorph social structure and the intelligence of the Queen. A conversation between Ripley and Bishop relates directly to our ability to assess potential intelligence:

RIPLEY: But these things come from eggs…so where are all the eggs coming from?
BISHOP: That is the question of the hour. We could assume a parallel to certain insect forms who have hivelike organization. An ant or

RIPLEY: termite colony, for example, is ruled by a single female, a queen, which is the source of new eggs.

RIPLEY: You're saying one of these things lays all the eggs?

BISHOP: Well, the queen is always physically larger than the others. A termite queen's abdomen is so bloated with eggs that it can't move at all. It is fed and tended by drone workers, defended by the warriors. She is the center of their lives, quite literally the mother of their society.

RIPLEY: Could it be intelligent?

BISHOP: Hard to say. It may have been blind instinct…attraction to the heat or whatever…but she did choose to incubate her eggs in the one spot where we couldn't destroy her without destroying ourselves. That's if she exists, of course.

This conversation spotlights both the possible tactical prowess of the Xenomorph Queen (at least) and the hive-like social organization of the species. The intelligence of the Queen is highlighted at the end of *Aliens* when the Queen orders other Xenomorphs not to attack Ripley after Ripley threatens to destroy her eggs.

Additionally, *Alien: Resurrection* and numerous examples from extra-filmic *Alien* literature suggest the presence of a Xenomorph hive mind and even telepathy. In such cases, Xenomorph intelligence is difficult to assess compared to human intelligence, as telepathy and hive-mind attributes are apples to the oranges of human capacities in relevant areas. As Xenomorph Queens clearly exhibit reason and agency *and* they dominate the hive mind, this may well mean that their intelligence is aggregated in ways that match or surpass human intellect.

All in all, we have incomplete information about the Xenomorphs. We certainly have evidence of apparently limited intelligence, or with animal-like qualities, but many of these examples are either relatively newborn (e.g., *Alien*) or born from lower species (e.g., Xenomorphs from dogs in *Alien*[3]). As Xenomorphs take on some physical traits from the species they hatch from (e.g., the tendrils of the PredAlien in *Alien vs. Predator: Requiem*), it stands to reason they may absorb the cognitive capacities (or limitations) of the host species to at least some degree. Simultaneously, many Xenomorphs born from sentient species who have aged past newborns have exhibited both tactics and intelligence. Moreover, the Queen exhibits intelligence, often at the human level. At the same time, the Queen's intelligence dominates the hive, and the presence of telepathy and hive-mind capabilities expand Xenomorph intelligence in relevant ways, which are capacities beyond the merely human. In short, even without a hive mind, evidence suggests that Queens and Xenomorphs from intelligent species likely exhibit many if not all the facets we associate with human intelligence. With a hive mind, they surely qualify. So, even though we don't have full details, it is highly likely that Xenomorphs have the traits identified by Sartre as elevating them above animals. Thus, they are worthy of agency, self-defense, and, in Sartre's analysis, resistance.

Stubborn Rejection of their Animal Condition

Ultimately, your average Xenomorph exhibits enough self-awareness and intelligence to defend itself against human aggression, hunt, hide, use tools, and even sabotage human tactical advantages in the course of its self-defense. Xenomorph Queens exhibit intelligence at least comparable to humans, while showing additional traits such as control of the hive-like mental connection with others of her species and possibly having telepathy. In short, our tendency to think of Xenomorphs as mere animals mostly stems from a combination of their unique circumstances and our own lack of understanding. Like the colonizers Sartre criticizes, we view the Xenomorphs as something less than full persons, and the fault is our own, not theirs. Xenomorphs likely meet the criteria that Sartre ascribed to personhood, the self-creation that begets moral value, and that ultimately legitimates resistance in the face of oppression.

Given this, what looks like alien aggression might really be alien self-defense, a refusal on the part of the Xenomorphs whose homes we invade, and whose bodies we try and take for science, to be hunted down or cornered as mere animals. We view the aliens as frightening because of our unfamiliarity, but consider this: the filmic evidence suggests that each intelligent species they encounter has sought to use, degrade, or murder them. Human corporations seek to use them for research, the military hunts them, and colonists build homes where they live (a literal colonial act). The Yautja (Predators) hunt them for sport. The Engineers use them as weapons of war. Never are they seen as beings who feel pain, have intrinsic value, or are worthy of autonomous self-determination. Meanwhile, Xenomorph Queens likely experience all these depravities via their connection to the hive mind. Under these circumstances, just as Sartre defends the revolutionary violence of the colonized in the process of decolonization, Sartre would defend Xenomorph attempts at self-defense. What looks like mindless aggression may be nothing of the sort. Indeed, we tend to interpret *Alien* as the story of unfortunate workers being preyed upon by an alien menace. But isn't it more literally the story of a newborn extraterrestrial being hunted by a pack of humans and, ultimately, dying at the hands of Ripley, our most gifted Xenomorph killer?

In short, Xenomorphs are justified in practicing revolutionary violence. They have sufficient intelligence to create themselves and their own destinies as a species, yet the other intelligent species in the universe continually hunt, kill, use, and abuse them. In this light, when they attack, it is usually either in the context of self-defense, or in opposition to further campaigns to use or destroy them. Sartre sees the human colonizer treat the human colonized as mere "beasts of burden," whose sometimes-violent resistance is both legitimate and the fault of the colonizer. Sartre would also (under these conditions) defend the Xenomorphs for their aggression against our species, and would chide us for demonizing and degrading them. Indeed, he would even likely abhor our *traditional* read of the *Alien* series—that the Xenomorphs are a deadly menace to the human species and the universe at large—and would argue that that very interpretation shows how deeply our view has been infected by a humano-centric ethos of colonizers of the stars.

Its Structural Perfection is Only Matched by its Autonomy

Sartre's philosophy highlights the fact that our traditional read of the *Alien* series is both anthropocentric and wrong. Xenomorphs very likely exhibit the cognitive capacity that Sartre identifies as central to human freedom, and as such they are worthy of their own autonomous self-determination, not extermination. Thus, Sartre's famous defense of revolutionary violence against a colonizing force applies to the Xenomorphs, and where we thought humans to be the protagonists of the *Alien* series, Sartre would point out the ways in which we are its true villains. Indeed, what does it say about us that we root for Ripley to torch the jealously guarded Xenomorph eggs in front of the Xenomorph Queen—their *mother*? Moving forward, it is my hope that we can recognize our kinship with the Xenomorphs, and instead of fearing and exterminating them, embrace them for the intelligent species they are. With true empathy for our Xenomorph siblings, I hope we find that little alien inside of all of us, just waiting to burst out.

Notes

1. Jean-Paul Sartre, *Nausea*, trans. Lloyd Alexander (New Directions, 1959), 156.
2. Jean-Paul Sartre, *Existentialism and Human Emotions* (Citadel Press, 1985), 43.
3. Ibid., 15.
4. Jean-Paul Sartre, "Preface," in *The Wretched of the Earth* by Frantz Fanon (Grove Press, 2007), lxix–l.
5. Ibid., li.
6. Ibid., lii.
7. Ibid.
8. O'Bannon, quoted in Ian Nathan, *Alien Vault* (Voyageur Press, 2011), cited from "The Eighth Passenger," *Strange Shapes* blog, https://alienseries.wordpress.com/2012/10/21/the-eighth-passenger/(accessed July 5, 2016).

Index

Alien and Philosophy: I Infest, Therefore I Am, First Edition.
Edited by Jeffrey Ewing and Kevin S. Decker.
© 2017 John Wiley & Sons Ltd. Published 2017 by John Wiley & Sons Ltd.